REFERENCE

33-2472   S   PN3355   95-4269 CIP

Henry, Laurie. **The fiction dictionary.** Story Press, 1995. 324p index ISBN 1-884910-05-X, $18.99

Henry's book intends "to focus on the myriad terms germane to the needs of most fiction writers"—types, elements, schools and theories of fiction—"to study how they have metamorphosed through the years and to better understand this art form." Compared to literary dictionaries published in the past decade—Frank Lentricchia's *Critical Terms for Literary Study* (2nd ed., 1995), Meyer Abrams's *A Glossary of Literary Terms* (6th ed., 1993), Jeremy Hawthorn's *A Concise Glossary of Contemporary Literary Theory* (1992), and Wendell Harris's *Dictionary of Concepts in Literary Criticism and Theory* (1992)—or Karl E. Beckson's earlier *A Reader's Guide to Literary Terms* (1960), Henry's is unique and comprehensive. In addition to definitions it provides synonyms, development of the terms, discussions, cross-references, and sample excerpts from fiction, selected mostly from female authors ("she" is used to refer to a writer or reader instead of the conventional "he"). Accepted terms such as "allegory" and "allusion" are juxtaposed to "technically contemporary" terms and techniques ("cyberpunk," "bubble-gum," "kmart," and "computer fiction"). An excellent index enhances this handsomely-bound, useful, and enjoyable work. Recommended for all types of libraries.—*P. Kujoory, University of the District of Columbia*

CHOICE JAN '96 ~ Vol 33, No 5   *©1996 American Library Association*

THE Fiction
Dictionary

THE Fiction Dictionary

Laurie Henry

STORY PRESS
CINCINNATI, OHIO

99 98 97 96 95   5 4 3 2 1

Library of Congress Cataloging-in-Publication Data

Henry, Laurie
    The fiction dictionary / Laurie Henry.
        p.   cm.
    Includes index.
    ISBN 1-884910-05-X
    1. Fiction—Technique. 2. Fiction—Dictionaries. I. Title.
PN3355.H43   1995
801'.953'03—dc20   95-4269
                                                                                      CIP

Designed by Clare Finney
Cover illustration by Tom Landecker

 The Fiction Dictionary is printed on recycled paper.

Laurie Henry holds graduate degrees in writing from Johns Hopkins University and the University of Iowa. Her work has appeared in *The American Poetry Review*, *Poetry*, *Missouri Review*, *Antioch Review*, *Kansas Quarterly* and elsewhere. A chapbook of poetry, *Restoring the Chateau of the Marquis de Sade*, was published by the Silverfish Review. She teaches English at Raymond Walters College in Cincinnati, and she is associate editor of *Story* magazine.

for John and Eric

FOREWORD

Defining fiction. How is that possible when people like Henry James and Virginia Woolf and E.M. Forster and John Barth and John Gardner redefine it every other decade? Fiction is constantly evolving. It's as dynamic as the people who write it, as disparate as the characters who dart across the pages of the stories and the novels etched in our memories.

But we can take a closer look at the types, elements, schools and theories of fiction to study how they have metamorphosed through the years and to better understand this art form. That is the goal of *The Fiction Dictionary*—to focus on the myriad terms germane to the needs of most fiction writers.

In this dictionary you will find a startling variety of entries, ranging from Aristotelian terms, such as "catharsis" and "mimesis," to contemporary ones, such as "narrative collage" and "Kmart fiction." Still more terms are indexed at the back of the book, because many exist in tandem with synonyms and near-synonyms. The writer looking for a definition of "self-reflexive fiction," for example, will not find it—but it's there, cross-indexed under its synonym, "metafiction."

The entries have several components. First, the term itself appears in bold print. Then, in parentheses, you will find synonyms for the term. Next, the definition is given, followed by a detailed discussion of the term. Within this discussion, you will notice that asterisks appear before words that are defined elsewhere in the book. Excerpts from fiction usually appear within or after the discussion to give you a clear sense of the term "in action"—how the great writers have employed it in their novels and short stories. Finally, at the end of the entry, you will often find cross-references to related entries.

The Fiction Dictionary makes for great browsing. It is meant to entertain and surprise you. We hope it also will provide valuable new insights into the lore and language of fiction.

Lois Rosenthal
Editor-in-Chief
Story Press

A

Abstract Language Words that express concepts or ideas. Some examples are "love," "happiness," "death" and "childhood." Almost everyone has experienced happiness, but no two people's ideas of it could be the same; that is what makes the idea of happiness an abstract one. A concrete word like "doorknob," on the other hand, will call up similar mental pictures in most people's minds.

The word "abstract" also is sometimes used to refer to general categories of objects rather than to the individual member of the category. "Animal" is a somewhat abstract concept, for example, since there are so many possible members of the category. "Three-toed tree sloth" is a concrete term: It refers to one specific species.

Most of the time, contemporary writers avoid the abstract in favor of the concrete. If too much is left to the reader's imagination by using words that are too general, the writer can lose control of the story: The reader may form a mental picture or idea entirely different from the one the writer wants to create.

Abstract language is also powerful, however, and is necessary to discuss some large, complicated topics adequately. Abstract language can be especially effective when combined with concrete *images. Here is Leo Tolstoy's description of Ivan Ilych's dying moment at the end of *The Death of Ivan Ilych*, which includes the abstract concepts of "time," "invisible force," "death," "agony," "conviction," "justification" and "life."

> For three whole days, during which time did not exist for him, he struggled in that black sack into which he was being

> thrust by an invisible, restless force. He struggled as a man condemned to death struggles at the hands of the executioner, knowing that he cannot save himself. And every moment he felt that despite all his efforts he was drawing nearer and nearer to what terrified him. He felt that his agony was due to his being thrust into that black hole and still more to his not being able to get right into it. He was hindered from getting into it by his conviction that his life had been a good one. That very justification of his life held him fast and prevented him from moving forward, and it caused him the most torment of all.

This important moment in Ivan Ilych's life could not be described using only concrete language; yet Tolstoy is careful as well to compare the indescribable, abstract feeling of approaching death with a more concrete image, the struggle of a prisoner at the hands of an executioner.

Absurdist Fiction *(existential fiction)* Fiction in which characters struggle with the notion that their very existence makes no sense, and that because no higher order justifies their existence, there are no criteria for knowing what actions are correct.

In the mind of the existentialist, God either does not exist or, if he does, has not given any indication of how human beings should live. In absurdist fiction, characters must either come to realize and accept that there are no answers to their problems, or they grimly continue against all odds to try to find answers.

Based on the philosophy of Martin Heidegger, Karl Jaspers, Jean-Paul Sartre, and novelist Albert Camus, existential fiction is a French form begun in the 1930s, related to the *philosophical novel.

Sartre's *Nausea* is written in the form of the journal of the protagonist, Roquentin, a historian, who feels a deep, constant sense of nausea. He comes to realize the nausea is caused by his feeling that there is no good reason for humans to exist—and yet they continue to do so in spite of themselves, despite the fact that human behavior is often ugly and disgusting.

Roquentin finally decides to try to escape the unbearable pointless-ness of existence through the creation of a literary work, as he thinks on the last page of the novel:

> A book. Naturally at first it would only be a troublesome, tiring work, it wouldn't stop me from existing or feeling that I exist. But a time would come when the book would be written, when it would be behind me, and I think that a little of its clarity might fall over my past. Then, perhaps, because of it, I could remember my life without repugnance. Perhaps one day, thinking precisely of this hour, of this gloomy hour in which I wait, stooping, for it to be time to get on the train, perhaps I shall feel my heart beat faster and say to myself: "That was the day, that was the hour, when it all started." And I might succeed—in the past, nothing but the past—in accepting myself.

The word "absurd" also is sometimes used as a synonym for irrea-list fiction, to describe work in which the insanity of human existence is pointed out through writing that confounds the conventions and the reader's expectations regarding plot, character, story and theme. *(See: gratuitous act, irrealist fiction, philosophical novel.)*

Academic Fiction   Fiction that is considered dry, verbose, old-fashioned, somewhat stuffy.

The term is related to the kind of visual art called academic, after the French Academy's conservative tastes, done in the late 1800s, before the impressionists and other modern artists began their reform of painting. Sometimes the word also is used to describe fiction that uses a lot of foreign terms and literary allusions that probably would be beyond a reader who is not a university student or faculty member.

An unnaturally formal style is sometimes adopted consciously as a characterizing device, often with comic or ironic intent, as in the open-ing paragraph of Graham Greene's *Travels With My Aunt*, where the fusty dignity of the language contrasts delightfully with the odd idea of being "agreeably excited" by one's mother's funeral:

> I met my Aunt Augusta for the first time in more than a half a century at my mother's funeral. My mother was approaching eighty-six when she died, and my aunt was some eleven or twelve years younger. I had retired from the bank two years before with an adequate pension and a silver handshake. There had been a takeover by the Westminster and my branch was considered redundant. Everyone thought me lucky, but I found it difficult to occupy my time. I have never married, I have always lived quietly, and, apart from my interest in dahlias, I have no hobby. For those reasons I found myself agreeably excited by my mother's funeral.

The term also is occasionally used as a synonym for *"campus novel," for those novels that are academic in that they take place on college campuses. *(See: campus novel, euphuism.)*

Action Plot *(adventure plot)*   A fast-moving, event-filled plot in which the main reader interest lies in the answer to the question, "What happens next?" rather than in, say, a universal theme or in characterization. At the conclusion of such a novel, the protagonist usually has not changed, and a sequel, full of similar adventures, is possible.

Action plots are found in genre fiction as well as in literary fiction—in comedy and farce in particular. The characters in an action plot can be fully developed and complex, and the adventures do not have to be earthshaking; take, for example, John Kennedy Toole's *A Confederacy of Dunces*, in which the characters embark on a series of deranged, misguided adventures. Here is Ignatius J. Reilly, who has taken a job selling hot dogs from a cart (although he usually ends up eating most of them himself):

> Lost in speculation about means for raising the money, Ignatius did not notice that for quite some time his cart had been traveling in a straight and unswerving line. When he attempted to pull closer to the curb, the cart would not incline to the right at all. Stopping, he saw that one of the bicycle tires had lodged in the groove of a streetcar track. He tried to bump the cart out of the groove; it was too heavy to be easily bounced. He bent and tried to lift the cart on

one side. As he slipped his hands beneath the big tin bun, he heard through the light mist the grinding of an approaching streetcar. The hard little bumps appeared on his hands, and his valve, after wavering for a moment of frantic decision, slammed closed. Wildly Ignatius pulled upward on the tin bun. The bicycle tire shot up out of the tracks, rose upward, balanced for a second in the air, and then became horizontal as the cart turned over loudly on its other side. One of the little lids in the tin bun opened and deposited a few steaming hot dogs on the street.

"Oh, my God!" Ignatius mumbled to himself, watching the silhouette of the streetcar forming a half-block away. "What vicious trick is Fortuna playing on me now?"

Aesthetic Distance   A term taken from the theater to describe the emotional closeness the writer, as well as the reader, feels toward the characters and situations in a story.

Writers sometimes face difficulties in creating a protagonist of whom they do not particularly approve, whom they feel great aesthetic distance toward. Yet the reader *should* feel more distance from fictional characters than from important people in his own life, or he will end up skipping sections that describe unpleasant events in their lives and will miss out on the complete experience of the novel.

Young (and nostalgic adult) readers of Louisa May Alcott's *Little Women*, for example, frequently skip the chapter when Beth March dies, because of their involvement with Beth and other grieving members of the March family:

> So the spring days came and went, the sky grew clearer, the earth greener, the flowers were up fair and early, and the birds came back in time to say good-bye to Beth, who, like a tired but trustful child, clung to the hands that had led her all her life, as father and mother guided her tenderly through the Valley of the Shadow, and gave her up to God.

Clearly, there is no single ideal aesthetic distance that a writer should create between himself and the work and between the reader and the work. Some writers want the reader to sink into a story completely; others put up roadblocks to keep readers from forgetting that they are reading a work of fiction.

Maintaining aesthetic distance is to some extent the reader's responsibility, but the writer can do much to ensure that the reader maintains the proper distance. Usually it is the writer's tone—his relationship toward his subject matter—that makes it clear how the reader is supposed to feel about the subject.

"Aesthetic distance" is sometimes used synonymously with "psychic distance"; the difference, to the extent that one exists, is that psychic distance refers to the relationship of the writer and reader with the characters, while aesthetic distance refers to the relationship of the writer and reader with all aspects of the work. *(See: frigidity, psychic distance.)*

Aesthetics The study of the problems inherent in deciding what comprises beauty—in other art forms as well as in literature.

In addition to judging what constitutes beauty in prose, aesthetics includes questions of what it is that people find beautiful, why people are drawn to what is considered beautiful, and why people feel drawn to create beautiful things.

The idea of aesthetic values is clearly in opposition to *moral fiction, in contrast to those who would consider the *theme of a piece of fiction—what it has to say—more important than how it is said. *(See: art for art's sake, moral fiction.)*

Aleatory Fiction *(chance fiction)* Fiction on any subject based on chance methods—either used by the writer in writing the fiction, or by the reader in deciding in what order to read the words.

Some examples are Italo Calvino's *The Castle of Crossed Destinies*, which was composed in part by the random placement of tarot cards, and Julio Cortàzar's *Hopscotch*, in which Cortàzar suggests an alternate order for the chapters than the published one:

> In its own way, this book consists of many books, but two books above all.
>
> The first can be read in a normal fashion and it ends with Chapter 56, at the close of which there are three garish little

stars which stand for the words *The End*. Consequently the reader may ignore what follows with a clean conscience.

The second should be read by beginning with Chapter 73 and then following the sequence indicated at the end of each chapter. In case of confusion or forgetfulness, one need only consult the following list: 73 - 1 - 2 - 116 - 3 - 84 - 4 - 71 - 5 - 81 - 74 - 6 - 7 - 8 - 93 - 68 - 9 - 104 - 10 - 65 . . .

In 1962, French writer Marc Saporta published his "factorial" novel, *Composition No. 1*, whose pages are not bound and can be read in any order. To organize his novel *Naked Lunch*, William Burroughs is said to have thrown the handwritten pages into the air, then typed them in whatever order he picked them up off the floor.

Producing fiction through random methods is often difficult and tedious by hand; more and more writers interested in aleatory fiction look to the computer to help them with the randomizing effort. *(See: algorithmic fiction, computer fiction, dada, hyperfiction, Oulipo.)*

Algorithmic Fiction Writing that uses techniques of substitution of one word in a text (generally a previously published, well-known text) for another, to create an entirely new work. Possibilities include random substitutions and substitutions by algorithms, which can range from simply substituting one noun for another to complex formulas.

French writer Jean Lescure's "S + 7 method" (substantive plus the seventh word that comes after it in the dictionary) is one fairly simple example. Here are a few sentences from John Cheever's "A Country Husband," followed by a changed version using Lescure's method, in which most of the nouns and adjectives have been replaced with the seventh noun or adjective following it in the dictionary:

> The Weeds' Dutch Colonial house was larger than it appeared to be from the driveway. The living room was spacious and divided like Gaul into three parts. Around an ell to the left as one entered from the vestibule was a long table, laid for six, with candles and a bowl of fruit in the center. The sounds and smells that came from the open kitchen door were appetizing, for Julia Weed was a good cook.

> The Weeds' dyadic color-coded houseguest was more laryn-geal than it appeared to be from the droopnose. The llama was Spanish and divided like a gavotte into throttled parts. Around an eluant to the left as one entered from the vetch was a loose-leaf tablemate, laid for six, with cane sugar and a bowling green of fry pans in the center. The sour cream and smiles that came from the opercular kneaded dorbeetles were applicable, for Julia Weed was a gooseberry coontie.

Generally, the aim of word substitution is not simply comic, but the creation of new meanings and images by juxtaposing apparently disparate ideas. Some writers try to create deliberately absurd effects that mirror the chaos and irrationality of contemporary society.

For reasons that should be clear, algorithmic methods are more popular in poetry than in fiction, although the quality of the new work in any genre depends on the quality of the original work, the size of the dictionary used, and the amount that the algorithmizer allows herself to cheat. *(See: aleatory fiction, computer fiction, dada, hyperfiction, Oulipo, surrealist fiction.)*

Allegory An old form related to the *fable or *parable, in which a story can be read at two or more levels. The first level is the literal level, in which some kind of literal story is told. At the second level, most of characters, places and events in the story are symbolic of larger concepts, and the whole story can be read as a parable for another, more universal story or lesson.

In Nathaniel Hawthorne's "Young Goodman Brown," for example, Faith is not only the name of the *protagonist's wife, but also a symbol of the protagonist's religious faith. At the moment when he is about to agree to become initiated into the devil-worshiping ceremony, Young Goodman Brown thinks of his wife and finally stands firm, exclaiming: "With Heaven above, and Faith below, I will yet stand firm against the devil!"

In John Bunyan's famous religious allegory, *Pilgrim's Progress*, a character named Christian travels toward the Celestial City while overcoming obstacles like the Slough of Despond, the Wicked-Gate, and the Valley of Humiliation. The story is an allegory for the struggle of all religious people to reach heaven while avoiding sin.

George Orwell's *Animal Farm* is a more contemporary allegory, in which a group of farm animals who seize control of their farm from the human farmer represent Stalin and other Bolshevik leaders of the Russian Revolution.

Allusion   A reference in a story to the proper name of a character, thing or setting from another literary work or from real life. This example comes from the first sentence of J.D. Salinger's *The Catcher in the Rye*, where Holden Caulfield alludes to a Dickens character:

> If you really want to hear about it, the first thing you'll probably want to know is where I was born, and what my lousy childhood was like, and how my parents were occupied and all before they had me, and all that David Copperfield kind of crap, but I don't feel like going into it, if you want to know the truth.

Writers have different reasons for using allusions. One motive might be simply to impress your reader with your character's (or your own) erudition.

Literary allusions to works familiar to most readers also can help a writer make a point quickly and economically in a kind of shorthand, in a way that does not necessitate lengthy explanation. In Barbara Pym's *No Fond Return of Love*, the *protagonist, Dulcie, is in love with Aylwin, who is in love with Dulcie's niece. Near the end of the novel, Aylwin suddenly realizes that it is Dulcie, not the niece, whom he loves. He worries for a moment that Dulcie may find his precipitous switch peculiar; then he muses:

> As for his apparent change of heart, he had suddenly remembered the end of Mansfield Park, and how Edmund fell out of love with Mary Crawford and came to care for Fanny. Dulcie must surely know the novel well, and would understand how such things can happen.

Since Barbara Pym's readers are surely familiar with the works of Jane Austen, this allusion helps the reader also find Aylwin's switch from the niece to Dulcie at the last moment appealing and believable. *(See: intertextuality, Kmart fiction.)*

Ambiguity The state that exists when there are several legitimate readings of a particular story or situation.

One good reason for being deliberately ambiguous is to explore a wide range of possibilities for the motivations behind people's actions, to make the point that, as in real life, it often is impossible to understand just what people are up to, and why.

The dark side of ambiguity, unfortunately, is vagueness, especially the vagueness often courted by a beginning, ungifted or lazy writer who leaves out information the reader needs to know to understand the story. Often, unintentional ambiguity occurs when the writer himself has not thought through the issue at stake in the story to the degree necessary to make things clear to the reader.

Often the way to achieve a positive, rich ambiguity, as opposed to vagueness, is to provide so much information that the reader simply knows too much to narrow his view of a character to a single idea. Readers, however, often feel frustrated by ambiguity that is created by withholding important information.

In this example, from Bobbie Ann Mason's "Big Bertha Stories," things are at last looking up for the protagonist, Jeannette. She's gotten a job, is reading, is seeing a therapist, and is finally coming to terms with her Vietnam veteran husband's post-traumatic stress disorder. Then, at the end of the story, after a neighbor tells her that her insides will be torn loose if she jumps on a trampoline too much, she dreams:

> That night, she has a nightmare about the trampoline. In her dream, she is jumping on soft moss, and then it turns into a springy pile of dead bodies.

That is the end of the story, and the dream's meaning remains ambiguous. Is Jeannette not doing quite as well as she (and we) had thought? Or is the dream a positive symbol of her finally coming to empathize with her husband, the significance of whose experiences she had trivialized earlier in the story. The answer is probably both—which makes this an example of rich, rather than impoverished, ambiguity.

Anachronism *(incongruity)* The portrayal of a character as existing—or of some event as taking place—at some time other than when it really did.

When they are not the result of sloppiness on the writer's part (the writer, say, has a character visit the Statue of Liberty in 1814, not knowing that the statue was constructed in 1886), anachronisms often are created out of comic impulse. They may also be ironic, as are those in John Fowles' *The French Lieutenant's Woman*, which, although taking place in 1867, makes frequent references to occurrences of a much later time period, jarring the reader out of a sense of the work as a piece of *realism. Here, it does so with an allusion to the Gestapo:

> And heaven also help the young man so in love that he tried to approach Marlborough House secretly to keep an assignation: for the gardens were a positive forest of humane mantraps—"humane" in this context referring to the fact that the great waiting jaws were untoothed, though quite powerful to break a man's legs. These iron servants were the most cherished by Mrs. Poulteney. *Them*, she had never dismissed.
>
> There would have been a place in the Gestapo for the lady; she had a way of interrogation that could reduce the sturdiest girls to tears in the first five minutes.

(See: historical fiction.)

Anecdote Short, penetrating stories about specific incidents, often told by one character to another. An anecdote generally takes place over a short period of time—a day, maximum—and does not involve a change of scenes, except in the popular case of an anecdote told as a *flashback.

Often the point of an anecdote is to reveal something about character, either the character telling the anecdote or the person it is being told about: It is a tool used to express a character trait not easily revealed through narrative. Here, in Tillie Olsen's "I Stand Here Ironing," the narrator, a harried mother, tells a worried social worker anecdotes about her daughter, who has been skipping school:

> "She did not get well. She stayed skeleton thin, not wanting to eat, and night after night she had nightmares. She would call for me, and I would rouse from exhaustion to sleepily call back: 'You're all right, darling, go to sleep, it's just a dream,' and if she still called, in a sterner voice, 'now go to sleep, Emily, there's nothing to hurt you.' Twice, only twice, when I had to get up for Susan anyhow, I went in to sit with her."

This anecdote shows not only the mother's exhaustion and desperation at the time when her children were small but also the guilt she feels now at having neglected her older daughter.

In a less realistic mode of fiction, of course—in a yarn, for example—the anecdote sometimes lives as an end in itself.

Anglo-Saxon Versus Latinate Words Latinate words are derived from Latin or from the Romance languages of French, Spanish and Italian (and, theoretically, Romanian). Anglo-Saxon words are those derived from the Germanic language used in what is now England before the Norman Conquest in 1066. Often, however, the term "Anglo-Saxon" is broadened to encompass all words that are not obviously Latinate and that do not derive from some non-Western language. A good dictionary, like the *Oxford English Dictionary*, usually will provide the derivation of important words. Here are some examples:

Latinate	*Anglo-Saxon*
disagreeable	nasty
miserable	wretched
detest	hate
odorous	stinky
prevent	thwart
embrace	hug

A reference to Latinate language in a work, oddly, is usually a negative one; the recent preference is toward the shorter, pithier, more consonant-filled Anglo-Saxon words than to the longer Latinates. The prejudice sometimes seems irrational; after all, there is a reason students study Latin in school and not Anglo-Saxon. Also, there is far more great literature in Latin than in Anglo-Saxon, and many Latinate words express more subtle ideas than the rough Anglo-Saxon ever could.

The problem with Latinate words is that they usually are more generalized and abstract than Anglo-Saxon words; many Latinate words make it hard for the reader to form a clear mental picture. "Fire," for example, creates a more instantaneous image than a "conflagration." Also, Latinate language is considered more lofty, even scholarly, than Anglo-Saxon language, so that a Latinate style is seen as pretentious or affected.

Antagonist   The person or force that tries to thwart the *protagonist, or main character, of a work.

Usually the antagonist is a person, but it does not have to be: It can be a force of nature (as in Jack London's "To Build a Fire," in which a man fights frigid weather while trying to light a fire from a single match to keep from freezing to death). A nonhuman antagonist also can be the stodgy morals of a rigid society that prevents him from doing something (as the dull smugness of small-town life in Sinclair Lewis' *Main Street* gradually destroys the creativity and rebelliousness of protagonist Carol Kennicott). The antagonist can even be some flaw inside the protagonist that prevents him from doing something (as Ivan Ilych is prevented from a peaceful death by his lack of trust in God in *The Death of Ivan Ilych*).

Note that the antagonist is not necessarily an evil or negative force—if the protagonist's goals are evil or negative, the antagonist will be the positive force trying to keep him from achieving his goals. The antagonists in Emily Brontë's *Wuthering Heights*, for example, are those who would keep Cathy from the fatal mistake she makes of having anything to do with the passionate, deranged Heathcliff.

Anthology   A collection of stories by different authors.

Anthologies often are used as teaching tools for college English classes and, as such, cover the widest possible range of styles and authors. Anthologies meant for the general reader outside the classroom usually will be built around some specific mission or theme;

some examples from the 1990s are *First Sightings: Contemporary Scenes of American Youth*; *The Literary Lover: Great Contemporary Stories of Passion and Romance*; and *A Literary Christmas: Great Contemporary Christmas Stories*. Other anthologies focus on particular ethnic groups or geographical location, like *Chicago Stories, Best New Stories From the South*, or *The Heinemann Book of Contemporary African Short Stories*. Annuals like *The Pushcart Prize, Prize Stories: The O. Henry Award* and *Best American Short Stories* exist to showcase what their editors have found to be the most exciting work of the year, primarily from literary magazines.

Anthropomorphism   The endowment of animals with the ability to have human thoughts and emotions.

In George Orwell's *Animal Farm*, animals expel the farm's drunken owner and, in a satire of the Russian Revolution, begin to do the farm work themselves. Before morally deteriorating at least to the level of the farmer, the animals write their declaration of independence:

> *The Seven Commandments*
> 1. Whatever goes upon two legs is an enemy.
> 2. Whatever goes upon four legs, or has wings, is a friend.
> 3. No animal shall wear clothes.
> 4. No animal shall sleep in a bed.
> 5. No animal shall drink alcohol.
> 6. No animal shall kill any other animal.
> 7. All animals are equal.

(See: pathetic fallacy, personification.)

Anticlimax   The state that occurs when, at the time of a story when suspense is at its highest and the reader anticipates that the writer is about to bring events to a clear conclusion, the plot instead either ends abruptly or just peters out, leaving the reader with the feeling that problems have not been resolved.

The anticlimax is a modern technique; its purpose—when it is used intentionally and is not the result of an insufficiently thought-out plot—is to make the story seem lifelike, in the sense that many of life's real problems tend not to resolve themselves conclusively.

Unlike in life, however, fictional anticlimaxes can often prove quite satisfying—if the reader does not feel cheated out of a genuinely *obligatory scene.

In "14 Stories," the first piece in Stephen Dixon's collection of thirteen stories called *Fourteen Stories*, Eugene Randall, despondent over the loss of his business and family, shoots himself in the mouth in a hotel room. He does not die immediately and knocks the phone off the hook, attempting to call for help. The story consists of his thoughts, along with the conversation of a couple who find his suicide note to his mother; the hotel telephone operator; the hotel detective; a boy outside who finds the bullet; and Anna, the maid who is called to clean up the room. The story ends, in fact, with the maid's request that she not be forced to clean up after the body is removed:

> "Call Harriet who works on the twelfth or that new girl on the fifteenth. They can come up or down on the elevator and use my cart. And I also don't know how to clean up dried bloodstains. Maybe that makes me a very bad chambermaid, Mr. Hire, but I never can stand the sight of blood. I can't even stand the sight of my own blood. I can't even hardly take care of my daughter when she gets hurt and spills lots of blood. Please take me off, Mr. Hire. I just can't do it."

Compared with the dead man, Anna seems like a minor character, and her desire not to clean the room is a minor crisis compared to Mr. Randall's suicide. The ending seems anticlimactic. Yet it is appropriate to the story, mirroring the ultimate indifference and selfishness with which all involved, except perhaps Mr. Randall's mother and children, are likely to view his suicide.

Antihero   A *protagonist who seems anonymous, perhaps even unlikable, yet whom you care for and support nevertheless—even though the character does not have the good points—like intelligence, strength of character, moral uprightness, and freedom from serious mental illness—you would expect from a conventional hero.

Although unsympathetic protagonists—the *picaro, for example—are not new, the antihero is a twentieth-century phenomenon. Despite his character flaws, the antihero is often true to some personal moral code outside those of mainstream society, and is admirable in a way for standing up, even if ineffectively and ineffectually, to the sometimes dangerous arrogance of the prevailing powers of contemporary society.

The term sometimes is used incorrectly to describe a protagonist whose character is so loathsome that he would be considered the antagonist of most novels—but "antihero" and "antagonist" are not at all synonymous.

Here is the antihero protagonist of Jeffrey Frank's *The Creep*, a man so worried about appearing unpopular that he asks the telephone operator to call his apartment and test his phone lines so people next door will think he has friends. Yet you've got to admire him, too, for his keen observations and, in this passage, his unwillingness to compromise by taking a boring job to end his loneliness, even though it is the only kind he might be qualified for:

> Bartholomew is lonely. The very worst thing about being lonely was that other people, especially the lonely ones, spotted it. No one hates a lonely person more than a lonely person, he knew. After a month in the city he tried to find a job, but there was nothing for him. The Executive Employment Agency let him fill out papers, but, sensing a $50 wkly. man, showed no great enthusiasm, perhaps also sensing he simply wanted to meet people, offering him finally a position as either counterman or messenger boy, the fate of those untrained legions, which he refused (without seriously damaging the Agency), being able to remain with the unprepared unemployed for the time being.

An antihero often is best written about by an author who is able to step back a bit and put some distance between the character and the reader: If the antihero is *really* unlikable (a Charles Manson type, for example), the book risks losing the reader's interest and sympathy.

Antirealistic Fiction *(irrealist fiction, surfiction)* Contemporary fiction in which the author departs from the conventional techniques of fiction—such as plot, character development, and realistic depiction of scenes—relying instead on absurdity and fantasy.

Here is the beginning of Ishmael Reed's *Mumbo Jumbo*, whose highly artificial, idiosyncratic language keeps it from seeming realistic:

> A True Sport, the Mayor of New Orleans, spiffy in his patent-leather brown and white shoes, his plaid suit, the Rudolph Valentino parted-down-the-middle hair style, sits in his office. Sprawled upon his knees is Zuzu, local doo-wack-a-doo and voo-do-dee-odo fizgig. A slatternly floozy, her green, sequined dress quivers.
>
> Work has kept Your Honor late.
>
> The Mayor passes the flask of bootlegged gin to Zuzu. She takes a sip and continues to spread crawl and behave skittishly. Loose. She is inhaling from a Chesterfield cigarette in a shameless brazen fashion.
>
> The telephone rings.
>
> The Mayor removes his hand and picks up the receiver; he recognizes at once the voice of his poker pardner on the phone.
>
> Harry, you'd better get down here quick. What was once dormant is now a Creeping Thing.
>
> The Mayor stands up and Zuzu lands on the floor. Her posture reveals a small flask stuck in her garter as well as some healthily endowed gams.
>
> What's wrong, Harry?
>
> I gots to git down to the infirmary, Zuzu, something awful is happening, the Thing has stirred in its moorings. The Thing that my Grandfather Harry and his generation of Harrys had thought was nothing but a false alarm.

Antirealistic fiction often relies for its effects on the same techniques used in *metafiction in general: *anachronisms, narrative collage and *typographical devices, for example. Unlike in more conventional fiction, the intent with antirealistic fiction often is to make sure that the reader does *not* come to identify and empathize with the characters in a realistic way.

Contemporary antirealistic fiction has its roots in the work of the French surrealists and in the early-twentieth-century work of Franz

Kafka and James Joyce—especially in their use of the concept of portraying the subconscious mind in words.

The word "surfiction," identical in meaning to antirealistic fiction, was conceived by writer Raymond Federman to describe works that are "deliberately illogical, irrational, unrealistic, non sequitur and incoherent." The word, which was more current in the 1980s than presently, generally is used to describe *metafiction of the 1960s, 1970s and 1980s. *(See: metafiction.)*

Anti-Utopian Novel A novel showing that life in some new social order, usually a communal society with rules sharply different from those of conventional capitalism, can be just as dreadful and demoralizing as conformity to a corrupt capitalist society. In an anti-Utopian novel, the *protagonist often is the person who refuses to go along with the rules of the new, supposedly ideal society.

Often the anti-Utopian novel is a reaction against the *Utopian novel, which describes in a hopeful light life in a new society. Examples of anti-Utopian novels are Samuel Butler's *Erewhon* (*Nowhere, backwards*); Aldous Huxley's *Brave New World*; and George Orwell's *Animal Farm* and *1984*.

More recent anti-Utopian works often center around the communal societies of the 1970s. Mark Vonnegut's 1973 nonfiction account of his mental deterioration on a commune in Canada, *The Eden Express*, and Joan Didion's nonfiction *Slouching Towards Bethlehem*, for example, vividly examine the potential problems of communal life. This passage is from Judith Rossner's novel *Any Minute I Can Split*, which shows the protagonist's increasing disillusionment with the commune she has joined, and how the characters, despite their freedom, do not find happiness:

> Starr had fallen madly in love with a fifteen-year-old boy, who was a student at the Putney School, and was spending a great deal of time away from the farm. Paul, looking as though he'd been hit by a ton of bricks, wandered around the house aimlessly when he wasn't taking care of the children . . . Carol and Jordan had both taken Paul's part in that argument, asking Starr what for Chrissake she wanted from the poor guy, who was always perfectly decent to his kids,

the result being that Starr wasn't speaking to either of them, although she was on polite terms with her husband. Jordan was making it with Butterscotch. Carol took great pains to let everyone know that was just fine with her because she'd really had it with men for the time being anyhow ... Carol did still spend a great deal of time with Hannah, although she began to be upset not so much by Hannah's ideas on women and drugs as by Hannah's comments on mother-hood. It was Hannah's opinion, for example, that any woman who intended to work after having babies would do the kind-est thing if she drowned the babies first, a view which caused Carol guilt and pain and terrific confusion because she wasn't absolutely certain that Hannah was wrong.

Apocalyptic Literature   Fiction whose main theme is the last judg-ment of humanity. The term, which takes its name from the books of the Bible that deal with the revelation of future events—in particular the books of Daniel and Revelations—is often broadened to include the presumed imminent end of the world in general, even when it is not presented in biblical terms.

Puritan writers of the colonial period, including Cotton Mather and Jonathan Edwards, are among the best-known American writers of apocalyptic literature, but the type tends to become popular during all periods of social upheaval and national crisis.

An example of apocalyptic literature is Albert Camus' *The Plague* (*La Peste*), published in 1947, in which the potential for the end of the world—or at least of humankind—is metaphorically presented by an epidemic of bubonic plague in twentieth-century Algeria. The citizens react with increasing fear, which causes increasing deterioration of civilization within the quarantined city.

The book, in which the plague is often also seen as a metaphor for Nazism, has as one of its *themes the encouraging idea that as long as human beings do not completely lose hope, as long as a con-certed effort is made to continue fighting against evil forces, human existence is likely to struggle on. At the end of *The Plague*, however, after the gates of the city have been opened and its residents are celebrating as if they have completely forgotten about the epidemic, the narrator points out ominously that the germs of the plague never die and may always come back.

Archetype   A character or image that has been in literature from the beginning and that regularly recurs in different literatures of different people.

The term comes from the work of psychologist Carl Jung and from anthropologist James G. Frazer, whose *The Golden Bough* discusses archetypes and myths as they appear similarly in different cultures. Jung felt that this recurrence of images and myths takes place because behind every person's "unconscious"—that part of the mind that does not reflect rational, conscious thought—there is a "collective unconscious" of "primordial images" that everyone shares, which may even encompass realities that occurred before human beings evolved as Homo sapiens.

It is this unconscious memory, Jung asserted, that accounts for the fact that these "primordial images" of our remote ancestors occur in myths, religion and literature. The "primordial image" from the distant past is what constitutes an archetype; it creates strong responses from readers that they are not really able to explain.

Some figures that are considered archetypes are, as Jung described them, the Mother, Father, Son, Daughter, Priest, Mentor, Magician and Authority Figure.

A writer who deals in archetypes is E.M. Broner, whose characters often have a larger-than-life, indescribably mythical feel, as the Russian woman does in this passage called "Bearers of the Dream," from a section of the novel *Her Mothers*:

> In the artist's village of Ein Hod she meets Ilana, a Russian potter. Ilana has a rounded belly, a rounded bottom, handles of arms.
> "Tell me your story, Ilana," says Beatrix.
> They have returned from a concert in the stone amphitheater of Ein Hod. Wild dogs had rushed across the stage while the chamber group bowed. A donkey with a scarred nose had walked this distance from an Arab village nearby and had brayed. A scorpion is crawling across the stage.

Ilana and Beatrix shiver in the night air, but yet it is warmer in Ein Hod than in Jerusalem, Tel Aviv, or Haifa. The days are sweltering. Beatrix cannot bear her clothes upon her body. Ilana works naked in the pot shop. The women sweat while the clay dries.

"I am the daughter of collectors," says Ilana. "My parents came from Leningrad with a shipload of furniture and with a large library. My father is a man of culture."

"And your mother?"

"My mother is paralyzed. She gave birth and saw it was a girl and never spoke again. She walks slowly with a cane. She writes her requests shakily. She sleeps separately."

Note how, although the character of the Russian woman seems to embody more than just the characteristics of a single individual, she is not a cliché. It is important that a writer work for good characterization—that the character appear first as a believable character rather than an archetype.

Architectonic Novel *(double plot)* A term first used by Henry James to describe a novel with more than one dominant plot, each of which involves, for the most part, separate characters and incidents.

An example is William Makepeace Thackeray's *Vanity Fair*, in which the lives of Amelia Sedley and Becky Sharp, friends at school despite remarkably dissimilar personalities, gradually become disengaged from each other only to become connected again later in their lives.

Becky Sharp, the poor daughter of a French teacher, is intelligent but often scheming in her desire to gain financial security. Becky's husband Rawdon Crawley is disinherited for marrying her, but she still lives very well, as she soon begins a romantic relationship with a good friend of her husband. Eventually, however, Rawdon Crawley realizes what is going on, and near the end of the book Becky is forced to live in virtual exile in France.

Amelia, credulous and a little stupid, the protagonist of the novel's other main plot, is the daughter of a rich businessman who loses his money through speculation. She marries a man who is killed at the Battle of Waterloo and is forced through lack of money to let her son be brought up by her dead husband's grandfather; thus her twenties and thirties are filled with hardships and difficulties.

The two former friends—and the two plots—do not truly intertwine again until the end of the long book, when Amelia, her son (who has inherited his great-grandfather's fortune), and Amelia's loutish brother, Joseph, meet up with Becky in France. At the end of the novel, Joseph begins to fall under the spell of Becky's charms, and Amelia is married to her first love, the decent but awkward William Dobbin.

The architectonic novel must generally be longer than a novel with a single plot, if each plot is to be fully developed. The writer of the architectonic novel must take care to consider carefully the relationship between the two (or more) plots: Too much of a parallel relationship between the plots can make the book seem overplotted and contrived; on the other hand, if the relationship between the two plots is totally distant, the novel easily can begin to seem uncontrolled and disorganized. *(See: chronicle novel, maximal fiction, systems novel.)*

Art for Art's Sake The idea that art—including, of course, fiction—ideally has no ulterior motive, such as being instructive, teaching a lesson, or suggesting a certain solution for a social problem; beauty is its own reward. The concept of "art for art's sake" rejects the idea of *moral fiction and social realism.

Oscar Wilde, a leading proponent of the philosophy, suggested that "the only beautiful things are the things that do not concern us" and that "lying, the telling of beautiful untrue things," should be the goal of all art.

"Art for art's sake" is related to the theoretical idea of the *pure novel, which ideally would not be "about" anything outside of itself, in the way that nonrepresentational art does not refer to real objects in the real world.

Still, the fact that words, unlike colors and shapes, have definite and indelible denotations as well as connotations, limits the possibility of truly nonrepresentational fiction, and the concept of art for art's sake in fiction generally stops well before reaching this extreme. *(See: aesthetics, moral fiction, pure novel.)*

Atmosphere   A work's dominant *mood, especially in regard to how it is established through its physical setting or landscape.

Atmosphere is more than setting, also encompassing the emotional feeling the reader derives from the work. Creating an atmosphere helps the reader to know what kind of story to expect—what kind of attitude she is likely to develop toward a story. It is clear from the beginning, for example, that *The Return of the Native*, by Thomas Hardy, will not show an easy, trouble-free environment with calm, rational characters, even before those characters have appeared:

> A Saturday afternoon in November was approaching the time of twilight, and the vast tract of unenclosed wild known as Egdon Heath embrowned itself moment by moment. Overhead the hollow stretch of whitish cloud shutting out the sky was as a tent which had the whole heath for its floor.
>
> The heaven being spread with this pallid screen and the earth with the darkest vegetation, their meeting-line at the horizon was clearly marked. In such contrast the heath wore the appearance of an instalment of night which had taken up its place before its astronomical hour was come; darkness had to a great extent arrived hereon, while day stood distinct in the sky.

The term "atmosphere" is often used when describing stories in which the prevailing mood is cold, bleak, ominous and frightening, but it can be applied to those with any type of mood, even a bright or sensuous one. *(See: mood, psychic distance, tone.)*

Author-as-Character   A concept put into words by critic Jonathan Wilson in an article in *The Literary Review*, to describe the effect created when the author of a fictional work with fictional characters includes himself as a character in the work.

Authors appear as characters all the time in *autobiographical fiction, of course. It is different, though, when the plot is not meant to reflect reality lived by the author—and the author who walks through the book purposely has been created to be a bit different from the one who really lives.

Including a real person in a fictional story forces the reader to become aware of the idea that fictional characters can take on an existence as "real" as that of real people.

In *Democracy*, by Joan Didion, for example, a character named Joan Didion appears as the narrator of the book, interacting freely with other characters who only exist on paper—flying with two fictional characters, the Victors, to Kuala Lumpur, and talking with them on the way.

Indeed, the second chapter of *Democracy* begins:

> Call me the author.
> Let the reader be introduced to Joan Didion, upon whose character and doings much will depend of whatever interest these pages may have, as she sits at her writing table in her own room in her own house on Welbeck Street.
> So Trollope might begin this novel.

Putting herself into the novel as a character, as Milan Kundera and W.P. Kinsella also have done, in one way makes the novel seem more *realistic. If Joan Didion, a verifiably living human being, exists in the novel, providing verifiable facts about her real self (for example, both the real Joan Didion and the character once worked at *Vogue*), it follows that other characters in the novel will seem more real as well.

On the other hand, including one's self as a character in fiction also serves to make the writer seem less like a real person, just as the other characters are not real people. If Joan Didion could not have flown to Kuala Lumpur with the Victors because the Victors do not exist, in some ways it seems less likely that Joan Didion herself exists.

Naturally, not all authors who include themselves as characters in fiction mean for their presence to raise questions of the reality of fiction and real life in the reader's mind, as Jonathan Wilson remarks in this article from *The Literary Review*:

> In 1938, Edmund Wilson wrote a highly favorable review of Henry Miller's *Tropic of Cancer*, among other things Wilson praised Miller for the skillful, ironic portrait of his protagonist ("Henry Miller"), for making the hero really live "and not merely in his vaporings or his poses." Miller gives us,

says Wilson, "the genuine American bum come to lead the beautiful life in Paris; and he lays him a way forever in his dope of Pernod and dreams." Miller was so incensed by Wilson's praise of his ironic distancing that he replied in a letter to the editor: "The theme is myself and the narrator, or the hero as your critic puts it, is also myself. . . . if he means the narrator, then it is me. . . . I don't use 'heroes' incidentally. . . . I am the hero and the book is myself."

(See: new journalism, nonfiction novel, passive characterization.)

Authorial Intrusion *(intrusive narrator)*   What occurs when the author seems to step out of the story and address the reader, as Anthony Trollope does even in the title of his novel *Can You Forgive Her?*, in which he asks the reader directly to forgive the behavior—which isn't really that bad—of one of his characters.

Authorial intrusion provides a change of pace; it can provide the reader with the pleasures of an entirely new voice, that of someone uninvolved in the plot and complications. It is also useful in the same way that summary is, to let the author (rather than the characters, who may be untrustworthy or otherwise unable to perform the task) cover a great deal of ground quickly.

Authorial intrusion was out of favor in the prose of the twentieth century until the 1970s, when it became one of the tools of *metafiction. In the third section of John Barth's "Life-Story," a story about a man in the process of writing a story, the author seems to address the reader directly:

> The reader! You, dogged, uninsultable, print-oriented bastard, it's you I'm addressing, who else, from inside this monstrous fiction. You've read me this far, then? Even this far? For what discreditable motive? How is it you don't go to a movie, watch TV, make amorous advances to the person who comes to your mind when I speak of amorous advances? Can nothing surfeit, saturate you, turn you off? Where's your shame?

It is important to remember that the authors who are intruding are *implied authors, not necessarily the actual voices of the people writing the story—even in nineteenth-century fiction, when the presumed voice of William Makepeace Thackeray tells the reader at the end of *Vanity Fair*:

> Ah! Vanitas Vanitatum! Which of us is happy in this world? Which of us has his desire, or, having it, is satisfied? Come, children, let us shut up the box and the puppets, for our play is played out.

Thackery probably is not talking to us in the same way he would write privately in his diary, where he would be more likely to reveal his true self. Often the writer will deliberately hide behind a *persona, a kind of mask, through which he can control the intimacy of the relationship between himself and the reader. *(See: psychic distance, tone, uninstrusive narrator.)*

Authorial-Omniscient Voice A term coined by John Gardner to describe a point of view in which a third-person narrator states what appear to be facts and reaches authoritative conclusions using neutral, transparent language and speaking, as Gardner says in *The Art of Fiction*, "with dignity and proper grammar, saying what any calm, dignified, and reasonable person would say."

This example of narration told in the authorial-omniscient voice comes from Leo Tolstoy's *War and Peace*:

> At the exact hour, the prince, powdered and shaven, walked into the dining-room, where there were waiting for him his daughter-in-law, Princess Marya, Mademoiselle Bourienne, and the prince's architect, who, by a strange whim of the old gentleman's, dined at his table, though being an insignificant person of no social standing, he would not naturally have expected to be treated with such honour. The prince, who was in practice a firm stickler for distinctions of rank, and rarely admitted to his table even important provincial functionaries, had suddenly pitched on the architect Mihail Ivanovitch, blowing his nose in a check pocket-handkerchief in the corner, to illustrate the theory that all men are equal, and had more than once impressed upon his daughter that

Mihail Ivanovitch was every whit as good as himself and her. At table the prince addressed his conversation to the taciturn architect more often than to anyone.

Gardner contrasts the authorial-omniscient voice with the *essayist-omniscient voice, which is much more personal. Using the essayist-omniscient voice, the narrator reveals something about his own sex and background, as well as about the scene he describes. Each essayist-omniscient voice is distinct from every other, says Gardner, whereas authorial-omniscient voices tend to sound more or less alike.

Autobiographical Fiction *(autonovel)*   Fiction based, whether or not the author acknowledges it, on the writer's own life.

As long as it satisfies this condition, autobiographical fiction can use either a *first-person or third-person narrator. Thomas Wolfe's first four novels (including *Look Homeward Angel*), which draw heavily from his own life, use a third-person narrator.

The line between autobiographical fiction and actual autobiography can be thin. The protagonist of Henry Miller's *Tropic of Cancer* and *Tropic of Capricorn* is himself named Henry Miller, and the fictionalization is not so much with the events he describes but in the poetic, lyrical language, such as the following from *Tropic of Capricorn*:

As a boy of six or seven I used to sit at my grandfather's workbench and read to him while he sewed. I remember him vividly in those moments when, pressing the hot iron against the seam of a coat, he would stand with one hand over the other and look out of the window dreamily. I remember the expression on his face, as he stood there dreaming, better than the contents of the books I read, better than the conversations we had or the games which I played in the street. I used to wonder what he was dreaming of, what it was that drew him out of himself. I hadn't learned yet how to dream wide-awake. I was always lucid, in the moment, and all of a piece. His daydreaming fascinated me. I knew that he had no connection with what he was doing, not the least thought for any of us, that he was alone and being alone he was free.

An autobiographical novel is different from actual autobiography in that the writer is free to change events to make them fit better into a conventional fictional structure, as well as simply to disguise details the writer would prefer not to reveal. In *A la recherche du temps perdu* (translated either as *In Search of Lost Time* or *Remembrance of Things Past*), Marcel Proust substitutes female characters for the author's actual male lovers.

An autobiographical novel also is different from a *roman à clef in that in a roman à clef, part of the reader's pleasure comes from recognizing well-known figures as characters with different names. Romans à clef also are autobiographical novels, but autobiographical fiction includes the much larger category of novels that uses real but not famous people as characters. *(See: author-as-character, roman à clef, simulated autobiography.)*

Automatic Writing *(free association, trance writing)*   Writing in which the words seem to come straight to paper from the subconscious mind.

The term is sometimes used to describe a process in which the writer puts on paper the first thing that comes to her mind, using techniques of free association, without trying to make sense of it or edit it. More often, however, "automatic writing" is used to describe what comes from a trancelike state into which a writer enters and tries to create without knowing what she is doing.

Real automatic writing, done by real people in a trancelike state, curiously, often is valued because it appears so lucid, as if a perfectly rational spirit voice has taken over the writer's hand and mind. Automatic writing done to produce fiction tends to be more ethereal, mysterious and dreamlike.

Here's Joan, in Margaret Atwood's *Lady Oracle*, preparing for an experiment in automatic writing:

> I stared at the candle in the mirror, the mirror candle. There was more than one candle, there were three, and I knew that if I moved the two sides of the mirror toward me there

would be an infinite number of candles, extending in a line as far as I could see . . . The candle was very bright, I was holding it in my hand and walking along a corridor, I was descending, I turned a corner, I was going to find someone. I needed to find someone.

There was movement at the edge of the mirror. I gasped and turned around. Surely there had been a figure standing behind me. But there was no one. I was wide awake now, I could hear a faint roar from the television in the next room, and the voice of the announcer, "He shoots, he scores! A blistering drive from the point. There may have been a re-bound. . . . Here comes the replay. . . ."

I looked down at the piece of paper. There, in a scrawly handwriting that was certainly not my own, was a single word:

Bow

Few writers can honestly say that they produced a novel entirely through automatic writing, although Jack Kerouac urged writing "without consciousness" and himself claimed to write works, including *On the Road*, as quickly as he could type them. Harriet Beecher Stowe claimed that *Uncle Tom's Cabin* was dictated to her by God.

Incidentally, Gertrude Stein, often accused of creating her more difficult works through automatic-writing techniques, vehemently denied this. *(See: improvisation, stream of consciousness.)*

Avant-Garde Fiction *(experimental fiction)* Writing that stands out from the prevailing style of its era in form, style or subject matter— in a way, needless to say, that does not seem obsolete or archaic. Contemporary avant-garde works often are considered difficult and challenging; generally the author does not make an effort to engage the reader by presenting a strong illusion of reality and a clearly moving plot.

The term "avant-garde" often is used to describe writers in the earlier part of the twentieth century who consciously tried new methods of fiction-writing, such as stream of consciousness, automatic writing, and absurd juxtapositions of images. These writers include Gertrude Stein, James Joyce, Samuel Beckett and Franz Kafka.

The term "avant-garde" also has been used, as Alain Robbe-Grillet points out in his essay "On Several Obsolete Notions" (in the influential *For a New Novel*), as a kind of ghetto-izing term, permitting conventional critics to reject innovative work:

> The word "avant-garde," for example, despite its note of impartiality, generally serves to dismiss—as though by a shrug of the shoulders—any work that risks giving a bad conscience to the literature of mass consumption. Once a writer renounces the well-known formulas and attempts to create his own way of writing, he finds himself stuck with the label "avant-garde."

Ironically, some writers using avant-garde techniques work from an impulse to get closer to the illusion of reality—by using techniques like *stream of consciousness, for example—rather than to eschew it. The innovators of the middle part of the twentieth century, like Robbe-Grillet and other *nouveau romanceurs*, often felt that the use of unconventional technique would make their work seem more honest and psychologically real than conventional devices. Other writers, of course, work from a different philosophy, feeling that conventional narrative simply cannot accurately capture the complexity of contemporary life.

Since the late 1960s, *metafiction—fiction whose real subject is the writing of fiction itself—like Steve Katz's 1968 *The Exagggerations of Peter Prince* (yes, three *g*'s) typifies fiction considered avant-garde. This novel includes pages with *x*'s through them that the author has apparently discarded or revised; pages with a variety of typefaces and strikeovers; pages filled with apparently meaningless language (one page nearly completely filled with the word "beep"); and constant references to the fact that the book is fiction and not a representation of reality.

Before a paragraph that begins, "Authorless, gleaming, Peter Prince felt fortunate so suddenly to have been removed, by some means (never mind) to the eleventh century where the noonday sun seemed somehow brighter and agreeably dry-hot ..." the narrator writes, referring to the real writers Ron Sukenick and Peter Schjeldahl:

Well I'm sorry for the delay after all my promises, but blame it on Sukenick. He said, "Just wait here for me, Katz, and I'll put you in my novel."

So I waited.

"That's why I haven't got Peter Prince from Italy to Egypt yet. I'm waiting just where he told me for Sukenick to put me in his novel, here on the street corner with the busted lamp. It can take some patience, because if he ever shows up at all he's usually late. And it's probably some little insignificant thing he's going to have me do, a little trip to Long Island, or a conversation with one of those characters of his who always wears tinted contact lenses. Even for the best friendship it's not worth neglecting Peter Prince, especially when he needs to go on a trip. Quality writing is measured by its transitions. But I promised, and I'll have to wait it out, that's all, and I beg for patience from anyone who is still around. In the meantime, as one of the feature presentations of this novel, I am proud to be able to present a paragraph by Peter Schjeldahl who has, among other things, been remarkable. The following paragraph is by PETER SCHJELDAHL: . . .

Other recent writers considered avant-garde include Kathy Acker, Stephen Dixon, Walter Abish and Charles Newman.

B

Background Description The illustration of the physical *setting, where a *scene occurs.

In an essay in *Collected Impressions,* novelist Elizabeth Bowen says that description of location "is only justified in the novel where it can be shown, or at least felt, to act upon action or character. In fact, where it has dramatic use." Other writers generally warn as well against the overuse of description—especially paragraphs of description uninterrupted by action or dialogue. Novelist Ivy Compton-Burnett points out also that no matter how careful and precise a writer is in painting a picture of the scene, the reader will inevitably form his own mental image of the scene, despite the writer's possible desires to the contrary.

Certainly, however, description often is used to help establish an *atmosphere in fiction. This example of successful background description, interlaced between details showing character and pushing the plot forward, comes from John Casey's *Spartina:*

> Dick Pierce swung the bait barrel off his wharf into his work skiff. He cast off and began to scull down Pierce Creek. He built his skiffs with an oarlock socket on the transom. He had to tell most buyers what it was for. In fact sculling was a necessity for him—this far up the creek it was too narrow to row and, except at high water, too shallow to put the outboard down.
>
> The tide was still dumping and he let her drift a bit. A spider's strand broke against his forehead. A light mist came

off the water but dissolved as soon as it got above the black banks. Dick loved the salt marsh. Under the spartina there was black earth richer than any farmland, but useless to farmers on account of the salt. Only the spartinas thrived in the salt flood, shut themselves against the salt but drank the water. Smart grass. If he ever got his big boat he might just call her Spartina, though he ought to call her after his wife.

He always started off these fair early-summer days in a mood as calm and bright as the surface of the water. Everything was lit up silver and rose—the dew, the spider's webs, the puffs of mist, even the damp backs of the dunes on the barrier beach that divided the salt ponds, the marsh, and the creeks from the sea.

Where Pierce Creek joined up with Sawtooth Creek he let the outboard down and cranked it up. He could see the breachways and through the breachway the horizon, a pale streak. . . .

(See: exposition.)

Bathos A negative term for the effect when a writer describes the emotions created by a genuinely tragic situation in such an exaggerated, *overwritten manner that the piece loses its tragic tone and becomes unintentionally melodramatic and comic.

An example of bathos comes from Mark Twain's *Huckleberry Finn*, in the bathetic poem "O'd to Stephen Dowling Bots, Dec'd," supposedly written by a morbid young girl who died soon after completing her opus:

> And did young Stephen sicken,
>   And did young Stephen die?
> And did the sad hearts thicken,
>   And did the mourners cry?
>
> No; such was not the fate of
>   Young Stephen Dowling Bots;
> Though sad hearts round him thickened,
>   'Twas not from sickness' shots.

No whooping-cough did rack his frame,
   Nor measles drear, with spots;
Not these impaired the sacred name
   of Stephen Dowling Bots.

Despised love struck not with woe
   That head of curly knots,
Nor stomach troubles laid him low,
   Young Stephen Dowling Bots.

O no. Then list with tearful eye,
   Whilst I his fate do tell.
His soul did from this cold world fly,
   By falling down a well.

They got him out and emptied him;
   Alas it was too late;
His spirit was gone for to sport aloft
   In the realms of the good and great.

A story crammed full of unrelated deaths and other tragedies is especially likely to be accused of bathos. The term is sometimes expanded to describe works of fiction in which the writer seems to expect the reader to weep—or includes hypersensitive characters who weep—over relatively small tragedies (the poignantly sad blue eyes of a dead opossum lying by the side of the road, for example).

Generally, bathos is a problem of description and style rather than of plot. The biblical Book of Job, for example, is full of tragedy and suffering, but no one would accuse it of being bathetic, because the writing is not melodramatic; Job's emotions seem entirely appropriate to his situation. It is important that a writer not forget that real life can be tragic, and that it usually is a mistake to leave out genuine emotion from a story in hopes of avoiding bathos. *(See: frigidity, overwriting, pathos, sentimentality, underwriting.)*

Beat Fiction A movement of the mid- to late 1950s and early 1960s by writers who consciously rebelled both against what they perceived as the staidness and smugness of the prevailing American culture, and against the dry, *academic writing of the era.

Beat writers were influenced by the improvisatory nature of jazz and by drug and alcohol use, as well as by the tenets of Zen Buddhism. Beat writers were convinced that personal experience absolutely was appropriate subject matter for fiction, although it was rejected by many writers of the day, in favor of overly symbolic themes.

The word "beat," out of which the word "beatnik" later emerged (which often is attributed to writer John Clellon Holmes, who described typically "beat" characters in his 1952 novel *Go*), has several meanings. In *On the Road*, Jack Kerouac often uses the word in the familiar sense of being tired, exhausted. However, the term also came to define a kind of sensibility—of being willing to go for broke, to hide nothing, to face life as honestly and nakedly as possible. In the sense that it is also related to Zen Buddhism and a general desire to escape from the restrictions of conventional society, it also is related to "beatific" and "beatitude."

The most important fiction writers among the beats were William Burroughs and Jack Kerouac. Kerouac's second novel, *On the Road*, written over about a three-week period in 1951, is the most important work of the movement.

On the Road deals autobiographically with several trips Kerouac made around the country with friends, living off of little money, devoting himself to his writing, eschewing comfort in favor of a kind of psychic purity. A fast typist, Kerouac wrote the novel on rolls of radio-teletype paper so he would not have to stop to change sheets of paper as he wrote. Calling his technique "spontaneous prose," he later refused to revise; his goal was to write as much as possible "without consciousness," almost as if in a trance.

Here is a passage from *On the Road*, a good example of the exuberance and spontaneity combined with sharp observation of the best beat writing:

> Along about three in the afternoon, after an apple pie and ice cream in a roadside stand, a woman stopped for me in a little coupe. I had a twinge of hard joy as I ran after the car. But she was a middle-aged woman, actually the mother of sons my age, and wanted somebody to help her drive to Iowa. I was all for it. Iowa! Not so far from Denver, and once

I got to Denver I could relax. She drove the first few hours, at one point insisted on visiting an old church somewhere, as if we were tourists, and then I took over the wheel, and though I'm not much of a driver, drove clear through the rest of Illinois to Davenport, Iowa, via Rock Island. And here for the first time in my life I saw my beloved Mississippi River, dry in the summer haze, low water, with its big rank smell that smells like the raw body of America itself because it washes it up. Rock Island—railroad tracks, shacks, small downtown section; and over the bridge to Davenport, some kind of town, all smelling of sawdust in the warm midwest sun. Here the lady had to go on to her Iowa hometown by another route, and I got out.

Beginning The first sentence or paragraph or page of a story: whatever goes on before the story's real *conflict is made clear. A story's beginning had better be compelling, because if it is not, a reader often will not get past it.

A good beginning introduces not only the characters and situation but also the *tone and *mood of a story. It often is said that a story's ending is implicit in its beginning, and this is true not so much because of its plot, but because its tone and mood tacitly suggest in a general way what kind of an outcome can be expected. The opening paragraph of John Steinbeck's "The Chrysanthemums" talks only about the California landscape, but the isolating fog and the lack of sunshine over the valley do not lead the clever reader to believe that a joyous ending is in the offing:

The high gray-flannel fog of winter closed off the Salinas Valley from the sky and from the rest of the world. On every side it sat like a lid on the mountains and made of the great valley a closed pot. On the broad, level land floor the gang plows bit deep and left the black earth shining like metal where the shares had cut. On the foothill ranches across the Salinas River, the yellow stubble fields seemed to be bathed in pale cold sunshine, but there was no sunshine in the valley now in December. The thick willow scrub along the river flamed with sharp and positive yellow leaves.

One difficulty with beginnings comes in knowing exactly where to start a story. In his essay, "To Begin, To Begin," Clark Blaise provides examples of beginnings that are unpromising in that they seem to start too late, in which the dramatic opening action appears *gimmicky because there's not sufficient explanation of the motivation for the character's behavior:

> Catelli plunged the dagger deeper in her breast, the dark blood oozed like cherry syrup.

> The President's procession would pass under the window at 12:03, and Slattery would be ready ...

Blaise also describes beginnings that start too soon, in which there is too much unnecessary exposition before the real action of the story begins, like the following:

> When I saw Bob in the cafeteria he asked me to a party at his house that evening and since I wasn't doing much anyway I said sure, I wouldn't mind. Bob's kind of an ass, but his old man's loaded and there's always a lot of grass around ...

Often, a writer chooses between beginning with expository summary or *in medias res, with dialogue. Probably the most common way to begin, however, is to set the scene, to describe the *situation of the story before the plot begins, before the story's complications begin to show themselves.

Bildungsroman *(apprenticeship novel, novel of education)*   A German term for a novel that shows the growth and development (or, sometimes, the deterioration) of the protagonist in relation to the society of her times, usually starting in childhood.

The term often is broadened to describe nearly any novel whose protagonist is a young person who grows to mental and emotional maturity during the course of the novel; in this sense it is an incredibly common type.

Charlotte Brontë's *Jane Eyre* is a bildungsroman in the sense that we watch Jane Eyre's growth from an emotional, sensitive child into a self-sufficient, self-denying adult.

When Jane Eyre learns that her employer, Mr. Rochester, whose marriage proposal she has accepted, is already married, Jane runs impetuously away into a new life as a schoolteacher in another town. Finally, however, she turns from a loveless marriage to her decent but cold cousin and returns to Mr. Rochester, whose wife has burned to death in Rochester's house. Attaining maturity, she realizes at last that love is more important to her than the selflessly decent but passionless life she has been living.

The term "education novel" is sometimes used as a synonym for a bildungsroman; other times, "education novel" has a different definition, as a *didactic form of the late eighteenth century, which presented in fictional terms an idealized method of intellectually and morally educating a young person.

A bildungsroman often is similar to a *story of initiation, but with a bildungsroman, it is not necessary that a character experience a specific, precise moment in time when she finally reaches the brink of maturity, as is likely in the case of a story of initiation. It is sufficient to follow the development even of a character whose adult traits are completely foreseeable in her childhood behavior. *(See:* künstlerroman, *story of initiation.)*

Biographical Novel   A novel that transforms the life of a famous person into fiction through the imagination of individual scenes meant to show what kind of person the subject is. A biographical novel usually will illustrate the daily life of the *protagonist as well as more dramatic moments.

A biographical novel will incorporate true biographical facts and will be historically accurate, although it also will include imagined dialogue and incidents. It is, of course, easier to write a biographical novel in which the protagonist is a celebrated person whose life has been full of drama and whose story will include more of the suspenseful aspects of a novel than most people's. Here is an example from *Lust for Life*, by Irving Stone, who also wrote biographical novels of the lives of Michelangelo and Sigmund Freud:

Dr. Felix Rey, young interne of the hospital of Arles, was a short, thickset man with an octagonal head and a weed of black hair shooting up from the top of the octagon. He treated Vincent's wound, then put him to bed in a cell-like room from which everything had been removed. He locked the door behind him when he went out.

At sundown, when he was taking the patient's pulse, Vincent awoke. He stared at the ceiling, then the white-washed wall, then out of the window at the patch of darkening blue sky. His eyes wandered slowly to Doctor Rey's face.

"Hello," he said, softly.

"Hello," replied Doctor Rey.

"Where am I?"

"You're in the hospital of Arles."

"Oh."

A flash of pain went across his face. He lifted his hand to where his right ear had once been. Doctor Rey stopped him.

"You mustn't touch," he said.

". . . Yes . . . I remember . . . now."

"It's a nice, clean wound, old fellow. I'll have you on your feet within a few days."

A biographical novel is different from *historical fiction in that in a historical novel characters may be invented and placed into a historical setting; in a biographical novel, all the characters will have lived. *(See: historical fiction, roman à clef.)*

Black Humor *(dark humor)* A term originating in the 1950s to describe a type of humor that combines a sense of the absurdity of life with farce and other low kinds of comedy, often targeting helpless victims as the ostensible butts of its jokes.

The goal of serious black humor in literature (as opposed to the simple gross-out joke) often is to express the ultimate senselessness and futility of contemporary life. There is no meaning to life, the black humorist often asserts; sometimes the simple observation of the horrible conditions under which human beings must live is all that literature can do.

Joseph Heller's *Catch 22* is a classic example of serious fiction that engages in black humor: Here, the protagonist is trying to sort out whether a fighter pilot who is insane will be forced to continue to fly:

> There was only one catch and that was Catch-22, which spec-
> ified that a concern for one's own safety in the face of dan-
> gers that were real and immediate was the process of a ratio-
> nal mind. Orr was crazy and could be grounded. All he had
> to do was ask; and as soon as he did, he would no longer be
> crazy and would have to fly more missions. Orr would be
> crazy to fly more missions and sane if he didn't, but if he
> was sane he had to fly them. If he flew them he was crazy
> and didn't have to; but if he didn't want to he was sane and
> had to. Yossarian was moved very deeply by the absolute
> simplicity of this clause of Catch-22 and let out a respectful
> whistle.

Bubble-Gum Fiction A term used by Jerome Klinkowitz in *The Practice of Fiction in America* to describe innovative fiction that, unlike much *metafiction, which has been accused of ignoring the reader to concentrate on language, also makes a concerted effort to appeal to the reader through creating engaging characters and exciting stories. The term does not at all have the negative connotations that "bubble-gum music" does.

Writers of bubble-gum fiction include William Kotzwinkle and Tom Robbins, who, like many metafictionists, try to keep their language as far away as possible from the conventions of realism—yet also to include elements that will appeal to a general readership.

An example is Kotzwinkle's *The Fan Man*, published as a paperback original in 1974. The narrator is Horse Badorties, a drug-addicted *antihero who often falls asleep for twenty-four hours at a time and loses things like the sink and the telephone—or if he does not, he does not remember what the phone is used for. Horse Badorties nev-ertheless remains likeable because of his engaging use of language, and his determination to make every lucid minute of his life part of an ongoing monologue he dictates into a tape recorder:

> I just woke up, man. Horse Badorties just woke up and is
> crawling around in a sea of abominated filthiness, man,

which he calls home. Walking through the rooms of my pad, man, through broken glass and piles of filthy clothes from which I shall select my wardrobe for the day. Here, stuffed in a trash basket, is a pair of incredibly wrinkled-up muck-pants. And here, man, beneath a pile of wet newspapers is a shirt, man, with one sleeve. All I need now, man, is a tie, and here is a perfectly good rubber Japanese toy snake, man, which I can easily form into an acceptable knot looking like a gnarled ball of spaghetti.

One chapter, called "It's Dorky-Day Once Again!" consists of the protagonist repeating the word "dorky" for paragraphs at a time.

The intention in *The Fan Man* is not to reveal the inner character of the protagonist, as is the intent of much stream-of-conscious writing, but to focus on language and its use. Still, the character is engaging enough to keep even most devoted realists reading.

Burlesque *(persiflage, travesty)* Derived from the Italian word for "mockery"; comedy whose style is purposely at odds with the subject matter.

In one type of burlesque, also called a travesty, the writer employs a dignified, even formal style to straight-facedly report a nonsensical issue, as Donald Ogden Stewart does in a section on pedestrian travel in his parody etiquette manual, *Perfect Behavior.*

> In the first place, it is always customary in a city for a young lady, either accompanied or unaccompanied, to walk on the sidewalk. A young "miss" who persists in walking in the gutters is more apt to lose than to make friends among the socially "worth while."
>
> Gentlemen, either with or without ladies, are never seen walking after dark in the sewers or along the elevated tracks.
>
> It is not *au fait* for gentlemen or ladies wearing evening dress to "catch on behind" passing ice wagons, trucks, etc.; the time and energy saved are doubtfully repaid should one happen to be driven thus past other members of one's particular social "set." . . .
>
> It is never correct for young people of either "sex" to push

older ladies in front of swiftly approaching motor vehicles or street cars.

A young man, if run over by an automobile driven by a strange lady, should lie perfectly still (unless dead) until an introduction can be arranged; the person driving the car usually speaks first.

In another type of burlesque, a serious subject is treated as if it were trivial, as in Donald Barthelme's "The Temptation of St. Anthony":

For this reason, in any case, people were always trying to see the inside of the saint's apartment, to find out if strange practices were being practiced there, or if you could discern, from the arrangement of the furniture and so on, if any had been, lately. They would ring the bell and pretend to be in the wrong apartment, these people, but St. Anthony would let them come in anyhow, even though he knew very well what they were thinking. They would stand around, perhaps a husband-and-wife team, and stare at the rug, which was ordinary beige wall-to-wall carpet from Kaufman's, and then at the coffee table and so on, they would sort of slide into the kitchen to see what he had been eating, if anything. They were always surprised to see that he ate more or less normal foods, perhaps a little heavy on the fried foods. I guess they expected roots and grasses.

(See: parody.)

C

Camp Fiction   A kind of frivolous, playful, fiction whose power depends on artifice, stylization and exaggeration in the subject and in the writing, rather than on the work's intrinsic content or moral sensibility.

Here, in Ronald Firbank's campy *Caprice*, the protagonist, Miss Sinquier, waits for a letter:

> In the gazebo at the extremity of the garden, by the new parterre, Miss Sinquier, in a morning wrapper, was waiting for the post.
>
> Through the trellis chinks, semi-circular, showed the Close, with its plentiful, seasoned timber and sedate, tall houses, a stimulating sequence, architecturally, of whitewash, stone and brick.
>
> Miss Sinquier stirred impatiently.
>
> Wretch!—to deliver at the Palace before the Deanery, when the Deanery was as near! . . .
>
> She waited.
>
> Through the Palace gates, at length, the fellow lurched, sorting as he came.
>
> "Dolt!"
>
> Coiled round and round like some sleek snake her future slumbered in it.
>
> Husband; lovers . . . little lives, perhaps—yet to be . . . besides voyages, bouquets, diamonds, chocolates, duels, casinos! . . .

She shivered.

"Anything for me, Hodge, to-day," she inquired, "by chance?"

"A fine morning, miss."

"Unusually."

It had come . . .

That large mauve envelope, with the wild handwriting and the haunting scent was from her.

Susan Sontag, in her famous essay "Notes on Camp," points out that camp is not only "the spirit of extravagance," but also involves a somewhat overdone, even vulgar quality, which may not be perceptible to its creator: "Camp," Sontag writes, "is a woman walking around in a dress made of three million feathers."

Truly excellent fiction with an exaggerated style and a less-than-serious subject usually is not considered camp; the term generally implies a certain failure on the part of the writer to attain a desired effect. Indeed, few writers say they want to create camp fiction; it is generally a term that is applied after the fact, by a less than completely impressed readership, although the reader may enjoy a work on "camp" terms. *(See: decadence.)*

Campus Novel   A work whose setting is a college or university.

The term often is narrowed to include novels with comic or satirical intent that are especially interested in showing the foibles of individual faculty members, students, and the university system itself. The campus novel form is similar to the *waiting-room fiction technique: a group of oddly assorted characters forced to interact in order to do their jobs.

The typical campus novel *protagonist is not a legitimate star in his field: Jim Dixon in Kingsley Amis' *Lucky Jim* primarily is interested in drinking and avoiding the attentions of a female colleague; the protagonist of Don DeLillo's *White Noise*, though head of the department of Hitler Studies at a respected college, does not speak German; the English professor protagonist in David Lodge's *Small World* does not know what the popular critical term "deconstruction" is because he did most of his studying in a TB sanitarium and did not have access to recent scholarship.

Still, the campus-novel protagonist is likely to be morally better and far more likeable than his fellow professors who take their fields of specialty very seriously. Here's Jim Dixon, answering the questions of a fellow instructor about why he became a specialist in medieval history:

> Dixon tried to laugh. ". . . the reason why I'm a medievalist, as you call it, is that the medieval papers were a soft option in the Leicester course, so I specialized in them. Then when I applied for the job here, I naturally made a big point of that, because it looked better to seem interested in something specific. It's why I got the job instead of that clever boy from Oxford who mucked himself up at the interview by chewing the fat about modern theories of interpretation. But I never guessed I'd be landed with all the medieval stuff and nothing but the medieval stuff." He repressed a desire to smoke, having finished his five o'clock cigarette at a quarter past three. . . .
>
> "Haven't you noticed how we all specialize in what we hate most?" Dixon asked, but Beesley, puffing away at his pipe, had already got up. Dixon's views on the Middle Ages themselves would have to wait until another time.

Canon The core works of literature that are commonly taught and written about, consisting of those that have been recognized over the years as important.

The concept of a canon of important writings was first conceived in the fourth century A.D., as it became necessary to decide which books would comprise the Bible.

Traditionally, a work becomes part of the canon by remaining influential to readers and to other writers over a period of time, usually about a hundred years. But in some instances, much less time has been necessary—in the cases of William Faulkner and Ernest Hemingway, for example.

Recent critics have pointed out that the literary canon is heavily weighted toward works by white men of European descent, to the exclusion of much work by women and minorities. Many now suggest that the canon either be expanded to include more work by women and minorities or that new, separate canons, comprising work by writers from different cultures, be created.

Card A term coined by Henry James to describe a memorable, vividly portrayed, eccentric minor character who does not change from the beginning of the work to the end. The card becomes unforgettable because she is so vividly portrayed, though the character is nearly always *flat and sometimes even a *caricature.

An example of a card is the charmingly obsequious and pompous Mr. Collins, from Jane Austen's *Pride and Prejudice*, who in his last appearance is as insensitive as he was in his first, writing a letter of condolence to his uncle over the fact that his daughter has run off with an improvident scoundrel, even living with him without the benefit of marriage:

> My dear Sir:
>
> I feel myself called upon by our relationship, and my situation in life, to condole with you on the grievous affliction you are now suffering under, of which we were yesterday informed by a letter from Hertfordshire . . . No arguments shall be wanting on my part that can alleviate so severe a misfortune, or that may comfort you under a circumstance that must be of all others most afflicting to a parent's mind. The death of your daughter would have been a blessing in comparison of this. And it is the more to be lamented because there is reason to suppose, as my dear Charlotte informs me, that this licentiousness of behaviour in your daughter has proceeded from a faulty degree of indulgence, though at the same time, for the consolation of yourself and Mrs. Bennet, I am inclined to think that her own disposition must be naturally bad, or she could not be guilty of such an enormity at so early an age.

Cards are not the *protagonists of their novels; part of their charm is how they, unlike most protagonists, never change; they remain the same no matter how far they are pushed. The card is not necessarily a completely comic character, of course; she can be a serious one, or even a sinister one. An example is old Miss Havisham, from Charles Dickens's *Great Expectations*, who, deranged after having been jilted on her wedding night, has not left her house in many years and dresses in her ancient, yellowed wedding gown. Miss Havisham has raised a young girl, Estella (with whom the protagonist Pip falls in love), and taught her to break men's hearts as revenge for her own abandonment so many years before.

Caricature   A work that exaggerates aspects or features of a character, generally for humorous or satiric purposes. The term is used less frequently in fiction than to describe certain kinds of visual art, such as cartooning.

The narrator of Jay McInerney's *Story of My Life* is a caricature of a rich girl who is empty-headed and selfish. It is unlikely that anyone in real life could appear so vapid:

> I try dialing Francesca but I'm getting this weird signal, then a computer-girl voice comes on and says, we're sorry, your service has been temporarily interrupted for nonpayment and I'm like, shit, not this again, fucking Jeannie. I don't know, this happens every other month, just about, and suddenly I'm cut off from all my friends and delivery service from the deli. Trauma city. Last time it happened we moved into a room at the Plaza for a couple of days and charged it to Jeannie's dad while we waited for the check to clear, but after he got that bill, he called the hotel and told them basically to shoot us on sight, or at least not let us charge to his corporate account. Between phone calls and room service I guess we did do some serious damage. Rebecca was in Paris for some reason, some guy, and we had the line open to France for most of the afternoon one time, taking turns with Becca while the other one went down to Trader Vic's for refills and all these fat out-of-town businessmen thinking we were hookers . . .

(See: burlesque, parody, satire.)

Catharsis *(sometimes katharsis)* A term taken from Aristotle's discussion of dramatic tragedy, describing the feeling a reader should have after viewing (or reading) a tragedy: not depression, but a kind of relief mixed with elation.

Ideally, catharsis can make the individual reader feel kinship with all of humanity and come to some kind of an understanding of the world's unavoidable sufferings. The concept is an abstract one, however, and the experience of catharsis will come more easily to an audience member at a theater, in the company of others, than to a lone reader. Sitting in a theater, crowded among other people, the concept of humanity must necessarily remain more immediate.

Even watching a video alone at home is a less private, personal experience than reading a book, since the characters in a movie can function almost in the same way other audience members can in a theater. After the senseless assassination of a singer on a stage in Robert Altman's *Nashville*, for example, the film ends with close-up shots of the stunned, silent faces of the members of the audience. It is easy for the viewer to feel like part of this audience, just another face in the crowd, enjoying the final song, "It Don't Worry Me," and at the same time feel a sense of guilt about forgetting the murder so quickly.

Practically speaking, a reader may be said to feel catharsis at the end of an unhappy story if she leaves feeling an emotion other than simple depression, or annoyance at the obstinance of limited or driven characters. A writer can help this along by preparing the reader for an unhappy ending early on, especially through *foreshadowing.

Center of Consciousness *(central consciousness, central intelligence, reflector)* The undramatized third-person narrator who tells a story.

Even when the reader also sees into the minds of one or more characters, there's still a narrator—someone different from the author—telling the story, through whose eyes events and details are filtered; who is, in fact, able to interpret the details of what is going on better than the character himself. Henry James called such narrators "reflectors," and their purpose often is to provide a unifying vision for a work of fiction.

Here's Michael Lewin, the unlikable protagonist of Dan Jacobson's "Led Astray" reflecting on the future life he sees for himself:

[His affair with Jill Stanlake, a college student he lives with] was something that Lewin intended one day—when he was married, settled, and successful—to look back on with pleasure, gratitude, and amusement. He often gave himself pleasure now by anticipating his emotions then. He doubted that the affair would come to an end as little as he doubted that he would one day be successful. He was a research student at King's College, London, having just come down from Oxford, and was supposed to be working for his Ph.D. on a grant he had received but he didn't intend making an academic career for himself. He was attracted by the idea of going into television, or journalism of the superior kind. If he had had money, he might have gone to the Bar. He was, anyway, on the lookout for openings, and was sure he would find one, eventually. He claimed to despise failure, and, indeed, looked down on Jill because she had failed to marry the man she wanted to marry and had accepted as a lover someone (himself) who had told her that he didn't love her.

We learn a lot about Lewin in this passage, but it is not Lewin who is giving us this information. It is a narrator who sees through and is able to convey to us the shallowness of Lewin's plans, and to let us know subtly that things will not turn out as he desires. *(See: implied author.)*

Chapter A significant, definite section or segment in the narration of a novel. New chapters usually begin on a new page; chapters usually are numbered and are sometimes titled, providing an easy way for the reader who pauses at the end of a chapter to remember where to begin reading the book again.

A chapter break often is the author's indication that the reader has reached a definite pause in the plot or thematic structure of a book. It often is called for when one scene has just ended and a new one is about to begin, for example, or if the writer is about to pass a considerable period of time without writing about it.

In *Henderson the Rain King*, Saul Bellow's narrator and protagonist, Gene Henderson, has gone to Africa on a kind of spiritual pilgrimage. Henderson's journey becomes more complicated when his new friend, the king of the tribe with whom he has been living, dies after being mauled by a lion.

The following chapter break, while it does not show a change of scene from one chapter to the next, shows a definite break in the action, moving from the objective description of the house where Henderson is taken after the king's death to a more thoughtful description of his thoughts about his life and his grief:

> The small house built of flat slabs had two wooden doors of the stockade type which opened into two chambers. His body was laid down in one of these. Into the other they put me. I scarcely knew what was happening anyway, and I let them lead me in and bolt the door.
>
> 21
>
> At one time, much earlier in this life of mine, suffering had a certain spice. Later on it started to lose this spice; it became merely dirty, and, as I told my son Edward in California, I couldn't bear it anymore. Damn! I was tired of being such a monster of grief.

However, authors sometimes try for other effects as they explore the relationships between the end of one chapter and the beginning of the next. An example of extreme continuity between chapters—the second chapter begins just a second or so after the first has ended—occurs much earlier in *Henderson the Rain King*, when the narrator describes a quarrel with his wife, one of the events that caused him to make the pilgrimage to Africa:

> ... when I saw tears I lost my head and yelled, "I'm going to blow my brains out! I'm shooting myself. I didn't forget to pack my pistol. I've got it on me now."
>
> "Oh, Gene!" she cried, and covered up her face and ran away. I'll tell you why.
>
> 2
>
> Because her father had committed suicide in that same way, with a pistol.

Sometimes writers use very short chapters to create special effects. For example, Joan Didion creates exaggerated discontinuity with her extra-short chapters in *Play It As It Lays*. The quick, hectic chapters work in part to characterize the deeply disturbed protagonist, Maria, mirroring the disconnectedness of her life. Here is chapter fifty-two (of eighty-four) in its entirety:

> Maria made a list of things she would never do. She would never: walk through the Sands or Caesar's alone after midnight. She would never: ball at a party, do S-M unless she wanted to, borrow furs from Abe Lipsey, deal. She would never: carry a Yorkshire in Beverly Hills.

Characterization   The techniques a writer uses to portray the people who perform the actions in a story.

Many contemporary writers consider characterization the most important element of fiction, in part because it is often how the events that take place in a story affect the characters—how they think and feel about those events—that really matters, rather than simply the fact that the events have occurred.

Techniques that help the writer characterize characters include *description, both physical and of the characters' actions; *dialogue; and *interior monologue.

Here, in *Of Mice and Men*, John Steinbeck uses a character's physical appearance as a tool to characterize her:

> She had full, rouged lips and wide-spaced eyes, heavily made up. Her fingernails were red. Her hair hung in little rolled clusters, like sausages. She wore a cotton house dress and red mules, on the insteps of which were little bouquets of red ostrich feathers.

In this passage from Somerset Maugham's "The Outstation" it is Mr. Warburton's reactions to what he sees that characterize him; his pride at the neatness of the guard characterizes him as a bit snobbish and persnickety. The passage also serves another function, however, helping to set the scene of colonial India in ways unrelated to characterization:

The new assistant arrived in the afternoon. When the Resident, Mr. Warburton, was told that the prahu was in sight he put on his solar topee and went down to the landing-stage. The guard, eight little Dyak soldiers, stood to attention as he passed. He noted with satisfaction that their bearing was martial, their uniforms neat and clean, and their guns shining. They were a credit to him. From the landing-stage he watched the bend of the river round which in a moment the boat would sweep. He looked very smart in his spotless ducks and white shoes. He held under his arm a gold-headed Malacca cane which had been given him by the Sultan of Perak.

It also is interesting to note that characters can reveal themselves in ways they do not mean to, as the college student Bonny Baginski does, pathetically, in her pretentious "Statement of Purpose" for a graduate school application in Charles Newman's *The Five-Thousandth Baritone*:

Scholastic Objectives
In going into Graduate study (M.A./Ph.D.) my field of concentration will be Post Modern Music and the teaching of Music Education. I myself am an actress, musician and singer, and am interested not only in all the Humanities and Social Sciences but in the way people influence and especially relate to one another. . . . While I intend to continue to perform I will also continue my researches into other relevant interdisciplinary fields, and learn Greek and Latin. I am interested in a realm of discourse where both forms and meanings achieve an autonomous existence, but which have also created a truly Western ill-definedness of role problems.

While many writers base characters on real people they have known, others create characters entirely through imagination. French writer André Gide remarked:

The creation of character does not depend upon the writer's having a good memory of fascinating people he has known.

If I spoiled the portrait of old La Perouse, it was because I clung too closely to reality. The difficult thing is inventing when you are encumbered by memory.

(See: antihero, protagonist.)

Charged Image A term coined by poet Ezra Pound to describe the dominant picture in a work, usually a visual picture that combines both an emotion and an idea. The charged image must be an important image that increases in significance during the course of the story. Ideally, all of the important elements of the story, especially theme and character, will come together in this single important image.

Charged images appear less often in fiction than in poetry, but they still are as important and can be as intense as in poetry. A charged image will be the picture that the reader is left with after completing the work, the one that will remain with him even after he has forgotten some of a book's details.

An example of such an image appears in F. Scott Fitzgerald's *The Great Gatsby*—the green light at the end of Daisy's dock, which Nick Carraway first notices early in the novel and observes Gatsby watching:

> I decided to call to him. Miss Baker had mentioned him at dinner, and that would do for an introduction. But I didn't call to him, for he gave a sudden intimation that he was content to be alone—he stretched out his arms toward the dark water in a curious way, and, far as I was from him, I could have sworn he was trembling. Involuntarily I glanced seaward—and distinguished nothing except a single green light, minute and faraway, that might have been at the end of a dock. When I looked once more for Gatsby he had vanished, and I was alone again in the unquiet darkness.

The green light is a symbol of the attitude Gatsby has taken throughout his quest for Daisy; in the end it becomes ironic, since he really didn't have a green light to go ahead and try to penetrate the social strata and win Daisy, as Carraway tells us at the end of the novel:

And as I sat there brooding on the old, unknown world, I thought of Gatsby's wonder when he first picked out the green light at the end of Daisy's dock. He had come a long way to this blue lawn, and his dream must have seemed so close that he could hardly fail to grasp it. He did not know that it was already behind him, somewhere back in that vast obscurity beyond the city, where the dark fields of the republic rolled on under the night.

Gatsby believed in the green light, the orgiastic future that year by year recedes before us. It eluded us then, but that's no matter—tomorrow we will run faster, stretch out our arms farther. . . . And one fine morning—

Chronicle Novel   A type of novel that spans a wide range of times and places and includes a huge number of characters whom the writer has specifically chosen to represent different aspects of the economic and social conditions of the time. Often there is no single protagonist.

The term often is used synonymously with "saga novel." However, there are differences. The chronicle novel is not likely to have a mythic, universal theme, but a saga does, with its origins in the medieval Scandinavian works. The chronicle novel is more likely to take place over a period of years rather than generations, as does the saga.

An example of a chronicle novel is John Dos Passos' *U.S.A.* trilogy, whose characters are carefully chosen to show how human beings exploit one another and are ultimately willing to give up their ideals, especially because of flaws in the capitalist system, although the trilogy also points out flaws in communism.

The trilogy's first book, *The 42nd Parallel*, follows characters ranging from a successful but corrupt entrepreneur, to a printer who keeps talking about joining the Mexican Revolution but never can bring himself to do so, to a young woman who feels that through her job she has grown beyond her own family and rejects the brother she had once adored. The book spans the globe, from various parts of the United States to Mexico and to France. *(See: family chronicle.)*

Circular Structure   A form in which a story's conclusion shows a return to the situation (generally an undesirable situation) that was present at the work's beginning.

An example is Ambrose Bierce's "An Occurrence at Owl Creek Bridge," which begins:

> A man stood upon a railroad bridge in Northern Alabama, looking down into the swift water twenty feet below. The man's hands were behind his back, the wrists bound with a cord. A rope closely encircled his neck. It was attached to a stout cross-timber above his head and the slack fell to the level of his knees.

The man, Peyton Farquhar, about to be hanged as a traitor in the Civil War, suddenly escapes the noose and makes his way back to his wife on his family plantation. When it seems that the story is about to end with Farquhar's being reunited with his wife, the scene suddenly shifts back to the bridge. We learn that Farquhar's escape has been a dream or hallucination, as the last paragraph makes clear:

> Peyton Farquhar was dead; his body, with a broken neck, swung gently from side to side beneath the timbers of the Owl Creek Bridge.

Other times, a plot's circular structure is meant to show that the *protagonist is destined to pass again through the same difficulties she has just weathered, because she has failed to make the kind of psychological or spiritual growth the reader has hoped for; she has learned nothing during the course of the plot and therefore is likely to relive the same dilemmas she has gone through before.

Hilma Wolitzer's *In the Flesh*, for example, opens with the characters, a young couple, moving into their first apartment. The couple, expecting a child, faces all kinds of emotional difficulties, separates for a while, and then reunites. At the end, reconciled, more mature, they think they're on the right track. Still, the book ends with the characters about to move into their first house—basically the same situation they were in at the beginning of the book—implying that they have not learned as much about themselves as they have hoped, that their troubles probably are not over.

The term also can be used to describe works in which young people seem destined to repeat the errors of their parents; often the circular plot shows the children's circle through rebellion right back to the undesirable behavior of their parents. This scene from Ira Levin's *The Boys From Brazil* ends with the scene of a boy painting a picture of a crowd watching a "really good person that they loved and respected" in a stadium:

> He bent his sharp nose closer to the paper and gave dot-mouths to the smaller people. His forelock fell. He bit his lip, squinting his deep blue eyes. Dot, dot, dot. He could hear the people cheering, roaring; a beautiful growing love-thunder that built and built, and then pounded, pounded, pounded, pounded.
> Sort of like in those old Hitler movies.

Unfortunately, the young artist is an actual clone of Adolf Hitler; the assumption is that society is destined to repeat the same mistakes it made early in the twentieth century. *(See: naturalism.)*

Cliché A word or phrase that has been used so many times that its original vitality has become lost through repetition.

"She was as quiet as a mouse" and "it was so hot you could fry eggs on the sidewalk" are obvious examples of clichés; they certainly contain kernels of truth, but they have been used in so many circumstances they have become trite. "Beads of sweat dripped down her forehead" is an example of a less familiar but still overused phrase.

It is possible, however, to play with well-worn phrases in new ways, a technique used frequently by *metafictionists. In Donald Barthelme's "The Falling Dog," a narrator contemplates the ramifications of having been knocked to the pavement by a dog that leapt on him from a high window. One *crot begins by listing some clichés relating to the word "dog":

> die like a
> dog-eat-dog
> proud as a dog in shoes
> dogfight
> doggerel
> dogmatic

The first two phrases on the list definitely are clichés, but they have been transformed and made almost new again by appearing in the unfamiliar context of Barthelme's story. The third phrase, "proud as a dog in shoes," is not a cliché but sounds as if it could become one someday, because it describes a concept so vividly that many people might want to use it.

Gordon Lish's "The Merry Chase," on the other hand, consists almost entirely of clichés that have been strung together for humorous effect, as is clear from this first paragraph:

> Don't tell me. Do me a favor and let me guess. Be honest with me, tell the truth, don't make me laugh. Tell me, don't make me have to tell you, do I have to tell you that when you're hot, you're hot, that when you're dead, you're dead? Because you know what I know? I know you like I know myself. I know you like the back of my hand. I know you like a book. I know you inside out. I know you like you'll never know.

(See: overwriting, stock character, stock situation.)

Climax *(turning point)*   The point in a story's action when tension is at its highest, generally a point close to the end of the work.

In William Carlos Williams' short story, "The Use of Force," the *narrator, a doctor, makes a house call at a home in which the patient is a little girl who refuses to open her mouth so he can make a diagnosis. Finally, enraged despite himself, the doctor forces the screaming, hysterical child's mouth open; the doctor's overwhelming, guilty rage at the sick child as he finally is able to see into her throat forms the climax of the story:

> But the worst of it was that I too had got beyond reason. I could have torn the child apart in my own fury and enjoyed it. . . .
>
> In a final unreasoning assault I overpowered the child's neck and jaws. I forced the heavy silver spoon back of her teeth and down her throat till she gagged. And there it was— both tonsils covered with membrane.

A climax will be followed, in a conventional story, by the *denoue-ment, the tying up of any loose ends at the end.

The term "climax" occasionally is used as a synonym for *crisis, but in fact, a work might have many crises and only one climax. *(See: crisis.)*

Comic and Grotesque Names   Names that are humorous in them-selves, regardless of the characters they describe.

Some examples of this type of name are Dr. Slop (from Laurence Sterne's *Tristram Shandy*), Brother Wrestrum (presumably pro-nounced "restroom," from Ralph Ellison's *Invisible Man*), William Faulkner's Montgomery Ward Snopes and Wallstreet Panic Snopes (and their relatives, Mink, Eck and Flem Snopes, from "The Hamlet" and "The Town"), and Recktall Brown (from William Gaddis' *The Recognitions*).

Comic and grotesque names may provide some easy amusement (although the joke can wear off quickly with repetition), but odd names for characters should serve more subtle functions as well. A comic name can give some immediate information about the family background of the character. (What kind of person would name a child "Wallstreet Panic"?) A comic name also can be a subtle reminder of the author's feelings about a character. The speaker in *Invisible Man*, for example, initially admires the self-assured, committed Brother Wrestrum; his name reminds the reader that the author does not share the speaker's view—and neither should the reader.

An out-of-the-ordinary name also has a subtle and not-always-intended purpose: It must at least for a moment take the reader out of the story, reminding him that he is reading a work of fiction, not actually becoming involved in someone's real life.

Comic Relief   The insertion of a comic scene or character into a work that generally is serious or even tragic.

Comic relief temporarily releases some of the tension the reader feels while reading the serious work and also can heighten the work's ultimate tragic effect, by showing the contrast between the humor of the moment and the sadness of the overall situation.

In this early scene from Leo Tolstoy's *The Death of Ivan Ilych*, the bit of comedy surrounding Peter Ivanovich's sitting down and Ivan

Ilych's insincere widow's getting her shawl caught on the table leg, coming in the middle of what would seem to be a very serious scene, takes the attention away from the death of Ivan Ilych and removes much of the tragic feeling from the scene:

> When they reached the drawing-room, upholstered in pink cretonne and lighted by a dim lamp, they sat down at the table—she on a sofa and Peter Ivanovich on a low pouffe, the springs of which yielded spasmodically under his weight. Praskovya Fëderovna had been on the point of warning him to take another seat, but felt that such a warning was out of keeping with her present condition and so changed her mind. As he sat down on the pouffe Peter Ivanovich recalled how Ivan Ilych had arranged this room and had consulted him regarding this pink cretonne with green leaves. The whole room was full of furniture and knick-knacks, and on her way to the sofa the lace of the widow's black shawl caught on the carved edge of the table. Peter Ivanovich rose to detach it, and the springs of the pouffe, relieved of his weight, rose also and gave him a push. The widow began detaching her shawl herself, and Peter Ivanovich again sat down, suppressing the rebellious springs of the pouffe under him. But the widow had not quite freed herself and Peter Ivanovich got up again, and again the pouffe rebelled and even creaked. When this was all over she took out a clean cambric handkerchief and begin to weep. The episode with the shawl had cooled Peter Ivanovich's emotions and he sat there with a sullen look on his face.

Another function of comic relief is as a method of avoiding *bathos: at least the writer is showing the reader he's aware of a certain amount of absurdity, of the potential for melodrama, in a situation. Comic relief also increases the distance the reader feels from the characters—after all, you're unlikely to become deeply involved with a character when you've just laughed at his funeral.

Computer Fiction Often used synonymously with *"hyperfiction" or "interactive fiction," the term describes fiction written in such a way that the computer is responsible for generating some of the material in the fiction—not, as is usual, just for word processing.

Computer programs to write fiction are much less common than those to write poetry; poetry-writing programs are easier to write, and the plotlessness and repeated words and images that often are a part of computer-generated work have more in common with certain types of poetry than with fiction. Still, software programs for fiction writers do exist.

In 1993, Carol Publishing published computer scientist Scott French's novel, *Just This Once*, which he wrote via a computer program. He crafted the program to create a book as much as possible in plot and language like the romances of Jacqueline Susann, author of *Valley of the Dolls*. According to *New York* magazine, however, the book had trouble finding a publisher because of threatened lawsuits by Susann's estate, which, indeed, did take place but were settled out of court.

Writers also have published traditionally generated novels through computer networks, and "computer fiction" sometimes is used to refer to these books. With more and more people logging onto on-line services like Prodigy and the Internet system, writers have a huge possible audience for their work without having to go through a traditional publisher. They just type in their work and hope someone downloads it.

Indeed, Greg Costikyan—who first "published" his science fiction series through the Prodigy on-line service—became the first writer, in 1993, to have his work move from on-line publishing to paper when his series, *By the Sword*, was published in hardcover by Tor Books. Computer publishing, indeed, is a possibility whose promise is just beginning to be explored. *(See: hyperfiction.)*

Confessional Novel A work of fiction whose main reason for being is to allow the first-person protagonist to confess to the reader a crime, transgression or sin, or a series of them—usually something potentially shocking or embarrassing.

The protagonist is not necessarily a stand-in for the author, as Moll certainly is not in Daniel Defoe's confessional work, *Moll Flanders*. On the other hand, the protagonist might have a close relationship with the author. This example comes from Erica Jong's *Fear of Flying*:

Of course it all began with my mother. My mother: Judith Stoloff White, also known as Jude. Not obscure. But hard to get down on paper. My love for her and my hate for her are so bafflingly intertwined that I can hardly see her. I never know who is who. She is me and I am she and we are all together. The umbilical cord which connects us has never been cut so it has sickened and rotted and turned black. The very intensity of our need has made us denounce each other. We want to eat each other up. We want to strangle each other with love. We want to run screaming from each other in panic before either of these things can happen.

And later:

I met my first "phallos" at thirteen years and ten months on my parents' avocado-green silk living-room couch, in the shade of an avocado-green avocado tree, grown by my avocado green-thumbed mother from an avocado pit. The "phallos" belonged to Steve Applebaum, a junior and art major when I was a freshman and art major, and it had a most memorable abstract design of blue veins on its Kandinsky-purple underside. In retrospect, it was a remarkable specimen: circumcised, of course, and huge (what is huge when you have no frame of reference?), and with an impressive life of its own.

Conflict   The struggle between two or more contrary forces that generally is at the heart of any fictional work's *plot. Without conflict, it is difficult for a work to develop the *suspense that very often is necessary for a reader to retain interest.

Generally, conflict arises out of the struggle of the *protagonist to achieve a definite goal, and the goal must be compelling enough that a reasonable protagonist would not simply walk away from the struggle that creates the conflict. It is easy for the reader to ask, "Why doesn't she just quit her job and get a new one?" say, in a boss-employee conflict. There must be sufficient motivation for the employee to keep the job. If we know, for example, that the character cannot leave her job because she already has left ten other jobs and is worried that she will never be able to get another one, the situation will seem believable and the conflict engrossing.

Conflict generally is divided into four categories:

- man against nature;
- man against man;
- man against society;
- man against some aspect of himself.

Another type of conflict that sometimes is cited is man against fate, or against the gods; in practice, however, this kind of conflict usually is accomplished through one of the first four categories of conflict.

In a novel, conflict rarely is limited to a single choice from the above list; there may either be a combination of more than one type of conflict, or more than one separate type may be brought into play.

In Jane Austen's *Pride and Prejudice*, for example, Elizabeth Bennet fights against the various characters who try to thwart her sister's search for happiness; against a flaw in her own character, i.e., the prejudice that prevents her from changing her first impression of Mr. Darcy; and against the society that rules that her father's estate be entailed on the odious Mr. Collins.

Connotation　The emotional associations a word has, as opposed to its dictionary meaning, which is its *denotation.

A skunk, for example, might be defined uninterestingly as a black-and-white mammal. When the word "skunk" is used, however, a reader thinks of someone who is conniving, tricky and low-down, because of the associations of a skunk's smell.

A heavy use of connotative, or suggestive, words will bring the style of a fictional work closer to that of poetry. Some writers known for their connotative language are Virginia Woolf, Jean Cocteau, J.P. Donleavy and Vladimir Nabokov. Here, Humbert Humbert, the narrator of Nabokov's *Lolita*, ponders the connotations of the name:

> Lolita, light of my life, fire of my loins. My sin, my soul.
> Lo-lee-ta: the tip of the tongue taking a trip of three steps
> down the palate to tap, at three, on the teeth. Lo. Lee. Ta.

She was Lo, plain Lo, in the morning, standing four feet ten in one sock. She was Lola in slacks. She was Dolly at school. She was Dolores on the dotted line. But in my arms she was always Lolita.

(See: denotation.)

Conspiratorial Mystique The relationship a reader feels with a piece of difficult fiction, generally contemporary *metafiction, which demands an intense amount of time and effort on the reader's part to sort out what is going on.

If the reader comes out of the book feeling the work has been worth it, the conspiratorial mystique effect probably has taken hold. There is also a sort of snob appeal—that this reader, unlike so many others, has had the patience and natural intelligence necessary to sort out the difficult work. By separating the reader from the many nonreaders of a difficult work, the book pulls the reader closer to it, emotionally, than a less difficult book might.

In this passage, the first few paragraphs from William Gaddis' *J.R.*, for example, the reader may feel as much confusion as the lawyer who is trying to get the two elderly characters to sign a document; completing the book can give a subtly satisfying feeling absent from coming out of, say, a work of popular fiction, in the same way that a runner might feel more satisfaction at completing a marathon than a shorter race:

> —Money . . . ? in a voice that rustled.
> —Paper, yes.
> —And we'd never even seen it. Paper money.
> —We never saw paper money till we came east.
> —It looked so strange the first time we saw it. Lifeless.
> —You couldn't believe it was worth a thing.
> —Not after Father jingling his change.
> —Those were silver dollars.
> —And silver halves, yes and quarters, Julia. The ones from his pupils. I can hear him now . . .
> Sunlight, pocketed in a cloud, spilled suddenly broken across the floor through the leaves of the trees outside.

—Coming up the veranda, how he jingled when he walked.

—He'd have his pupils rest the quarters that they brought him on the backs of their hands when they did their scales. He charged fifty cents a lesson, you see, Mr. . . .

—Coen, without the h. Now if both you ladies . . .

—Why, it's just like that story about Father's dying wish to have his bust sunk in Vancouver harbor, and his ashes sprinkled on the water there, about James and Thomas out in the rowboat, and both of them hitting at the bust with their oars because it was hollow and wouldn't go down, and the storm coming up while they were out there, blowing his ashes back into their beards.

Control   The idea that the writer in every case knows exactly what he will do next with his story, that no effects are accidental. A book giving the impression of control certainly will not seem improvised, or loose—unless that is the impression the writer wants to give. The difficulty is that a controlled novel can give the impression of seeming mechanical or contrived.

The concept of control includes the idea of *le mot juste*, that the writer must be in control of every word, that he cannot let sloppiness rule his words.

Some writers, indeed, are suspicious of the idea of control, feeling that too much control will make the work seem contrived, that conscious control can close the work to different types of improvisation and subconscious inspiration. Other writers—those drawn to *surrealism, for example—feel that writing with control will seem dishonest, that the controlled writer will never be able to reach the true heart of his story. *(See:* le mot juste.)*

Conventions   Basic aspects of a work that readers accept, although in real life such premises might seem improbable.

In real life, it is unlikely that a character stands and tells her story to a listener without pausing, in great detail, for what would amount to hundreds of pages at a time. But this is exactly what happens in most novels with first-person narrators, like, for example, Mark Twain's *The Adventures of Huckleberry Finn*:

> You don't know about me, without you have read a book by
> the name of The Adventures of Tom Sawyer, but that ain't
> no matter. That book was made by Mr. Mark Twain, and he
> told the truth, mainly. There was things which he stretched,
> but mainly he told the truth. I never seen anybody but lied,
> one time or another, without it was Aunt Polly, or the widow,
> or maybe Mary. Aunt Polly—Tom's Aunt Polly, she is—and
> Mary, and the Widow Douglas, is all told about in that
> book—which is mostly a true book; with some stretchers,
> as I said before.

In the *epistolary novel, for example, we must take for granted that a real person would write constant letters to another, and that these letters would be coherent enough for an outside party to understand. In Samuel Richardson's *Pamela*, we accept the fact that a servant girl would be educated enough to write such literate letters—and so very frequently. *(See: donnée.)*

Crisis   A point in a story in which tension is high because a character is forced to make an important, or even—if the story has that much at stake—potentially life-changing decision.

A novel may well contain a number of crises, but it is difficult for a short story to develop more than one in a relatively small amount of space. The final crisis before the story's resolution, presumably at a point in which the character faces the greatest amount of *conflict and difficulty, is called the *climax.

In Frank O'Connor's "First Confession," the first crisis comes early:

> When Mother was at work and my grandmother made the
> dinner I wouldn't touch it. Nora once tried to make me, but
> I hid under the table from her and took the bread-knife with
> me for protection. Nora let on to be very indignant (she
> wasn't, of course, but she knew Mother saw through her, so
> she sided with Gran) and came after me. I lashed out at her
> with the bread-knife, and after that she left me alone. I stayed
> there till Mother came in from work and made my dinner,
> but when Father came in later Nora said in a shocked voice:
> "Oh, Dadda, do you know what Jackie did at dinnertime?"

Then, of course, it all came out; Father gave me a flaking; Mother interfered, and for days after that he didn't speak to me and Mother barely spoke to Nora. And all because of that old woman! God knows, I was heart-scalded.

The next crisis occurs when the narrator, Jackie, must make his first communion and fears he has broken all ten commandments by his hatred of his grandmother. He is afraid of the priest and at the same time worries that if he makes a "bad confession," something terrible will happen to him.

The climax of the story does not come until nearly the end, when the boy finally confesses everything to the priest, and the priest takes his side against his sister, commenting that, "Someone will go for her with a bread-knife one day, and he won't miss her." This example points out what is easy to miss from the dour *connotations of the word "crisis"—that a crisis can mark a happy turn of events, rather than an unhappy one. *(See: climax.)*

Crot A term used in John Gardner's *The Art of Fiction* to describe one of the short, discrete sections of text separated by white space (or occasionally by asterisks) that form the type of story sometimes called a *narrative collage. Crot stories often take their effectiveness from their reflection of the disconnectedness, chaos, and absurdity of contemporary life, and from the odd juxtapositions of time and place that the reader makes as he reads from crot to crot.

The most common length for a crot seems to be a couple of paragraphs, and the individual crots may not at first seem to relate to each other closely: The movement from one to the next is abrupt, often transitionless. In addition to asterisks, crots also can be separated by numbers, or even titles, which William Gass uses in "In the Heart of the Heart of the Country," and which make the story look like a miniature novel with short but fully developed chapters.

Tom Wolfe writes of the crot: "In the hands of a writer who really understands the device, it will have you making crazy leaps of logic, leaps you never dreamed of before." The danger is that the story will degenerate into a series of thematically unrelated anecdotes whose logical organization never becomes clear.

Here are two crots from Donald Barthelme's 1970 story, "Views of My Father Weeping":

*

My father throws his ball of knitting up in the air. The orange wool hangs there.

*

My father regards the tray of pink cupcakes. Then he jams his thumb into each cupcake, into the top. Cupcake by cupcake. A thick smile spreads over the face of each cupcake.

(See: narrative collage.)

Cyberpunk   A type of science fiction especially prevalent in the 1980s, usually set in the near future and focusing on the relationships among human beings and computers and other forms of advanced technology.

This example comes from William Gibson's 1984 *Neuromancer*, which generally is considered the first and most influential work of cyberpunk. This passage deals with a typical cyberpunk theme, that of human beings who have been physically altered by new technology:

> Julius Deane was one hundred and thirty-five years old, his metabolism assiduously warped by a weekly fortune in serums and hormones. His primary hedge against aging was a yearly pilgrimage to Tokyo, where genetic surgeons re-set the code of his DNA, a procedure unavailable in Chiba.

Cyberpunk protagonists tend to be isolated, rebellious male *anti-heroes from the margins of society (the "punk" part of the word), drifting through a kind of meaningless, shattered world. The *tone tends to be cool, calculatedly anti-sentimental, as in this excerpt from *Neuromancer*.

> Case was twenty-four. At twenty-two, he'd been a cowboy, a rustler, one of the best in the Sprawl. He'd been trained by the best, by McCoy Pauley and Bobby Quine, legends in the biz. He'd operated on an almost permanent adrenaline high,

a byproduct of youth and proficiency, jacked into a custom cyberspace deck that projected his disembodied consciousness into the consensual hallucination that was the matrix. A thief, he'd worked for other, wealthier thieves, employers who provided the exotic software required to penetrate the bright walls of corporate systems, opening windows into rich fields of data.

Cyberpunk is popular even with readers not usually interested in science fiction and often is considered to transcend the bounds of "hard" science fiction because it uses many of the techniques of *postmodernist fiction and concerns itself with postmodernist issues: how human beings can respond to the increasingly fragmented, uncertain and impersonal society. Indeed, writers of cyberpunk tend to be influenced as much by writers like William Burroughs and Thomas Pynchon as by earlier science fiction writers.

Cyberpunk differs from postmodernist fiction, however, in the way that it emphasizes the interconnectedness of humans and machines, giving the machines as much emphasis as the humans, with the boundaries between humans and machines, between reality and irreality, frequently effaced.

The term "cyberpunk" also is in general use outside of its science fiction context, with cyberpunks equated with "hackers" and others who perpetrate more-or-less malicious computer crimes.

D

Dada A literary movement, begun in Zurich by poet Tristan Tzara in 1916, which flourished until the early 1920s. Its influence lingers in contemporary experimental fiction.

The dadaists, whose group included visual artists as well as writers, believed in using art to protest what they felt were the increasingly irrational conventions of life during the violence and destruction of World War I and the twentieth century in general. The dadaists' goal, indeed, was to destroy conventional art forms, to show the irrationality of contemporary human existence. Dada artist Hans Arp said of the dada movement:

> Dada aimed to destroy the reasonable deceptions of man and recover the natural and unreasonable order. Dada wanted to replace the logical nonsense of the men of today by the illogically senseless. . . . Dada gave the Venus de Milo an enema and permitted Laocoön and his sons to relieve themselves after thousands of years of struggle with the good sausage Python.

The word "dada" was chosen at random from a dictionary, and in dada art and fiction, objects were combined at random without consideration of logic or sense.

Louis Aragon's 1920 *Anicet*, which also includes the unforgettable line, "A taxi will easily hold five, but when the fifth is a dead body, it is not a simple matter to force yourself to slip your legs beneath the seat," is the best of the few dadaist novels. It begins:

Anicet remembered nothing of his secondary-school studies but the rule of the three unities and the relativity of time and space; these comprised his knowledge of art and life. He remained firm to these like iron, and they shaped his conduct. The result of this was some bizarrenesses that did not alarm even his family until the day when he proceeded on a public road to the indecent outskirts: he understood then that he was a poet, a revelation that first stunned him, but which he accepted simply, with modesty, with the conviction of not being able to cut loose from it. His parents, without a doubt, fell in with the universal opinion before doing what all parents of poets did: they called their son an ingrate and encouraged him to travel. He took care not to resist them, since he knew that neither railroads nor steamers would change his Noumenon.

Eventually less extremist writers absorbed the techniques and attitudes of the dadaists, and the group is now appreciated in particular for its influence on the surrealists and on playwrights of the theater of the absurd.

Dead Metaphor   A figure of speech that has been used so often that the literal part of the image is not even considered; the metaphorical meaning is the only one the reader appreciates at all.

When a person is described as a windbag, no one forms the mental image of a bag full of wind; the mental picture formed is of a stuffy, pompous person who will not stop talking and pontificating. When someone says we live in a "dog-eat-dog" world, adults understand the phrase without picturing dogs eating each other. Writers, however, must be careful not to create inappropriate images through the use of dead metaphors, as the image of a dog eating another dog might be inappropriate in a story that had nothing to do with violence.

"Dead metaphor" often is used as simply a synonym for *cliché, and can include figures of speech other than metaphors. *(See: cliché.)*

Decadence   A derogatory term used to describe fiction whose qualities include extreme self-consciousness and stylization, bizarre themes, exaggerated theatrical qualities, and, sometimes, a mixture of various genres. Used in its larger meaning, "decadence" describes the period of decline that follows a great era, as the third and second centuries B.C. are considered somewhat decadent in Greek art after the brilliance of the fourth century.

While the fiction of the *metafictionists of the 1960s and 1970s seems to fit the definition of decadence in some ways, it is important to remember that the term "decadent" is sometimes used by conventional critics to berate *avant-garde works in general. Indeed, work that once was called decadent—the work of the impressionist painters, for example, and of writers like James Joyce and William Faulkner—often later becomes part of the established *canon. *(See: camp fiction.)*

Deconstructive Fiction   A kind of fiction either consciously or unconsciously related to the philosophical and critical movement called deconstruction, which enjoyed particular popularity among U.S. scholars in the 1970s and 1980s.

Deconstruction, which is based on the ideas of the French thinker Jacques Derrida, calls for an extremely close examination of even the smallest passages of a work, with the aim of pointing out that the *connotations of language often give words different meanings from their literal ones. Deconstruction calls for taking apart both passages from a work and entire works of art, with the hope of discovering these hidden connotations.

This example of the deconstructive technique comes from a speech by Derrida reported in *The New York Times Magazine*, in which Derrida takes a closer-than-usual look at the inner meanings of the phrase "keynote address":

> I deserve less than ever to give a "keynote address," because I want to recall that a "key" can always get lost, and an "address" always fail to reach its "address."

The purpose of this deconstruction often is to point out the impossibility of a writer ever creating a work that will be completely clear to every reader, because every reader approaches a work with different expectations and preconceptions. In addition, the idea of deconstruction asserts that many subjects—death, for example—are inevitably impossible to understand through language alone.

John Gardner expands on the idea of deconstruction to describe it as fiction that "tells the story from the other side or from some queer angle that casts doubt on the generally accepted values handed down by the legend." Gardner does that himself in *Grendel*, in which he retells part of the story of Beowulf from the monster's point of view:

> It wasn't because he threw that battle-ax that I turned on Hrothgar. That was mere midnight foolishness. I dismissed it, thought of it afterward only as you remember a tree that fell on you or an adder you stepped on by accident, except of course that Hrothgar was more to be feared than a tree or snake. It wasn't until later, when I was full-grown and Hrothgar was an old, old man, that I settled my soul on destroying him—slowly and cruelly. Except for his thanes' occasional stories of seeing my footprints, he'd probably forgotten by then that I existed.

In this sense of the meaning of deconstructive fiction, much *parody, especially parody of literary works, seems to fit the definition. *(See: literature of exhaustion, parody.)*

Denotation   The dictionary definition of a word, without its emotional, psychological or subconscious implications.

Problems in finding a word with the desired meaning often are solved with the help of a good dictionary. While a thesaurus also can be useful in locating an appropriate word, the thesaurus usually will offer synonyms without supplying a word's *connotations—the emotional responses the word calls forth in the mind of the reader. The denotations of "fool," "blockhead," "clod," "oaf," "simpleton" and "turkey" are roughly the same, for example, yet the words are not interchangeable. *(See: connotation.)*

Denouement   *(falling action, resolution)*   The part of a story that comes after the climax, after the story's main problems are solved, in which remaining loose ends, if any, are tied up.

In Richard Yates' *A Good School*, the denouement comes at a point after the protagonist and his classmates have graduated from an expensive but eccentric boarding school that is about to be shut down due to lack of funds, just at the onset of the United States' involvement in World War II. After graduation, in an *epilogue, the narrator describes what has happened to his classmates over the years:

> Pierre Van Loon died of shrapnel wounds inflicted by German artillery in the last week of what came to be known as the Battle of the Bulge.
>
> A month later, on the other side of the world, Terry Flynn was killed in the second or third assault wave on the beach of Iwo Jima.

Later, the narrator talks about his gratitude toward his father for sending him to Dorset Academy, where:

> I learned to write by working on the Dorset *Chronicle*, making terrible mistakes in print that hardly anybody ever noticed. Couldn't that be called a lucky apprenticeship? And is there no further good to be said of the school, or of my time in it? Or of me?

Contemporary fiction is less likely than older work to include a recognizable denouement; indeed, one common complaint about the work of recent writers like the *minimalists is that their stories end before reaching a true climax. The contemporary, nonminimal denouement usually contains some sort of "resonant twist," in which the writer steps back from the story while at the same time opening it out a bit, so that it speaks to a larger, more general theme, relating to readers in general as well as to the characters of the story.

Another alternative to a conventional tying-up denouement is to allow the story to move even further away from the command of the narrator than it was at first, a technique used in Tom Wolfe's *Bonfire of the Vanities*. Sometimes the denouement, instead of resolving anything, shows a kind of circular pattern, suggesting that although this particular problem has been solved, nothing has really been learned, and the cycle that led to the complications of the story is destined to repeat itself.

Kurt Vonnegut's "Harrison Bergeron" is a "what-if" story about what could happen if laws required that all people be absolutely equal in all their abilities. The Bergerons' fourteen-year-old son, Harrison, has been taken to prison for, among other reasons, refusing to wear his handicap radio, which shoots distracting sounds into his brilliant mind, causing him to lose his concentration. The climax of the story comes when the Handicapper General of the United States shoots and kills Harrison while he is dancing with a ballerina on television without the artificial handicaps that limit his strength. Afterward, Harrison's mother, who is naturally stupid, and his father, who wears a handicap radio, comment on what they have seen:

> George came back in with the beer, paused while a handicap signal shook him up. And then he sat down again. "You been crying?" he said to Hazel.
> "Yup," she said.
> "What about?" he said.
> "I forget," she said. "Something real sad on television."
> "What was it?" he said.
> "It's all kind of mixed up in my mind," said Hazel.
> "Forget sad things," said George.
> "I always do," said Hazel.

Ironically, the parents have forgotten their son's death just moments after it happens. This denouement shows that George and Hazel are destined to forget forever, that the cycle of forgetting will occur again and again. *(See: circular structure, reversal.)*

Description The words in a story that paint a picture of the physical aspects of a scene's location, characters, and any other important objects.

Writers use a lot of concrete nouns as well as adjectives in their description; they also use comparison and contrast and analogy to make a description vivid, as Jane Austen shows at the beginning of *Northanger Abbey* in her description of Catherine Morland:

> A family of ten children will always be called a fine family, where there are heads and arms and legs enough for the number; but the Morlands had little other right to the word, for they were in general very plain, and Catherine, for many

years of her life, as plain as any. She had a thin awkward figure, a sallow skin without colour, dark lank hair, and strong features;—so much for her person;—and not less unpropitious for heroism seemed her mind. She was fond of all boys' plays, and greatly preferred cricket not merely to dolls, but to the more heroic enjoyments of infancy, nursing a dormouse, feeding a canary-bird, or watering a rose-bush. Indeed she had no state for a garden; and if she gathered flowers at all, it was chiefly for the pleasure of mischief—at least so it was conjectured from her always preferring those which she was forbidden to take.—Such were her propensities—her abilities were quite as extraordinary. She never could learn or understand any thing before she was taught; and sometimes not even then, for she was often inattentive, and occasionally stupid.

Ideally, description will do more than just paint a picture; it will advance the plot, just as dialogue and action do. Description should provide necessary information, and the details of the descriptive passages should affect the characters in the story and not merely exist for the reader's edification.

Description by a character in a story told from the first-person point of view can be particularly significant in that presumably we are learning only what the character himself is choosing to tell us.

Details The information, particulars, minutiae and nuances that generally are included in fiction to make the stories in which they appear seem more real.

David Madden's "No Trace" is a story made up almost entirely of the detailed description of the narrator's son's dorm room. Gordon, the son, has just committed suicide by shooting himself on stage, while giving a speech at his graduation. The father persists in believing that everything he considers unsavory in the son's room really belongs to Gordon's roommate Carter:

As he rifled through the numerous letters, folded hastily and slipped or stuffed into pigeonholes, Ernest felt he was getting an overview of liberal and left-wing activities, mostly student-oriented, over the past five years, for Carter's associations began in high school. He lifted his elbow off Gordon's scrapbook—birthday present from Lydia—and flipped through it. Newspaper photo of students at a rally, red ink enringing a blurred head, a raised fist. Half full: clippings of Carter's activities. AP photo: Carter, bearded, burning his draft card. But no creep—handsome, hair and smile like Errol Flynn in "The Sea Hawk."

While realistic detail is the bread and butter of *realistic fiction, writers of other kinds of fiction have more ambiguous feelings about these kinds of specifics.

The mundane description of the grocery store in Don DeLillo's *White Noise*, observed by a man who has been exposed to toxic chemicals, makes the situation seem reassuringly normal, yet the detail also seems bizarre in this case, since the situation is so definitely abnormal. Much of the plot of *White Noise* rests on this shopper and his wife's desperate desire to obtain a secret, experimental drug that has been designed to help humans overcome their fear of death:

> The supermarket is full of elderly people who look lost among the dazzling hedgerows. Some people are too small to reach the upper shelves; some people block the aisles with their carts; some are clumsy and slow to react; some are forgetful, some confused; some move about muttering with the wary look of people in institutional corridors.
>
> I pushed my cart along the aisle. Wilder sat inside, on the collapsible shelf, trying to grab items whose shape and radiance excited his system of sensory analysis. There were two new developments in the supermarket, a butcher's corner and a bakery, and the oven aroma of bread and cake combined with the sight of a bloodstained man pounding at strips of living veal was pretty exciting for us all.
>
> Dristan Ultra, Dristan Ultra.

Deus ex Machina Literally, "a god from a machine," coming from ancient Greek drama to describe a point at the end of a play when,

just as things seem most bleak, an actor playing a god is lowered by a mechanical device onto the stage to right everything.

Since much more fiction—even realistic fiction—ends happily than you would expect if fiction were a mirror of real life, it would seem the "deus ex machina" technique must be in constant use. The term, however, generally is used now to suggest unnatural, strained coincidences, where characters are removed from difficulties through acts having nothing to do with their own skills or actions.

In a story, to avoid the appearance of contrivance, writers often make sure the gods that come down from the machine are relatively small ones.

In Anne Tyler's story, "Average Waves in Unprotected Waters," the narrator is Bet, a young woman who has decided to place her son in a state institution for the mentally retarded. Knowing that taking him from her town to the institution by train will be heartbreaking, she arranges her schedule so that she will not have to wait in the station for the train that will take her home after she drops her son off.

Her train home is twenty minutes late, however, and Bet is distraught to find that she must spend the extra time in the train station. Her problem is solved by a deus ex machina in the form of the town's mayor, who arrives suddenly and decides to try out on her a twenty-minute speech he is going to give, helping her pass the time before the train comes so she does not have to think about what she has just done.

Dialect   The distinctive habits of speech used by a particular race, class or regional group. "Y'all," for example, is an example of southern dialect. The comment of the "woman with the snuff-stained lips" in Flannery O'Connor's "Revelation" is a wonderful example:

> "You want to know wher you can get one of themther clocks?" she asked in a loud voice. . . . "You can get you one with green stamps," the woman said. "That's most likely wher he got hisn. Save you up enough, you can get you most anything. I got me some joo'ry."

The invented word "themther" (the "ther" rhymes with "were"); the quirky colloquialism of the phrase "save you up enough, you can get you almost anything," with its repeated "you"; and the speaker's mispronunciation of "joo'ry" all come together to make it easy for the reader to hear this woman as she speaks in the doctor's waiting room. Indeed, effective dialect in general will be composed of a combination of techniques, expressing the rhythms of entire sentences rather than simply substituting standard English words with colorful regionalisms.

One interesting exercise is to invent a dialect for a people who do not exist. Here are the opening sentences of Russell Hoban's *Riddley Walker*, which takes place in England sometime in the distant future.

> On my naming day when I come 12 I gone front spear and kilt a wyld boar he parbly ben the las wyld pig on the Bundel Downs any how there hadn't ben none for a long time befor him nor I aint looking to see none again. He dint make the groun shake nor nothing like that when he come on to my spear he wernt all that big plus he lookit poorly.

Note that this passage also contains *eye dialect: "wernt" and "ben" are pronounced the same as normal English words but are spelled differently. The point of the dialect in this novel is to show how written English, as well as spoken English, has deteriorated in this world of the future. *(See: eye dialect.)*

Dialogue The conversation among the story's characters. Edith Wharton once said, "Only the significant passages of their talk should be recorded," and it generally is accepted that, like description, dialogue should carry along the action of the story and be distinctive enough to show something about the speaker through her voice. If you use dialogue to show the sparkling wit of the characters, it is important that the wit really does sparkle, or the result can be painful.

In *realistic fiction, much of the delight of dialogue comes from making the speech sound as much as possible like the way people talk. If the reader loses track of who is talking in the middle of a conversation, that is usually a sign that the characters sound too similar to each other. It also is good to remember that what a character does not say can be as important as what she does say.

Note that the term "dialogue" also includes the narrator's *summary of dialogue (Frank told his wife he considered her no better than a tramp, and not only on account of her night with Rudy at the Ramada Inn), as well as direct dialogue, in which we hear only the actual words of the characters, sometimes without even the usual "he saids." Here is a bit of conversation between two café waiters watching their last drunken customer, in Hemingway's "A Clean, Well-Lighted Place":

> "Last week he tried to commit suicide," one waiter said.
> "Why?"
> "He was in despair."
> "What about?"
> "Nothing."
> "How do you know it was nothing?"
> "He has plenty of money."

It also is possible to combine indirect and direct discourse for clarity and variety:

> Frank told his wife that he never wanted to hear her voice again, and that he doubted that this most recent affair had been her first. "You're a tramp, and you've always been a tramp, you lying tramp!" He shut the bathroom door so the twins wouldn't hear him and threw Suzette's towel to the floor. "What do you have to say for yourself now, tramp?"

Contemporary writers generally avoid overusing alternatives to "said," such as "snarled," "hissed," and even the relatively innocuous "remarked." These synonyms tend to call attention to themselves, which the simple "said" and "asked" do not.

Diary Fiction Fiction written in the form of a character's journal or diary. Diary fiction shares a lot with *epistolary fiction (a story made up of letters) in that the author tries to create the illusion that the story was written by one of the characters.

The diary form is particularly effective at showing the workings of a troubled and/or self-deluding mind. At the beginning of the diary that comprises Alison Lurie's *Real People*, the self-satisfied fiction writer-protagonist, delighted to have gotten away from the husband she believes is unworthy of her, plans to use her stay at a writer's colony to work on a "ghost story." At the beginning the entries are glib, almost smug. As the illusions that have figured in her life begin to fall away, however, the writing becomes more disjointed, and by the end of the novel the main character faces the self-deceptions of her life much more honestly than before.

Usually the fictional diary, like its real-life counterpart, is meant to be a private document, but sometimes a great deal of tension in the story can come from the question of whether the diary will be found by someone who is not intended to read it (as happens in *Lolita*, when Humbert Humbert's wife finds his journal and learns of his passion for her daughter). Other times, the tension comes from the question of how we, the reader, come to be reading it (as with diaries that come to light after the author's death). The tape-recorded diary of "Offred" in Margaret Atwood's *The Handmaid's Tale* is being discussed at a scholarly symposium many years after its abandonment and rediscovery; we never learn what happened to the woman who made it.

The diarist also has the opportunity of lying flagrantly even in a diary meant for herself alone, as the narrator of Bel Kaufman's *Love, etc.*, does. The writer also can reread earlier diary entries and reflect on them, as Adrian Mole does in Sue Townsend's *The Adrian Mole Diaries*:

> *Thursday February 3rd*
> During the Month of March 1982 it would seem that both my parents were carrying on clandestine relationships, which resulted in the birth of two children. Yet my diary for that period records my childish fourteen-year-old thoughts and preoccupations.
>
> I wonder, did Jack the Ripper's wife innocently write:
>
> 10:30 P.M. Jack late home. Perhaps he is kept late at the office.
>
> 12:10 A.M. Jack home covered in blood; an offal cart knocked him down.

Didactic Fiction   A usually pejorative term describing fiction whose goal is to teach the reader something.

The word "didactic" is used to describe fiction that tries to teach the reader to feel a certain way about some subject, rather than to impart objective information. The form has much in common with all types of *thesis novels.

To call a story or novel "didactic" is considered an insult, implying either that its lesson is stated so baldly that its characters seem to be hollow clichés, used by the author as pawns to get across some specific opinion, or that the lesson itself is inappropriate for the fictional form.

However, there are plenty of good examples of fiction that teaches. Harriet Beecher Stowe's *Uncle Tom's Cabin*, for example, instructed many readers about the evils of slavery, encouraging the people of the North to begin to take more vigorous action to do away with the institution. *(See: thesis novel.)*

Diegesis   Derived from an ancient Greek word meaning "narration," the term has only within the past ten years or so been revived into the language of literary critics. Diegesis includes the speech and actions of characters as they are reported by the narrator, rather than by the characters themselves through *dialogue.

In diegetic fiction, the words are filtered through the narrator's viewpoint, which may show events in a light different from how the reader would perceive them if he heard the speaker say the words directly.

In this scene from Cynthia Ozick's "An Education," the protagonist, Una, is awestruck by the cleverness of two new friends. Visiting their apartment, she learns how they have done most of the decorating themselves. She must have learned this by hearing them tell her, but instead of being dramatized, the scene is told in indirect discourse, through diegesis. The use of this technique somehow subtly lets us know right away that we are not expected to admire Clement and Mary as much as Una does:

> Instead of pictures on the walls, there were two brightly
> crude huge rectangles of tapestry, with abstract designs in

them. Clement had sewn them. On the inside of the bathroom door, where vain people stupidly hang mirrors, Mary had painted a Mexican-style mural, with overtones of Dali. And all along the walls, in the kitchen and the bedroom and the living room and even in the little connecting corridor, were rows and rows of bookshelves nailed together very serviceably by Clement. Clement could build a bookcase, Mary said, in two hours flat.

The use of diegesis was not common among the *modernists, who wanted as little distance as possible between the reader and the character; but its use has become more common in recent fiction since the work of *metafictionists. *(See: center of consciousness, mimesis, narration, showing versus telling, summary.)*

Digression Material inserted into a novel that is not closely related to the main theme of the work. Digression rarely is appropriate in the short story.

Writers use the technique on purpose for two reasons. The first is for comic effect, as in Laurence Sterne's *Tristram Shandy*. At the beginning of the novel, Tristram Shandy recounts the events that led up to his birth. On the evening when he is to be born, instead of describing the birth, which is what the reader expects and probably hopes for, Tristram Shandy digresses by recounting in great detail irrelevant conversations between his father and uncle about military glories of the past and long, tedious philosophical speculations—for example, about the complexities of women's psychology. Tristram Shandy's birth does not actually occur until halfway through the novel.

Digressions also can exist simply to be informative, to heighten the effect of the theme, as do Herman Melville's factual chapters interspersed throughout *Moby Dick*, about the activity of whaling and the varieties and lives of whales. The facts about whales certainly are not directly related to the action of the novel, but they add depth and scope to the novel and help the reader further ponder the *symbolism of the whale.

Sometimes what initially appears to be a digression from the plot really is not, because it exists specifically to comment on some theme of the work. This often is done in contemporary fiction. Near the end of Raymond Carver's "Where I'm Calling From," the story of the narrator's life in a rehabilitation center for alcoholics is abruptly interrupted by his reminiscence about an incident years before, when he was in bed with his wife and then got up, naked, and came face to face in the window with his landlord. While this incident has nothing to do with life at the rehab center, it relates thematically with the story—making the point that the narrator is beginning to heal and think that joy might again be possible in his life—and so does not really fall into the "digression" category. *(See: narrative collage.)*

Documentary Novel *(paraliterary fiction)* Fiction that is formed partly or wholly through the use of documents—newspaper clips, medical reports, memos, legal briefs, music lyrics and even photographs.

The documents involved can be either real documents or documents created by the author. If a lot of documents are included, the effect draws nearer to that of the *nonfiction novel or *new journalism categories than to wholly imagined fiction.

Indeed, even writers who include just a few documents, as Ann Beattie and other *minimalists often do by using actual lyrics from popular songs, often do so for the purpose of creating a feeling of verisimilitude.

Up the Down Staircase, by Bel Kaufman, is a popular example of a documentary novel that consists solely of documents invented by the author to show the sad state of the innercity high school where a naïve young teacher has begun her career. The documents include senseless bureaucratic memos from the office, inane teaching notes left on the blackboard, illiterate book reports written by students, and letters from the English teacher protagonist to a friend to describe her days at school.

Another well-known example is from John Dos Passos' *The 42nd Parallel*, part of his *U.S.A.* trilogy, which opens with a section called "Newsreel." The section is composed of a selection of popular songs, headlines and political speeches carefully chosen to try to recreate the national mood of the country at the beginning of the twentieth century. *(See: pastiche novel, rap novel.)*

Donnée *(premise)*   From the French, for "given"; the basic *scene, idea, characters and *theme a writer begins with. The term, introduced by Henry James, is based on an analogy to the kind of geometry problem in which certain data are provided, from which the mathematician must work out the problem's solution.

In William Faulkner's *As I Lay Dying*, we accept that the Bundrens would go to the trouble of taking the dead wife and mother to be buried in her home community where she has asked to be buried, despite the great physical difficulties and despite that the father in particular seems unquestionably shiftless and unlikely to go to the trouble. If the family did not make the journey, after all, there would be no novel. At the end of the novel, we accept that there really would be another woman stupid enough to marry Anse Bundren.

A story, like Graham Greene's "The Destructors," might have as its theme the idea that envy of someone else's possessions will likely lead to attempts to destroy them, which not everyone would agree with, out of the context of a particular story.

In general, however, the reader grants the writer his donnée and questions not the likelihood of certain events occurring but the way in which the writer (if that is his goal) tries to convince the reader that the donnée is reasonable and possible. *(See: convention.)*

Doppelgänger *(double)*   From the German, for "double goer"; a common figure in literature referring to a kind of mysterious double, someone whose appearance or behavior seems oddly like that of the protagonist (or some other character) in the work, despite differences in their appearance, station in life, sex, race, etc. This parallel must be recognized by the reader, of course, but the characters themselves do not necessarily see it.

The protagonist in Joseph Conrad's "The Secret Sharer" is very aware that he has a "double." He is a ship's captain who has just taken his first command; he is rather unsure of himself and awkward with his men. One night while on watch, he allows Legatt, the first mate of another ship who has swum away from his ship after killing another man, to climb aboard.

The captain feels an instant bond with Legatt, who coincidentally comes from the same place in England as he does and is just a few years younger. Sacrificing the respect of the men under his command who find his secretive behavior eccentric, the captain agrees to hide Legatt in his room. The two men can speak to each other only in whispers but find a great satisfaction and mutual closeness in exchanging the stories of their lives and shared difficulties. The narrator seems amazed by the closeness he feels to his double:

> It occurred to me that if old "Bless my soul—you don't say so" (the first mate) were to put his head up the companion and catch sight of us, he would think he was seeing double, or imagine himself come upon a scene of weird witchcraft; the strange captain having a confabulation by the wheel with his own grey ghost.

At the end of the story, the captain orders the ship to travel dangerously close to an island so that the secret-sharer, his double, will be able to swim safely to it. The first mate is sure that the ship has run aground, but the captain believes he will be able to steer the ship away from the shallow water. Looking in the water for something to gauge whether the ship is moving, the captain sees his own hat, which the secret sharer had been wearing when he went into the water. The narrator feels hurt that Legatt did not take the hat with him, but somehow he feels more confident than previously, able to command the ship with authority:

> Walking to the taffrail, I was in time to make out, on the very edge of a darkness thrown by a towering black mass like the very gateway of Erebus—yes, I was in time to catch an evanescent glimpse of my white hat left behind to mark the spot where the secret sharer of my cabin and of my thoughts, as though he were my second self, had lowered himself into the water to take his punishment: a free man, a proud swimmer striking out for a new destiny.

Another example of a doppelgänger is in Robert Louis Stevenson's *The Strange Case of Dr. Jekyll and Mr. Hyde*, in which the decent but overly proud scientist Dr. Jekyll formulates a drug to bring out "the lower elements in [his] soul," one that turns him into the unspeakably evil killer Mr. Hyde. Yet, as Stevenson points out again and again, the two characters remain two sides of the same coin, two aspects of the same personality.

Double Entendre   From the French, for "double meaning"; a statement with two possible meanings, one of which is potentially crude and, sometimes, lascivious.

In *Lolita*, by Vladimir Nabokov, Lolita, on the road for the second time with her lecherous stepfather Humbert Humbert, receives a letter from a friend about a school play that Lolita is missing:

> As expected, poor Poet stumbled in Scene III when arriving at the bit of French nonsense. Remember? Ne manque pas de dire à ton amant, Chimène, comme le lac est beau car il faut qu'il t'y mène. Lucky beau! Qu'il t'y—what a tongue-twister!

The French phrase, which can be translated "Do not neglect to tell your lover, Chimène, that, because the lake is beautiful, he must bring you there," seems an improbable bit of dialogue but provides information about the romantic sensibility of the play.

The double entendre, which Humbert fails to understand but Lolita certainly does, is in the phrase "Qu'il t'y," since the name of Lolita's lover, Humbert Humbert's rival of whom he at this point is completely unaware, is "Quilty." *(See: polysemous language.)*

Double Voicing   A term from contemporary literary criticism describing words spoken in dialogue that the speaker has consciously taken from another source—generally a quotation from a well-known authority, but occasionally simply the words of another character—with a different meaning than the speaker intended.

In Barbara Pym's *An Unsuitable Attachment*, the character Penelope, meaning to mock a rather irritating older woman, Sister Dew, who is on a tour of Italy with Penelope's family and friends, remarks somewhat sarcastically as the group enters a restaurant:

> "I wonder if pussy was at that fish," said Penelope, in Sister Dew's manner. "I shouldn't fancy it after that."

The reader, ideally, will appreciate both the original meaning of whatever is spoken, and the "double-voiced" meaning—the one intended by the speaker—at the same time.

*Parody and *lampoon are the most noticeable examples of double voicing, but the term includes any situation when it is clear to the reader that one character is speaking in the words of another. In *The Recognitions*, for example, William Gaddis puts many exact and inexact quotations from well-known literary works into his characters' mouths, as when one of his characters quotes Macbeth after another character has cut his hand in a fall:

> "Yes, who would have thought the old man to have had so much blood in him . . . ?"

(See: allusion, intertextuality.)

Dreams   Generally used nowadays in fiction to show aspects of a character's psychological, subconscious, or emotional state that the character is not able to put into words to tell the reader directly. They're also an excuse for a writer to include lush, impressionistic imagery and to make odd combinations that might not suit the style of the rest of the work.

Dreams, of course, also are the staple fare of beginning writers who end their fantastic stories with "and then I woke up." Always a mistake.

In Isaac Bashevis Singer's "Gimpel the Fool," the dreamer is the foolish, naïve, constantly humiliated Gimpel, whose dream about his dead wife at the end of his story—near the end of his life—gives him comfort (which is ironic, since in life his wife had cared nothing for him). Gimpel, however, is much happier in his dream world than in the real one, and the dream at the end shows how pervasive this other world is to him:

> It is many years since I left Frampol, but as soon as I shut my eyes I am there again. And whom do you think I see? Elka. She is standing by the washtub, as at our first encounter, but her face is shining and her eyes as radiant as the eyes of a saint, and she speaks outlandish words to me,

strange things. When I wake I have forgotten it all. But while the dream lasts I am comforted. She answers all my queries, and what comes out is all that is right. I weep and implore, "Let me be with you." And she consoles me and tells me to be patient. The time is nearer than it is far. Sometimes she strokes and kisses me and weeps upon my face. When I awaken I feel her lips and taste the salt of her tears.

Dynamic Character *(changing character, kinetic character)* A character who changes in some important internal way between the beginning of the story and the end.

One dynamic character is the unnamed narrator in Ralph Ellison's *Invisible Man,* who early in his life hears his grandfather's deathbed words:

> "Son, after I'm gone I want you to keep up the good fight. I never told you, but our life is a war and I have been a traitor all my born days, a spy in the enemy country ever since I give up my gun back in the Reconstruction. Live with your head in the lion's mouth. I want you to overcome 'em with yeses, undermine 'em with grins, agree 'em to death and destruction, let 'em swoller you till they vomit or bust wide open."

As a boy, the narrator is confused by this statement; he finds himself following his grandfather's advice without thinking of it as treacherous: indeed, he gives a high school graduation speech in which he "showed that humility was the secret, indeed, the very essence of progress."

Though he claims not to believe this statement, he feels superior to the other young black men gathered at a smoker for the entertainment of white business leaders in his town and is uncritically grateful for their gift of a college scholarship.

By the end of the novel, after many disillusionments, however, he has become cynical, far less optimistic about others' motives toward him. Finally, he is living in a basement, his hopes for a conventionally successful future gone, getting pleasure out of cheating the electric company by illegally wiring hundreds of electric lights throughout his room, something he never would have considered as a young man. He's a changed—and therefore a "dynamic"—character.

Note that a superficial change in condition is not enough to make one a dynamic character: Cinderella changes from a poor girl to a rich one, but even when her fortune is made, when the prince puts the glass slipper on her foot, she still is the same person inside that she always was.

The term "dynamic character" frequently is confused with "round character," but the two are not quite the same. A dynamic character, who changes over the course of the story, always will be a round character; but a round character, although she has many different character traits, does not necessarily have to be a dynamic one. *(See: round character, static character.)*

E

Editorial Omniscience   The effect created when a third-person narrator adds his own remarks, presumably representing the ideas and opinions of the author, into the narrative. Editorial omniscience rarely occurs in realistic fiction, or in the fiction of the twentieth century in general—except, oddly, in *metafiction.

Here is the beginning of Jakob and Wilhelm Grimm's *tale, "Godfather Death":

> A poor man had twelve children and worked night and day just to get enough bread for them to eat. Now when the thirteenth came into the world, he did not know what to do and in his misery ran out onto the great highway to ask the first person he met to be godfather. The first to come along was God, and he already knew what it was that weighed on the man's mind and said, "Poor man, I pity you. I will hold your child at the font and I will look after it and make it happy upon earth." "Who are you?" asked the man. "I am God." "Then I don't want you for a godfather," the man said. "You give to the rich and let the poor go hungry." That was how the man talked because he did not understand how wisely God shares out wealth and poverty, and thus he turned from the Lord and walked on.

The editorial omniscience, which X.J. Kennedy points out in his anthology, *Literature*, occurs in the last sentence, when the narrator points out the stupidity of the poor man for not understanding God's wisdom.

Effaced Narrator   A third-person narrator who at times during a story is so closely identified with the *protagonist that the effect is nearly the same as with a *first-person narrator. The effaced narrator, however, also has the option, when necessary or desired, of showing the *scene with more sophistication and perception than the character would be able to.

The effaced narrator is especially important when the protagonist is less than brilliant intellectually or emotionally—when the narrator needs a way of showing what is going on without stepping back too far from the character.

The technique, though probably used unconsciously by many writers, was first verbalized by Gustave Flaubert about *Madame Bovary*. Flaubert wanted the reader to be able to hear Emma's voice vividly, but he also wanted to be able to explain aspects of Emma's character that Emma did not have the self-knowledge to explain. He moves in and out of Emma's consciousness as it seems necessary; in this example, Emma is unlikely to have been consciously able to come up with the "shipwrecked sailor" metaphor:

> At the bottom of her heart, however, she was waiting for something to happen. Like shipwrecked sailors, she turned despairing eyes upon the solitude of her life, seeking afar off some white sail in the mists of the horizon. She did not know what this chance would be, what wind would bring it her, towards what shore it would drive her, if it would be a shallop or a three-decker, laden with anguish or full of bliss to the portholes. But each morning, as she awoke, she hoped it would come that day; she listened to every sound, sprang up with a start, wondered that it did not come; then at sunset, always more saddened, she longed for the morrow.

Emma probably would be capable only of expressing a vague dissatisfaction. It is Flaubert's ability to extrapolate on her feelings to create the metaphor that gives her unhappiness such a sense of weight and reality.

Emblematic Name (redende *name)*   Names that are significant because they make some kind of serious, literal statement about a character's nature and values. In Katherine Anne Porter's "The Jilting of Granny Weatherall," Granny's name emphasizes the fact that the protagonist is tough. She has lived through a lot, barely ever resting; she has not always been delirious on her sickbed as she is in the story. Another example comes from Charles Dickens' *Little Dorrit*, in which a family of bureaucratic parasites is called the "Barnacles."

Emblematic names are used far less in the second half of the twentieth century than they were earlier, as they seem nowadays a bit heavy-handed, lacking the subtlety and understatement that marks much contemporary fiction. Even the *comic or grotesque name—like "Fanny Assingham" in Henry James' *The Golden Bowl*—is used more often than those chosen specifically to comment on a character's personality or moral traits. *(See: comic and grotesque names.)*

Ending *(conclusion)*   Whatever comes at the end of the piece of fiction—the last chapter in a novel; the last page in a story.

There are basically three types of endings: those in which the reader's desires for the character are satisfied (happy endings); those in which they are not (unhappy endings); and those in which something happens to let the reader know that her desires for the character will neither be satisfied nor disallowed.

The first two types of endings describe a resolution that occurs when everything has happened that we have wanted to know about, and either our hopes or our fears for the protagonist have been realized. With the third type of ending, there is no resolution, and we may learn that the character's (and perhaps our own) desire for a resolution was misguided in some way. Or we learn that although this problem may seem to be solved, it is not, for the characters have learned nothing and will soon embark on another similarly futile quest like the one they have just ended.

In Margaret Atwood's *Cat's Eye*, the narrator has wondered obsessively throughout the novel what happened to an old school friend of hers, a girl who first tormented her and then came to depend on her. During a visit to her home town she is convinced she will see her old friend again. The meeting never takes place, however, and in the end the narrator realizes it was unrealistic to believe it ever would. *(See: denouement.)*

Epic Fiction   While "epic" occasionally is used simply to describe a very long novel, most epics also have certain elements in common, including a plot involving characters whose actions create national or international consequences and settings encompassing a variety of locations.

The word "epic" originally was used to describe poems such as Homer's *Odyssey*, which were passed along orally and involved the great deeds of celebrated historical figures. But there are marked differences between oral epic poetry and epic fiction. The fictional epic is often, although not always, humorous, and its characters and plot generally are invented, rather than based on mythology or history.

Leo Tolstoy's *War and Peace* is an example of a fictional epic. Although it is not humorous, it is very long—more than five hundred pages in most editions—and includes a huge cast of characters, ranging from peasants to Russian nobility and the Emperor Napoleon.

The center of the plot is Napoleon's 1812 invasion of Russia, and the Russian people's rebellion against his rule, but other plots exist: the search by the book's two main male characters, Prince Andrey Bolkonsky and Pierre Bezukhov, to find meaning in life, either through an intellectual understanding or through the more emotional approach espoused by Tolstoy; the female *protagonist Natasha Rostova's emotional growth from girlhood to maturity; and various romantic attachments and *subplots among the characters. The variety of the scenes, plots and themes in the book come together to paint a vivid picture of Russia in the early nineteenth century. *(See: chronicle novel.)*

Epigram   A short, pithy, usually humorous saying that states something the writer hopes to present as a general truth.

An example from Dorothy Parker is "Men seldom make passes at girls who wear glasses." Oscar Wilde defines a cynic as "a man who knows the price of everything and the value of nothing." Often epigrams rhyme and are presented in lines, like poetry, such as the following by Sir John Harrington:

Of Treason
Treason doth never prosper; what's the reason?
For if it prosper, none dare call it treason.

In many ways, however, epigrams have more in common with fiction than with poetry, and their creation can be a useful exercise for a writer not used to thinking in terms of brevity—expressing a *theme, while omitting *characterization and *plot.

Epigraph   The inscription on the title page of a book, often a quotation but possibly an original saying by the author, which serves to call attention to the theme of the book.

One epigraph, which appears in E.M. Forster's *Howard's End*, is "Only Connect," which calls attention to the theme that human beings, and especially people from different social classes, are morally obligated to try to form connections among each other.

Ernest Hemingway begins "The Snows of Kilimanjaro" with a bit of information about the mountain that also relates to the story itself:

> Kilimanjaro is a snow covered mountain 19,710 feet high, and is said to be the highest mountain in Africa. Its western summit is called by the Masai "Ngàje Ngài," the House of God. Close to the western summit there is the dried and frozen carcass of a leopard. No one has explained what the leopard was seeking at that altitude.

Often writers use epigraphs, with attribution, from works they find personally meaningful and presumably relevant to the work they are writing. The danger is, as John Barth points out in *The Friday Book*:

> If you must lay on an epigraph, take it from some neutral text of a sort entirely different from your own. . . . But to preface your text with an epigraph from a superior author in the same genre is to remind the reader that he might better spend his time with that author than with you.

Epilogue *(afterword, periscope ending)*   A summing-up statement at the end of a book, in which the reader learns what happens to the characters after the book's conclusion.

John Irving's epilogue in *The World According to Garp*, for example, briefly describes the remainder of each character's life after Garp's death, which marks the end of the plot:

Donald Whitcomb would never sleep with Helen, despite rumors among the envious would-be biographers who longed to get their hands on Garp's property and Garp's widow. . . .

Ellen James would grow up to be a writer. She was "the real thing," as Garp had guessed. . . .

Florence Cochran Bowlsby, who was best known to Garp as Mrs. Ralph, would live a life of larkish turmoil, with no substitute for sex in sight—or, apparently, in need. She actually completed a Ph.D. in comparative literature and was eventually tenured by a large and confused English Department, whose members were only unified in their terror of her. . . .

Bainbridge Percy, who was best known to Garp as Pooh, would live a long, long time. The last of a train of psychiatrists would claim to have rehabilitated her, but Pooh Percy may simply have emerged from analysis—and a number of institutions—too thoroughly bored with rehabilitation to be violent anymore.

The concept of a summing-up epilogue originates with drama in the late seventeenth and eighteenth centuries and is less common in twentieth-century fiction.

Epiphany A word coined by James Joyce, defining a sudden moment of insight when a character discovers some truth important to the story. An epiphany usually occurs near the end of the story, when the plot demands some moment of truth for the story to conclude. Often the epiphany comes from a visual image, something that a character sees, that forces her to some important realization.

There is an epiphany at the end of "Araby," by James Joyce, in which a boy has gone to a bazaar in hopes of buying a gift for a neighbor girl he barely knows but loves so deeply that each morning he lies on the floor of his house and watches her leave for school. At the bazaar, the boy finds nearly all of the booths closed and nothing worth buying. He is disappointed but not devastated. At the end of the story, however, the lights go off, and the boy has an epiphany: Not only has the trip to the bazaar been in vain, but his whole love for the shadowy sister of his friend has been a delusion, perhaps a way to escape from the dreary reality of his home. "Gazing up into the darkness," he thinks later, "I saw myself as a creature driven and derided by vanity, and my eyes burned with anguish and anger."

Episode *(incident)* A happening that is dramatized in a story without a break for extensive *summary, or for commentary by the narrator. Usually a series of episodes will come together to form the entire work.

The term "episode" usually is differentiated from *"scene" in that an episode does not necessarily include *dialogue, while a scene generally does.

Eudora Welty's humorous story "The Petrified Man," for example, consists of only two episodes, although a lot of individual incidents take place in each.

In the first episode, we hear Leota, a beautician, telling her client Mrs. Fletcher, that her friend Mrs. Pike thinks that Mrs. Fletcher looks pregnant. Leota also tells Mrs. Fletcher that she and Mrs. Pike have been to a county fair and seen a character billed as the petrified man, a freak whose joints are slowly turning to stone. We get the feeling that Leota has a great deal of admiration for Mrs. Pike, who with her husband rents Leota's spare room. The episode (and the scene) concludes with the end of Mrs. Fletcher's hair appointment.

The second episode begins a week later, back at the beauty salon, with Mrs. Fletcher brooding about how she now looks pregnant even when sitting down. She is still angry that Mrs. Pike has spread word of her pregnancy around town and mentions casually that she has not yet told her husband that she is pregnant.

In this episode, Leota reveals that she has quarreled terminally with Mrs. Pike because Mrs. Pike saw an announcement offering a reward for the capture of an accused rapist in one of Leota's magazines, *Startling G-Man Tales*, and has realized that the rapist is in fact the petrified man she'd seen at the fair a week before. Leota is furious because Mrs. Pike will be able to collect the $500 reward for finding the man even though the reward offer was in Leota's magazine. This second episode ends when Leota and Mrs. Fletcher catch Mrs. Pike's son, who has been hanging around the beauty salon, and Mrs.

Fletcher spanks him, exclaiming: "You bad, bad boy, you! I guess I better learn how to spank little old bad boys."

The word "episode" sometimes is used in another sense, to denote a scene that simply describes the setting or develops character and that does not particularly advance the plot. *(See: anecdote, scene.)*

Episodic Structure A form of plot in which the individual scenes and events are tied to each other more through a simple chronology than through any particular cause-and-effect relationship. In general, the scenes in a book with an episodic structure could be rearranged almost at random without hurting the work as a whole.

An example is Daniel Defoe's *The Fortunes and Misfortunes of the Famous Moll Flanders, &c. Who was Born in Newgate, and during a Life of continu'd Variety for Three-score Years, besides her Childhood, was Twelve Year a Whore, five times a Wife (whereof once to her own Brother), Twelve Year a Thief, Eight Year a Transported Felon in Virginia, at last grew Rich, liv'd Honest, and died a Penitent. Written from her own Memorandums*, whose title is also a *summary of the plot, which moves chronologically through the seventy years of Moll Flanders' life. While the ending is definite and happy, most of the events that take place in Moll Flanders' life are related only chronologically, rather than through some more complicated scheme.

The *picaresque novel is an example of a novel type that uses an episodic structure, although a novel with an episodic structure does not necessarily deal with the barely legal adventures of the typical rogue-protagonist of the picaresque novel. *(See: picaresque novel, picaro.)*

Epistolary Novel A novel written in the form of letters—either all by one character or among characters. Although earlier examples exist, the originator of the epistolary novel in English is considered to be Samuel Richardson, in whose 1740-1742 *Pamela*, a household servant writes a series of letters home about her relations with her employer, who kidnaps and tries to seduce her but eventually marries her.

Alice Walker's 1982 *The Color Purple* is a more recent epistolary novel, divided into two sections of letters written by two sisters. The older sister is a semi-literate, abused woman who over the course of the story finds love and self-respect. The younger sister is adopted by a missionary family and writes about her life in Africa. The two sisters write letters—the older one to God and the younger one to her sister—for about thirty years, describing the major events in their lives.

John Barth's *Letters* is another epistolary novel, in this case written in the form of letters to and from the major characters in his previous books.

The writer of the epistolary novel lacks some of the options of a regular novel (dialogue, except recollected; often the element of surprise, since the event is being remembered and written about after it is over), but epistolary fiction does offer a few unique sources of tension. Will the letters be answered? Will they be intercepted by others? Will the writer of the letter later regret mailing it? In Alice Walker's *The Color Purple*, for example, the older sister discovers near the end of the novel that her husband has been hiding her younger sister's letters to her for years; she reads them all at once, not knowing if her sister is now alive or dead.

Essayist-Omniscient Voice A term used by John Gardner to describe a third-person narrator who, although not a character in the work, is much more personal than the anonymous *objective or *authorial-omniscient narrator.

Gardner points out, "Though we do not know the name and occupation of the speaker [in such a work], we sense at once that the voice is old or young, male or female, black . . . or white." Often, though not necessarily, this third-person narrator will have much in common with the author.

Mark Twain's "The Man That Corrupted Hadleyburg" is an example of a work whose narrative voice is so distinctive—with its odd words like "unsmirched," the hint of hyperbole in the idea that even babies in the cradle are being taught to be honest—that it could only have been written by Twain:

> It was many years ago. Hadleyburg was the most honest and upright town in all the region around about. It had kept that reputation unsmirched during three generations, and was prouder of it than of any other of its possessions. It was so proud of it, and so anxious to insure its perpetuation, that it began to teach the principles of honest dealings to its babies

in the cradle, and made the like teachings the staple of their culture thenceforward through all the years devoted to their education. Also, throughout the formative years temptations were kept out of the way of the young people, so that their honesty could have every chance to harden and solidify, and become a part of their very bone.

The opposite of the essayist-omniscient voice, the *authorial-omniscient voice, Gardner says, is carefully neutral, speaking always with "dignity and proper grammar, saying what any calm, dignified, and reasonable person would say." *(See: authorial-omniscient voice.)*

Euphuism   The most formal, affected, artificial, pedantic style possible in fiction, based on a style popular in sixteenth-century England, which takes its name from John Lyly's 1578 *Euphues*.

Nowadays the term is used to describe writing marred by excessive rhetorical questions, figurative language and references to mythology. It is hard to imagine a contemporary work using euphuism that does not have comic intent, as does this first paragraph from John Barth's *The Sot-Weed Factor*, called "The Poet is Introduced, and Differentiated from His Fellows":

> In the last years of the Seventeenth Century there was to be found among the fops and fools of the London coffeehouses one rangy, gangling flitch called Ebeneezer Cooke, more ambitious than talented, and yet more talented than prudent, who, like his friends-in-folly, all of whom were supposed to be educating at Oxford or Cambridge, had found the sound of Mother English more fun to game with than her sense to labor over, and so rather than applying himself to the pains of scholarship, had learned the knack of versifying, and ground out quires of couplets after the fashion of the day, afroth with Joves and Jupiters, aclang with jarring rhymes, and string-taut with similes stretched to the snapping-point.

(See: academic fiction.)

Exercise   A small, well-defined writing task that a writer or writing student undertakes, either for a class assignment or on his own initiative, meant to help the writer improve his technique in some aspect of the creative process.

The advantage of working on an exercise rather than on something that the writer finds personally meaningful is that when the writer is relatively indifferent to the material and is only trying to solve a writing weakness of some kind, he can concentrate on the problem at hand—developing character, say—without relying on his preconceived notions of what character should be, or focus on characters he's already invented.

One often-used exercise is "random words," in which the writer chooses three random words from a dictionary and proceeds to write a short-short-story incorporating all of these words.

Another, "smoke," described in John Gardner's *The Art of Fiction*, is played in a group in which one member thinks of a famous person and then tells the others, "I am a living Asian" or "I am a dead American" or whatever. The other players then try to guess the name of the character by asking questions such as, "What kind of weather are you?" or "What kind of smoke are you?" The players must use their intuition, more than their intellect, to think about what kind of character would be more likely, say, to smoke a Winston cigarette than a Marlboro or to chew tobacco rather than smoke.

Exposition Details, usually imparted in *summary form, that give the readers the background information they need to understand the story.

Here is the second paragraph of Saul Bellow's *Seize the Day*, in which the reader continues to learn facts about the *protagonist (he's unemployed, desperately trying to impress his father) and his surroundings. The main part of the exposition in this short novel seems to end with this paragraph, and the main action of the story—events exploring Tommy Wilhelm's impulsive nature and his bad relationships with his ex-wife and with his father—begins:

> Most of the guests at the Hotel Gloriana were past the age of retirement. Along Broadway in the Seventies, Eighties, and Nineties, a great part of New York's vast population of old men and women lives. Unless the weather is too cold or wet they fill the benches about the tiny railed parks and

along the subway gratings from Verdi Square to Columbia University, they crowd the shops and cafeterias, the dime stores, the tea-rooms, the bakeries, the beauty parlors, the reading rooms and club rooms. Among these old people at the Gloriana, Wilhelm felt out of place. He was comparatively young, in his middle forties, large and blond, with big shoulders; his back was heavy and strong, if already a little stooped or thickened. After breakfast the old guests sat down on the green leather armchairs and sofas in the lobby and began to gossip and look into the papers; they had nothing to do but wait out the day. But Wilhelm was used to an active life and liked to go out energetically in the morning. And for several months, because he had no position, he had kept up his morale by rising early; he was shaved and in the lobby by eight o'clock. He bought the paper and some cigars and drank a Coca-Cola or two before he went in to breakfast with his father. After breakfast—out, out, out to attend to business. The getting out had become the chief business.

Exposition often appears at the beginning of a story, but it can be interspersed throughout the piece, between or within,*episodes that more actively carry the plot. In some stories, of course, a long period of exposition is not particularly crucial, as in Hemingway's "A Clean, Well-Lighted Place," where the scene is set, for the most part, in this short paragraph and another one a little later:

It was late and every one had left the café except the old man who sat in the shadow the leaves of the tree made against the electric light. In the day time the street was dusty, but at night the dew settled the dust and the old man liked to sit late because he was deaf and now at night it was quiet and he felt the difference. The two waiters inside the café knew that the old man was a little drunk, and while he was a good client they knew that if he became too drunk he would leave without paying, so they kept watch on him.

(See: details, description.)

Eye Dialect An author's misspelling of a word to indicate that it is being spoken by an ignorant or non-native speaker of the language—even though, if the word were actually pronounced the way it has been misspelled, the pronunciation would be the standard, correct one. In the sentence, "Ah cain't kum raht naow," "kum" is eye-dialect spelling.

On the first page of Mark Twain's *Adventures of Huckleberry Finn*, Huck says:

> The Widow Douglas, she took me for her son, and allowed she would sivilize me; but it was rough living in a house all the time, considering how dismal regular and decent the widow was in her ways; and so when I couldn't stand it no longer, I lit out.

In this example, the word "sivilize" is eye dialect.

F

Fable A short tale, one of the earliest forms of fiction, told to illustrate a moral of some kind, in which the characters often are animals whose character traits symbolize human traits.

The most well-known writer of fables is Aesop, a Greek slave who lived about 600 B.C., who wrote most of the fables we know today—like the story of the hungry fox who tried to reach a succulent cluster of grapes hanging from a vine too high for him to reach and, after failing, convinces himself that the grapes probably were not ripe anyway. Aesop offers the moral to this one: "In the same way some men, when they fail through their own incapacity, blame circumstances."

Another noted writer of these moral tales is Jean de La Fontaine, a seventeenth-century French writer noted for his wit. Readers also have enjoyed the parodies of James Thurber, including "The Little Girl and the Wolf," which retells the story of Little Red Riding Hood but has the girl shoot the wolf with an automatic rifle at the end and offers the moral: "It is not so easy to fool little girls nowadays as it used to be."

"What You Can't Hang Onto," the first of William Maxwell's "Three Fables Written to Please a Lady," is a contemporary fable. It begins conventionally: "Once upon a time there was an old woman who lived in a house by a river," but contains plot twists that could only take place in a contemporary story. An English woman, the last surviving member of her family, has become tired of friends coveting her possessions. She decides to will her beloved house and furniture to some casual acquaintances, an American couple who seemed to love it without asking for anything. At first she makes the condition in her will that the couple must live in her house; then she removes this requirement.

After the old woman's death, the American couple walks through her house "without touching anything, and then sat down in the cold little parlor." They sell the house and when they come back to see it two years later, they find it sadly changed, with a "no fishing or trespassing" sign by the river, curtains in the window, and the garden full of weeds. The American woman says sadly, "I keep thinking that there was surely something we could have done." It is the river itself that offers the fable's moral:

> No, there was nothing. The collecting of beautiful objects has to end ultimately in their dispersal. The old woman would have found the curtains odious, as indeed they are, but fortunately she doesn't know. What you can't hang onto you must let go of—that is the principle on which I operate, on my way to the sea.

Fables are close to *parables in many respects; the difference is that while a parable often will remain mysterious and open to interpretation at its conclusion, the moral of a fable generally will be announced clearly and in such a way that it is easily understood.

Fabulation Contemporary nonrealistic fiction, including *parables, tales and *fables.

While the term often is used simply to refer to any unconventional contemporary fiction, it also is related to the word "fable"—stories that offer to their readers definite morals, in that contemporary fabulation as well is much less concerned with the representation of external reality than with a deeper, more internal truth.

An example is Thomas Pynchon's *Gravity's Rainbow*, which postulates a post-World-War-II world dominated by a group that controls everything through nuclear weapons. The protagonist, Lt. Tyrone Slothrop, is looking for a mysterious missile strangely numbered 00000. The theme of the novel concerns the way in which the contemporary world seems to be headed toward total destruction through its technological progress.

This paragraph comes from a section early in the book; Teddy

Bloat is a spy who plans to use his minicamera to photograph the random items on Slothrop's desk:

> Teddy Bloat's on his lunch hour, but lunch today'll be, ack, a soggy banana sandwich in wax paper, which he's packing inside his stylish kangaroohide musette bag and threaded around the odd necessities—midget spy-camera, jar of mustache wax, tin of licorice, menthol and capsicum Meloids for a Mellow Voice, gold-rim prescription sunglasses General MacArthur style, twin silver hairbrushes each in the shape of the flaming SHAEF sword, which Mother had Garrard's make up for him and which he considers exquisite.
>
> His objective this dripping winter noon is a gray stone town house, neither large nor historic enough to figure in any guidebook, set back just out of sight of Grosvenor Square, somewhat off the official war-routes and corridors about the capital. When the typewriters happen to pause (8:20 and other mythical hours), and there are no flights of American bombers in the sky, and the motor traffic's not too heavy in Oxford Street, you can hear winter birds cheeping outside, busy at the feeders the girls have put up.

Faction Fiction whose appeal is based on the research the writer has done on the factual subjects with which the work is concerned.

In *I Married a Best Seller,* Sheila Hailey, wife of best-selling novelist Arthur Hailey, describes her husband's interviews with doctors of different specialities, and with other health-care workers to assure that the details in his novel would be correct.

This scene from *The Final Diagnosis,* in which a doctor reviews the X rays of a nursing student (whose leg is ultimately amputated on the orders of a once great but now incompetent pathologist), shows how Hailey has used his research:

> Without speaking Coleman took the first slide again. He went over it once more, patiently and carefully, then repeated the process with the other seven. The first time around he had considered the possibility of osteogenic sarcoma; now he did so again. Studying the red- and

blue-stained transparencies which could reveal so much to the trained pathologist, his mind ticked off the pros and cons. . . . All the slides showed a good deal of new bone formation—osteoblastic activities with islands of cartilage within them. . . . Trauma had to be considered. Had trauma caused a fracture? Was the new bone formation a result of regeneration—the body's own attempt to heal? If so, the growth was certainly benign. . . . Was there evidence of osteomyelitis? Under a microscope it was easy to mistake it for the more deadly osteogenic sarcoma. But no, there were no polymorphonuclear leukocytes, characteristically found in the marrow spaces between the bone spicules. . . . There was no blood-vessel invasion. . . . So it came back basically to examination of the osteoblasts—the new bone formation. It was the perennial question which all pathologists had to face: was a lesion proliferating, as a natural process to fill a gap in the body's defenses? Or was it proliferating because it was a neoplasm and therefore malignant?

"Faction" is different from the *nonfiction novel, with which the term can easily be confused: While the facts upon which the faction novel rests are true, the characters are entirely the inventions of the writer. In the nonfiction novel, both the documentary facts and the characters and plot are based on real people and incidents.

Family Chronicle *(family saga)* A novel telling the story of a large family, often covering a period of many years or even generations. The intention often is realistic: As in life, some family members prosper; others fail; there are many falling-outs and occasional reconciliations. Often, *multiple narrators are used. The genre is popular in other media as well as in fiction, as the success of the PBS series "Upstairs, Downstairs" shows.

An example is John Galsworthy's massive series of three trilogies, *The Forsyte Saga*, *A Modern Comedy* and *End of the Chapter* (a total of nine novels), which follows the progress of a wealthy family between 1886 and World War I. The character who ties the family chronicle together is the beautiful, strong-willed Irene, who originally is married to one of the Forsytes, then has an affair with the fiancé of a second and is divorced by the first, and finally marries the cousin of her original husband. *(See: chronicle novel.)*

Farce A type of low comedy that includes bizarre coincidences, slapstick, patent absurdities and puns. Often farce includes some parody elements, with the humor being how far the situation gets from the normal, clichéd situation.

In Evelyn Waugh's *Decline and Fall,* an innocent schoolteacher has been sent to prison for his unwitting involvement in a prostitution ring. When his fiancée, who was really in charge of hiring the prostitutes, bribes Paul's jailers, the results are farcical:

> That evening at supper Paul noticed without surprise that there were several small pieces of coal in his dripping: that kind of thing did happen now and then; but he was somewhat disconcerted, when he attempted to scrape them out, to find that they were quite soft. . . . He examined his dripping more closely. It had a pinkish tinge that should not have been there and was unusually firm and sticky under his knife. He tasted it dubiously. It was paté de foie gras. . . .
>
> On another occasion the prison doctor, trotting on his daily round of inspection, paused at Paul's cell, examined his name on the card hanging inside his door, looked hard at him and said: "You need a tonic." He trotted on without more ado, but next day a huge medicine bottle was placed in Paul's cell. . . . Paul could not quite decide whether the warder's tone was friendly or not, but he liked the medicine, for it was brown sherry.

This farcical example from Frank Sullivan's 1940 "The Jukes Family," a parody of the radio soap operas that were popular at the time, mocks outlandishly the *clichés of the genre:

> The matriarch is Ma Jukes, a friendly old party of forty-five who has brought fifteen or twenty children into the world and has learned to take things as they come. She does the best she can to manage her unruly brood, each

of whom has some characteristic that sets him or her apart from the herd. . . .

The fourth child, Slim, age twenty-two, has a penchant for bigamy which frequently brings upon him the good-natured raillery of the rest of the family. Another of the boys, Timmy, is doing a stretch in Sing Sing, and Mayzetta, the third girl, is in her sophomore year at the Dobbsville Home for Delinquent Females. But the glamour girl of the Jukes Family is Babs—tall, striking, with dark, flashing eyes and a head of hair five and a half feet long. And every single strand of it a natural emerald green! Ma Jukes' family (she was a Cabot) all had hair of vivid yellow. Pa's folks' hair had been Alice blue. Nature's alchemy had combined the two colors happily in Babs.

Ficelle *(confidante)*   A term coined by Henry James to describe the protagonist's confidant(e), whose purpose is to draw out the protagonist through questioning, causing the main character to reveal necessary information to the reader. Taken from the French, *ficelle* literally refers to the strings a puppeteer uses to control a marionette.

In Jane Austen's *Pride and Prejudice*, the character of Charlotte, the protagonist's best friend, at first serves primarily as someone to listen to Elizabeth talk about her views of what marriage and love should be. In this role she is a *ficelle*. Later, however, she develops into something more, when she accepts the proposal of the repellent Mr. Collins (a man Elizabeth previously has rejected), out of desperation and a desire to get away from home.

A *ficelle* usually is found in a novel with a first-person narrator or a third-person narrator so closely identified with a protagonist that it is impossible for the narrator to step back and reveal information about the protagonist, if the protagonist does not have some particular reason or desire to reveal it.

Fictional Biography   A biography of a real person, fleshed out with imagined scenes and dialogue to add dramatic interest.

A fictional biography is different from a *simulated biography, which describes the life of a fictional person. The term is close in meaning to *biographical novel; if there is a difference, it is that the fictional biography is more likely than the biographical novel to be self-reflexive, to make it clear to the reader that the work is not really history.

Writers of fictional biographies are likely to realize the inherent difficulties with the genre and to go out of their way to make it clear that the biography has been fictionalized. Kate Millett does just that in *The Basement*, a fictionalized account of the real trial of Gertrude Baniszewski, a woman who murdered one of her children. The biography intersperses the imagined soliloquies of her psychotic subject with more objective reporting:

> I get old. Burned out. No man ever look at me if this goes on. Thirty-seven's pretty close to forty. And then it's over. They don't have to put up with that but we do. Look at them old geezers even in church. And you see plenty goin around on the street with young gals. Or that insurance man. Nothin stops 'em, if they got two dimes to rub together they can get it up. Who's to know anyway? They're Mr. and Mrs. Polite quick enough. Who knows what goes on in everybody's bedroom. I've had thirteen pregnancies and six miscarriages and I'll bet I still got lots to find out.

(See: faction, new journalism.)

Fictional Truth   The universal truths about the world or about life in general that a story reveals. Fictional truth should not be confused with literal truth: Just because something really happened does not mean that it necessarily resonates with some larger truth.

Often, it is the fictionalization of a true event, the rearrangement of detail, the emphasis on some *theme, that lets the fictional truth come out, as Amy Hempel says in a *Columbia Magazine* interview about her story, "In the Cemetery Where Al Jolson Is Buried": "I'd failed my best friend . . . when she was dying. I wrote that story. . . . There is not a word of dialogue in that story that either one of us ever said, yet it is a true story."

A literally true story about the death of a friend certainly would ramble; the feelings might be more chaotic than a short story can reasonably be expected to handle. It is in fictionalizing the episode that a writer should be able to, as John Gardner said, show something about how the world works, and how some problems that all human beings share can be resolved. *(See: theme.)*

Fictionist   A name for writers of experimental fiction, usually *meta-fiction. Not often used in the 1990s, the term has begun, to many, to sound a bit precious and gimmicky.

Fictions   A term that some writers of experimental or *antirealistic fiction prefer to use instead of "stories."

A "fiction," in general, is a short story or novel in which the attempt is not to suspend the reader's disbelief in the characters and plot, but to take advantage that the reader can never completely forget that she is reading about something that did not actually happen, to point out the arbitrariness and artificiality of society.

The idea behind the decision to call a story a fiction often lies in the writer's concept of life as something without form, full of coincidence and inexplicable events. Since most writers do not want to reflect this formlessness simply by making their stories formless, they work their plots into some kind of artificial structure, emphasizing some things, omitting others, for the sake of order and unity. This mental structure imposed by the author is what makes the work a fiction.

The word "fiction," indeed, is used in the same sense outside of literature, to describe things people generally know to be false but accept to avoid disruption and disorder. Jorge Luis Borges is an example of a writer of fictions; his most well-known collection of stories is, in fact, titled *Ficciones. (See: fabulation, metafiction.)*

First-Person Point of View   *(dramatized narrator, participant narrator)*   The "I" (or occasionally "we") that serves as the *narrator of a story. The first-person narrator can be a major character in the story (in which case he sometimes is known as the narrator-agent) or he can be a minor one. He also can be someone who barely exists as a character at all, who appears simply as an observer, as the "we" voice in William Faulkner's "A Rose for Emily" shows:

When Miss Emily Grierson died, our whole town went to her funeral: the men through a sort of respectful affection for a fallen monument, the women mostly out of curiosity to see the inside of her house, which no one save an old manservant—a combined gardener and cook—had seen in at least ten years.

While the voice of the narrator who seems to be speaking for the entire town in "A Rose for Emily" turns out to have a somewhat mild, eccentric personality, the first-person observer voice in this story sounds very much like a third-person, undramatized narrator.

First-person narrators often are flawed in some way—either *unreliable or *naïve—and some of the joy of many first-person narrations is the *irony between what an unreliable narrator sees and says, and what we, the more savvy readers, observe. In this passage from Ring Lardner's *You Know Me Al*, it is clear that the narrator is not as indifferent to Hazel Levy's marriage as he would like to think:

Al I got a surprise for you. Who do you think I seen last night? Nobody but Hazel. Her name now is Hazel Levy because you know Al she married Kid Levy the middleweight and I wish he was champion of the world Al because then it would not take me more than about a minute to be champion of the world myself. I have not got nothing against him though because he married her and if he had not of I probily would of married her myself but at that she could not of treated me no worse than Florrie. . . .

Al I am certainly glad I throwed Hazel over because she has grew up to be as big as a horse and is all painted up. I don't care nothing about them big dolls no more or about no other kind neither. I am off of them all. They can all of them die and I should not worry.

Flash Fiction Complete short stories of between 250 and 750 words—the limit suggested by James Thomas in his anthology, *Flash Fiction*.

The real question is how short a story can be and still be satisfying, and writers of flash fiction maintain that their pieces have all the elements of a short story; they're not simply snippets or *slices of life. Still, a story this short must necessarily move quickly, which is part of the genre's charm, and either compress the action or limit character development—or both.

Gary Burnham's "Subtotals" is an example of a very short story that spends little time with plot, concentrating on creating a vivid, strange character through apparently random details:

> "Number of refrigerators I've lived with: 18. Number of rotten eggs I've thrown: 1. Number of finger rings I've owned: 3. Number of broken bones: 0. Number of Purple Hearts: 0. Number of times unfaithful to wife: 2. Number of holes in one, big golf: 0; miniature golf: 3. . . ."

Bruce Eason's "The Appalachian Trail," which condenses the difficulties of maintaining a relationship to the wife's desire to walk the Appalachian Trail and the husband's reluctance to make the trip, is able to include apparent *digression and still fall within the word limit:

> "Here now," I say, pen working, setting numbers deep into the paper. "Let's say you walk, on average, some twenty miles a day. That's twenty into two thousand, right? It goes one hundred times. And so, one hundred equals exactly one hundred years. It'll take you one hundred years!"
>
> "Don't be stupid," she says. "One hundred days, not years."

The author is able to do this because he never veers into other aspects of the couple's relationship; he sticks to the short period of time they argue about the Appalachian Trail before the husband decides to go along. *(See: short-short story.)*

Flashback A way for a writer to include information that occurred before the opening of the story, to show the reader something that happened in the character's past or to give an indication of what kind of person the character used to be.

Laurie Colwin's *Family Happiness* begins with a description of a family breakfast in which everyone seems to depend on the grown daughter, Polly Solo-Miller, for everything from emotional support to sandwich-making. Polly seems to sail gracefully through the meal, satisfying her parents, husband, siblings and children. Only at the end of the book's second chapter do we see Polly's relief upon leaving her parents' apartment, her desire to head downtown to meet her lover, Lincoln, who appreciates her.

> "Put your arms around me and tell me everything you've thought or felt since Friday." He held her close. "I really do love you to pieces."
> "I love you to pieces, too," said Polly. "Isn't it sad?"

The chapter then flashes back to a time around a year earlier, when Polly and Lincoln met for the first time:

> Polly and Lincoln had met once the year before, at a group show that included a series of his landscapes in oil, and then again in Lincoln's one-man show the first week in September. . . .
> She realized, as she moved from picture to picture, that Lincoln Bennett had been in the back of her mind since she had met him in the spring. She had had an impulse to send him a letter—a fan letter—and she had composed it over and over in her mind but had never written it.

Flashbacks can be related, like this one, by the narrator through *summary, or they can be told as *anecdotes narrated by the characters themselves.

Flashforward   A sudden movement in a story from the present to the future, where the narrator reveals an event that has not yet occurred as far as the "now" of the story is concerned. After the flashforward, the narrator usually switches back to the present, as if nothing unusual had happened, and continues the narration.

An example comes from William Faulkner's "Barn Burning." This story begins when the protagonist, ten-year-old Colonel Sartoris Snopes, observes his father being tried for arson at a makeshift court in a general store. After the trial, in which Sarty's father is found not guilty for lack of evidence, Sarty's father hits Sarty on the side of the head, perceiving that the son would have testified against him, had he been called to the stand. After hitting him, Ab Snopes tells his son:

> "You're getting to be a man. You got to learn. You got to learn to stick to your own blood or you ain't going to have any blood to stick to you. Do you think either of them, any man there this morning, would? Don't you know all they wanted was a chance to get at me because they knew I had them beat? Eh?" Later, twenty years later, he was to tell himself, "If I had said they wanted only truth, justice, he would have hit me again."

The flashforward at the end of this passage to a period twenty years later shows that Colonel Sartoris Snopes survives his escape from his family—no easy task for a ten-year-old. The flashforward also suggests that he is destined to become an educated, thoughtful adult—something the reader could not necessarily have taken for granted either, considering that at ten he is completely illiterate.

Flat Character *(type, caricature)*   A term coined by E.M. Forster in *Aspects of the Novel* to describe a character constructed around a single quality or personality trait, whose personality traits usually can be summed up in a single sentence. Forster gives the example of Mrs. Micawber in Charles Dickens' *David Copperfield*. Married to an erratic, impecunious husband, Mrs. Micawber nevertheless stands by him; everything we know about her character can be expressed in her remark: "I will never desert Mr. Micawber." Forster comments: "There is Mrs. Micawber—she says she won't desert Mr. Micawber, she doesn't, and there she is."

It is tempting to disparage flat characters for their shallowness, to consider them something for a writer to avoid. Flat characters, however, possess some real advantages. For one thing, they are easily recognized as soon as they enter the scene because they're simple; readers often have seen their kind before. Another advantage is that they're easy for the reader to remember after they've left the story because they do not change. It is satisfying to a reader to recognize a familiar *type. In any case, it would be impractical for a short story to contain more than a small number of fully developed characters—or the story would cease to be a short story. *(See: card, stock character, type.)*

Fool Literature *(folly literature)*   A type of *satire that focuses on those aspects of human behavior that seem ridiculous. Fool literature aims to expose certain types of nonsensical or ignorant human behavior rather than deal with an entire society, as a satire often does. The term is related to "folly literature," a genre of the fifteenth through seventeenth centuries.

The form is not necessarily a comic one. Despite its title, Katherine Anne Porter's *Ship of Fools* is sad and thoughtful, the story of a varied group of ship passengers traveling from Mexico to Germany in 1931, blind to the imminent disaster of the war.

Each character is deluded in some way: There is a drunkard, a deluded religious zealot, a German couple who treat their dog like a human being, and an American couple who alternately torment and adore each other. The book explores the prejudices and emotional problems the characters exhibit, and by illustrating their personal cruelty to one another, show a definitely base side to humanity. *(See: satire.)*

Foreshadowing   The technique of giving the reader a subtle hint of some important event that will occur later in the story—especially a surprising or shocking event.

Often foreshadowing is used to let the reader know not to expect a happy ending. In Flannery O'Connor's "A Good Man Is Hard to Find," for example, a basically harmless, if soulless, family heads south from Georgia on a vacation to Florida. Nothing particularly ominous happens during the first part of the trip: The family stops to eat at a roadside restaurant, then heads on a detour to see a house the grandmother thinks she remembers. After an auto accident on the dirt road, however, as the family members gather, "The Misfit," a psychotic escaped prisoner, comes upon them and, after expounding on his confused philosophy of life, murders the entire family.

Without foreshadowing, the murder of the family would seem grotesquely out of place in this story, which seems to be written to mimic reality as closely as possible and whose tone, until the end, has been fairly humorous and light. But Flannery O'Connor sets up the reader for the ending in several subtle ways: by having the grandmother, who had not wanted to go to Florida, use the initially farfetched idea that the family might run into the Misfit as evidence that vacationing in Tennessee would be the right choice. Then, at the roadside restaurant, the owner mentions the Misfit (though not as the main subject of conversation), keeping his name subtly in the reader's mind, not letting anyone forget his existence, although he has not yet become part of the story. *(See: life imitating art.)*

Foreshortening A word coined by Henry James that refers to the effective but brief presentation of some situation or detail that is required to keep a work substantive and interesting but that need not be dramatized. The writer must make it clear what the important information is without dwelling on it unnecessarily.

Henry James uses as an example of foreshortening his own long story, "Julia Bride," which he says is:

> "foreshortened," I admit, to within an inch of her life; but I judge her life still saved and yet at the same time the equal desideratum, its depicted full fusion with other lives that remain undepicted, not lost.

The problem that Julia Bride faces is that she already has been engaged six times, and her mother has been divorced twice and is on the verge of her third divorce. Now wanting to become engaged to a seventh man from a higher class of society than she is used to, one who disapproves of divorce, Julia Bride searches out one of her previous romantic connections in hopes of having him vouch for her good behavior—and her former fiancé's bad behavior—in their relationship.

The foreshortening in this story comes from the fact that the reader learns practically nothing about Julia's six previous fiancés, her relationships with them and with her mother, and her reasons for having so many engagements and breaking them all off—only that this kind of louche behavior obviously is to be expected from the daughter of such a mother. It is vitally important to the story that Julia have rather a shocking past; it is not so necessary that the exact details of this past be known, and so they have been foreshortened. *(See: panoramic method, summary.)*

Foreword An introduction at the beginning of a novel, before the story begins. Often the term is used synonymously with *preface. If there is a difference, it is that a foreword generally is written by someone other than the novelist, to explain some aspect of the work that the writer of the foreword (rather than the writer of the novel) deems important.

Here is the last paragraph of Cassandra Austen's foreword to *Northanger Abbey*:

> One trait only remains to be touched on. It makes all others important. She was thoroughly religious and devout; fearful of giving offence to God, and incapable of feeling it towards any fellow creature. On serious subjects she was well-instructed, both by reading and meditations, and her opinions accorded strictly with those of our Established Church.

Note that the writer of the foreword does not have to be a real person, as is the case in Thomas Berger's *Little Big Man*, in which the writer creates a character who dictates the story of his life to another character while in the hospital:

> It was my privilege to know the late Jack Crabb—frontiersman, Indian scout, gunfighter, buffalo hunter, adopted Cheyenne—in his final days upon this earth. An account of my association with this remarkable individual may not be out of order here, for there is good reason to believe that without my so to speak catalytic function, these extraordinary memoirs would never have seen the light of day. This apparently immodest statement will, I trust, be justified by the ensuing paragraphs. . . .

(See: preface.)

Form An abstract concept, often mistakenly used synonymously with *structure, describing the way in which a work's shape is related to its theme and content. In a story that achieves its ideal form, it would be impossible to change one element (the location from Alabama to Missouri, for example; the length of the *protagonist's childbirth scene from three chapters to one) without destroying the work's emotional power. As Chekhov said, "Cut a good story anywhere, and it will bleed."

A work containing supernatural elements, for example, with larger-than-life characters reaching unusual heights of passion, might do better in the form of a *gothic *romance, for example, rather than as a novel, with its traditional emphasis on the day-to-day exploits of ordinary people. A story with discombobulated, disoriented characters might find its ideal form as a *narrative collage, in which the discontinuity of the narrative would match and mirror the confusion of the characters.

In this example, from Kurt Vonnegut's *Breakfast of Champions*, the narrator as well as the characters feel despair and confusion about the purpose of life in general, which is mirrored in the narrative, making the narrative collage a particularly appropriate form:

> While my life was being renewed by the words of Rabo Karabekian, Kilgore Trout found himself standing on the shoulder of the Interstate, gazing across Sugar Creek in its concrete trough at the new Holiday Inn. There were no bridges across the creek. He would have to wade.
>
> So he sat down on a guardrail, removed his shoes and socks, rolled his pantlegs to his knees. His bared shins were rococo with varicose veins and scars. So were the shins of my father when he was an old, old man.
>
> Kilgore Trout had my father's shins. They were a present from me. I gave him my father's feet, too, which were long and narrow and sensitive. They were azure. They were artistic feet.

Form can come not only from subject matter but also from the work's *tone. The form of a *lyrical novel, whose primary purpose is the expression of feeling and emotion, will be different—much less linear, probably more digressive—than that of a novel with an *action plot, for example. *(See: structure.)*

Fragrant Character A Henry James term for a character who, although she may seldom appear directly, exerts great influence on the other characters, on the plot, and on the reader. An example comes from Carolyn Chute's *LeTourneau's Used Auto Parts*, in which virtually all the characters have been affected by "Big Lucien" LeTourneau, who has by the end of the novel assumed almost mythical proportions. On the next-to-last page of the book, "Big Lucien" finally appears, however, and is described as:

> An ordinary man. A man you'd never ever notice on a city street. He has thinning hair. Work clothes. He has narrow cringing shoulders like he's ducking a thrown shoe. Weak-looking shoulders. A small man. What some would call a "shrimp."

Frame Story *(nested narratives)* The "outer shell" of a story within a story, the one that comes at the beginning of the work, before one of the characters sits down beside another and says, "Let me tell you a story."

One practical reason for using the "frame" device is as a way of including a lot of interesting stories within a single work, as occurs in Boccaccio's *Decameron*, in which ten men and women from Florence, Italy, decide to escape the risk of bubonic plague in the city by staying together in a small nearby town, where they tell each other stories for ten days—and the stories they tell each other form the bulk of the book.

Some frame stories become more complicated by having more than one frame: A character tells a story about another character who tells a story, etc.—and the stories themselves become more complicated through the individual voices of the tellers. This strategy is used in Flann O'Brien's *At Swim-Two-Birds*.

In Anton Chekhov's "The Man in a Case," we learn that a veterinarian and a schoolteacher, out hunting, are sleeping in a shed and telling each other stories. After three short paragraphs of introduction, the schoolteacher begins to tell the central story of the frame story— about a Greek teacher so rigid and timid in his ways that he gave up the chance for love over a trifling disagreement with his fiancée. This story lasts for about eighty paragraphs, and then the scene shifts back to the schoolteacher and the veterinarian, who wonders if his life is not, in its own way, as empty as the Greek teacher's in his friend's story.

In a sophisticated frame story like this, the teller is not just the bland voice through which the story is filtered, but a complicated character in his own right. His reasons for telling the story, his relationship with the person to whom he tells the story, and his relationship to the story and its characters all become important. *(See:* mise en abîme, *novel-within-a-novel.)*

Freitag's Triangle *(Freitag's Pyramid)* A concept invented by German critic Gustav Freitag in his 1894 *Technique of the Drama* to represent the conventional flow of the *plot of a play, starting with *rising action in which complications develop, a *climax, and finally a *denouement.

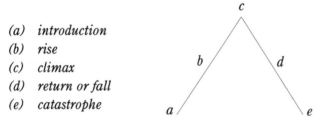

(a)   *introduction*
(b)   *rise*
(c)   *climax*
(d)   *return or fall*
(e)   *catastrophe*

Others, notably John Barth, have suggested that a variation of the diagram, including exposition, is more suitable to the conventions of fiction.

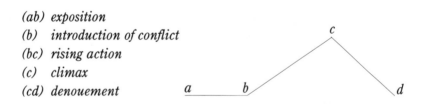

(ab) *exposition*
(b)   *introduction of conflict*
(bc) *rising action*
(c)   *climax*
(cd) *denouement*

Frigidity The writer's inability to care sufficiently about her characters, even when they are in desperate situations. Originally identified by the ancient Greek literary critic Longinus, "frigidity" is described in John Gardner's *The Art of Fiction.*

Frigidity usually reveals itself through some kind of inappropriate tone during a serious situation, which suggests that the writer is less involved in her characters and the situation than a normal reader, who has become deeply involved with the story, would be.

Gardner gives this example:

> Suppose the writer is telling of a bloody fistfight between an old man and his son, and suppose that earlier in the story he has shown that the old man dearly loves his son, though he can never find an adequate way to show it, so that the son, now middle-aged, still suffers from his belief that his father dislikes him, and wishes he could somehow turn the old man's dislike to love. Suppose, further, that the writer has established this story of misunderstandings with sufficient power that when the fistfight begins—the old man's blow to the side of his son's head, the son's astonished raising of his arms for protection, the old man's second blow, this time to the nose, so that the son in pain and fury hits the old man on the ear—our reaction as we read is horror and grief. We bend toward the book in fascination and alarm, and the writer continues: "The old man was crying like a baby now and swinging wildly—harmlessly, now that he'd been hurt—swinging and crying, red-faced, like a baby with his diapers full." "Yuk!" we say, and throw the book into the fire.

The problem here is that the writer has forgotten—or is not aware—that the reader realizes the genuine *pathos of this situation and needs time to reflect on it, while the writer has moved on to the inappropriate dirty-diaper image, a distraction at best. *(See: bathos, underwriting.)*

G

Genre Fiction *(category fiction)* Fiction that belongs to categories including action/adventure, science fiction, romance, western, mystery and horror. Some genres include subgenres; within the broad genre of romance, for example, we find historical romance, gothic romance, contemporary romance, romantic suspense, and various levels of erotic romance.

Gimmickry A term to describe plots or premises that are built on wildly unlikely coincidences (a would-be philandering husband, say, puts a personal ad in a sleazy newspaper that is answered by his wife) or upon trick endings (in which, for example, the reader learns at the last minute that the *protagonists, whom they have believed to be human beings, are in fact dolphins at a zoo).

Whether gimmicky stories invite rereading depends both on how believable the "gimmicks" are and on how good the writing of the story, apart from the gimmicky elements, is.

In Guy de Maupassant's "The Necklace," the protagonist loses a necklace lent her by a wealthy friend and spends the next ten years working to repay for the necklace, losing her beauty and wasting much of her life on hard work. At last she and her husband have amassed enough to repay the loan for the replacement necklace they have bought and given the friend. She finally tells the friend what she has done:

> Mme. Forestier had stopped.
>
> "You say that you bought a necklace of diamonds to re-place mine?"

"Yes. You never noticed it, then! They were very like."

And she smiled with a joy which was proud and naïve at once.

Mme. Forestier, strongly moved, took her two hands.

"Oh, my poor Mathilde! Why, my necklace was paste. It was worth at most five hundred francs!"

The gimmick—the revelation that the necklace was not worth much—is satisfying because the characterization seems so consistent throughout. The protagonist, despite her rather superficial desire to appear fine, seems like a person who would work for the rest of her life to pay back society for the wrong she has committed (losing the necklace). *(See: surprise ending.)*

Gothic Novel   A type of novel dating back to the late eighteenth century, whose plots deal with mystery, the supernatural and chivalry.

Today's gothic novels are characterized by a lot of dark, foreboding, desolate gloom in the atmosphere; a setting in a huge country house in the eighteenth or nineteenth centuries; often a hint of supernatural involvement, real or merely suspected; real danger and menace; and a plot involving a love relationship with a major strain of combativeness.

Although generally relegated to the genre shelves, the gothic novel sometimes, if it is unusually well written, develops a more general appeal. Joyce Carol Oates' *Bellefleur* achieves that, as can be seen from these paragraphs from the first chapter:

> Bellefleur Manor was known locally as Bellefleur Castle, though the family disliked the name: even Raphael Bellefleur, who built the extraordinary house many decades ago, at an estimated cost of more than $1.5 million, partly for his wife Violet and partly as a strategic step in his campaign for political power, grew vexed and embarrassed when he heard the word "castle"—for castles called to mind the Old World, the past, that rotting graveyard Europe . . . and when Raphael's grandfather Jean-Pierre Bellefleur was banished from France and repudiated by his own father, the Duc de Bellefleur, the past simply ceased to exist. "We are all Americans now," Raphael said. . . .

By the time Mahalaleel came to the manor, however, it was much changed. All but a very few of the staff of thirty-five servants had been dismissed over the decades, and a number of the rooms were closed off, and the wine cellar was badly depleted, and the marble statues in the garden were crudely weather-stained.

Other good writers who have added elements of the gothic to their fiction include Charlotte and Emily Brontë, Mary Wollstonecraft, Shirley Jackson, Edgar Allan Poe and Margaret Atwood. *(See: grotesque, melodrama.)*

Graphic Novel   Novels that resemble comic books in that they contain comiclike drawings and captions, but whose subjects are much more related to conventional fiction than to the lives of superheroes. Graphic novels often deal with personal experience and universal themes.

While the genre has been popular in China and Japan for many years, it was Art Spiegelman's best-selling *Maus*, which won a Pulitzer Prize in 1992, and its sequel *And Here My Troubles Began*, that brought the genre to the public eye in the United States, taking it beyond the usual comic-book readership of teenage boys and collectors.

Maus is the story of Auschwitz survivor Vladek Spiegelman, as told to his son Artie, the narrator, who appears to bear a close relationship to the author. Artie has trouble getting along with his father and finds it difficult to adjust his perceptions of his often harsh father with the stories he tells about surviving life in the concentration camp. The title, *Maus*, relates to the way in which Spiegelman has substituted mice characters for Jews and cats for Germans.

Gratuitous Act   *(Acte gratuit)*   An action performed by a character without obvious cause or motivation.

The term originated with the existentialists and generally is associated with *absurdist fiction. An example of a gratuitous act occurs in André Gide's *Lafcadio's Adventures*, in which one character, Lafcadio, murders another, Fleurissoire (who turns out, coincidentally, to be the brother-in-law of his mentor) by pushing him under a train car for no particular reason. Here, Lafcadio, alone in the train compartment with Fleurissoire before the murder, contemplates his next action:

> "A crime without a motive," went on Lafcadio, "what a puzzle for the police! As to that, however, going along beside this blessed bank, anybody in the next-door compartment might notice the door open and the old blighter's shadow pitch out. The corridor curtains, at any rate, are drawn. . . . What a gulf between the imagination and the deed! . . . And no more right to take back one's move than at chess. Pooh! If one could foresee all the risks, there'd be no interest in the game! . . . Between the imagination of a deed and . . . Hullo! the bank's come to an end. Here we are on the bridge, I think; a river. . . ."
>
> The window-pane had now turned black and the reflection in it became more distinct. Fleurissoire leant forward to straighten his tie.
>
> "Here, just under my hand the double fastening—now that he's looking away and not paying attention—upon my soul, it's easier to undo than I thought. If I can count up to twelve, without hurrying, before I see a light in the country-side, the dromedary is saved. Here goes! One, two, three, four (slowly! slowly!), five, six, seven, eight, nine . . . a light! . . ."

Gide felt that people inside and outside fiction perform gratuitous acts out of a deep-felt private need to express their individuality, that the gratuitous act is the only kind that truly reveals a character's inner essence.

Great American Novel   A theoretical, nonexistent type of novel that would, ideally, record the national psyche of the United States and pronounce the country's true goal, meaning and mission.

One novel that perhaps comes close to portraying—and criticizing—the American ideal in the first half of the twentieth century is F. Scott Fitzgerald's *The Great Gatsby*. Gatsby's sloughing off of his gauche North Dakota past to become a sophisticated New York party-giver, and his rise from poverty to wealth, mirror the idea of the

American dream. Ironically, Gatsby's attainment of the American dream proves hollow: His wealth has been gained illegally; and his love for Daisy, the woman for whom he has made the most dramatic of the changes in his life, is pathetically shallow.

Although Philip Roth has written a novel entitled *The Great American Novel*, the great American novel concept nevertheless remains hypothetical. As the idea of the United States as a melting pot of many peoples who share a single dream for the country becomes less and less a reality or a goal, the concept of the great American novel is less and less frequently invoked.

Grotesque   A work that includes characters who are physically, mentally or emotionally deformed in some way, and who act in ways that appear abnormal and bizarre to the average reader.

Grotesque elements in fiction can be used simply for comic effects, as they are in Eudora Welty's "The Petrified Man," in which a patron at a hair-styling shop recounts the anger she felt when a friend discovered that the petrified man they had seen together at a freak show actually was an escaped convict—and turned him in for reward money that she then did not share. More often, though, the humorous aspects of the grotesque are combined with more serious purposes on the part of the writer. Or the intent may be totally tragic, without a comic element at all.

The term "grotesque" came into use in the eighteenth century but most often is applied to twentieth-century works and often is seen as resulting from the modern view of the world as irrational and cruel. It also can be used, as Flannery O'Connor said, to show ways in fiction in which "man [is] forced to meet the extremes of his own nature."

Sherwood Anderson subtitled his *Winesburg, Ohio*, "The Book of the Grotesque," and defined a grotesque character as a person who "took one of the [many] truths to himself, called it his truth, and tried to live by it."

This passage from Anderson's 1920 story, "The Egg," is an example of grotesque imagery itself and also comments on the appeal of the grotesque to us as human beings and readers:

> On a chicken farm where hundreds and even thousands of chickens come out of eggs surprising things sometimes

happen. Grotesques are born out of eggs as out of people. The accident does not often occur—perhaps once in a thousand births. A chicken is, you see, born that has four legs, two pairs of wings, two heads or what not. . . .

At any rate he [Father] saved all the little monstrous things that had been born on our chicken farm. They were preserved in alcohol and put each in its own glass bottle. These he had carefully put into a box and on our journey into town it was carried on the wagon seat beside him. . . . All during our days as keepers of a restaurant in the town of Bidwell, Ohio, the grotesques in their little glass bottles sat on a shelf back of the counter. Mother sometimes protested but father was a rock on the subject of his treasure. The grotesques were, he declared, valuable. People, he said, liked to look at strange and wonderful things.

(See: black humor.)

H

Historical Fiction   Fiction that takes place during a definite, recognizable period in the real past. Historical fiction generally involves important political or social events of the day, as well as the daily lives of ordinary people.

The form also includes fiction that uses actual historical figures as characters, such as George Garrett's *Death of the Fox*, about the last days of Sir Walter Raleigh, and E.L. Doctorow's *Ragtime*, in which fictional characters interact with Admiral Peary, Harry Houdini, Emma Goldman and Henry Ford, among others.

There is a lot of overlap between the categories of fictional biography and historical fiction; when the terms are differentiated, the focus in historical fiction is more on plot than on character.

This example comes from George Garrett's *Death of the Fox*, which attains the ideal of historical fiction in its combination of rich, fresh language and historically accurate detail. The thoughts are those of Sir Walter Raleigh, imprisoned in the Tower of London:

> Here in the walls of the Tower the earth stands still.
>
> Sometimes, though, a whiff of the river's air brings with it the feeling of the tide running, comes into clouds of fever and rouses him with a palpable belief that he is aboard ship somewhere, now or years ago.
>
> He has lived in closer quarters with less comfort many times before. Has lived well enough out of a cedar chest that two men can lug. Has slept harder and rougher than on this narrow frame, slung with ropes and padded with thin

mattresses. Has more than one time found a place for himself in straw, or upon cold ground and stones. To waken stiff—and thorn-jointed, heavy-limbed as a lead doll. Many a pallet and bed, made in length and breadth for men of ordinary stature, has been too small for him.

Contemporary historical fiction often falls into the *metafiction mode (sometimes also called "mockhistorical," "antihistorical," "pseudohistorical," "fiction histories" or "historiographic metafiction"). The term "historiographic metafiction" was coined by critic Linda Hutcheon to describe works like E.L. Doctorow's *Ragtime*, Gabriel García-Márquez's *One Hundred Years of Solitude*, and Umberto Eco's *The Name of the Rose*—works that intermingle real people with fictional characters, works whose intentional anachronisms call attention to the fact that the story is fiction inspired by history, not history enlivened with fakery. *(See: fictional biography.)*

Hollywood Novel A novel dealing with the American film business, often set in Hollywood, California. The Hollywood novel typically contrasts a society apparently dedicated to the idea of film as an art with the greed and profit behind it.

In the Hollywood novel, as in movies themselves, things are not what they seem, as is clear in this passage from early on in Nathanael West's *The Day of the Locust*:

> A talent scout for National Films had brought Tod to the Coast after seeing some of his drawings in an exhibit of undergraduate work at the Yale School of Fine Arts. He had been hired by telegraph. If the scout had met Tod, he probably wouldn't have sent him to Hollywood to learn set and costume designing. His large, sprawling body, his slow blue eyes and sloppy grin made him seem completely without talent, almost doltish in fact.

F. Scott Fitzgerald's unfinished *The Last Tycoon* takes a more serious and sympathetic look at the world of stars and motion pictures, telling the story of Monroe Stahr, a movie director, and his love affair with a young woman who has never been inside a studio.

While the disparity between appearance and reality is an important element, part of the pleasure of this book is the apparent "insider's view" that the novel gives about what goes on in a studio, which Fitzgerald would have been in a position to know:

> There is never a time when a studio is absolutely quiet. There is always a night shift of technicians in the laboratories and dubbing rooms and people on the maintenance staff dropping in at the commissary. But the sounds are all different—the padded hush of tires, the quiet tick of a motor running idle, the naked cry of a soprano singing into a nightbound microphone.

Hyperfiction   Fiction written to be read on a computer screen, differentiated here (although not always elsewhere) from computer fiction, in that computer fiction is written partly by a computer but meant to be printed on paper and read in the usual way. Part of the impulse to write hyperfiction may be similar to that of a science fiction/fantasy magazine editor in the 1980s who published only on microfilm, with the motto, "because microfilm is the wave of the future and the future is now": a desire to produce fiction with the most technologically advanced methods available.

You lose something by not being able to hold a book in your hands, but hypertext does offer some possibilities not available with printed media. The computer's random-number generator is at the bottom of hyperfiction's ability to reassemble its plot differently each time the program is run—which can mean a new and different reading experience every day. Of course, reassembling a story divided into pieces in different order for different effects is not new to fiction, but it is much easier with computer software.

New computers, especially those with CD-ROM capabilities, offer sophisticated graphics; another perspective about hyperfiction is that, unlike a book but like life, you never know how long it will be. It is impossible to anticipate the approach of a conclusion, as is usually possible with conventionally printed material. *(See: aleatory fiction, computer fiction.)*

I

Image A word or phrase that creates a sensory picture in the mind of the reader. While most images are visual, images involving the other senses certainly are possible and often desirable. While almost all concrete nouns are capable of producing a mental image of some kind, the term frequently is used to describe the pictures created through the use of figurative language like similes and metaphors.

This example of imagistic fiction comes from John Hawkes' *The Lime Twig*:

> I noticed a pink reflection in the sky west of the station. The airplanes were bombing Highland Green. I saw the humps of dead geraniums and a wooden case of old stout bottles black and glistening against a shed. I had not moved. I felt the snow wet on my shoulders and on the rims of my ears.
>
> Large, brown, a lifeless airplane returning, it was one of our own and I saw it suddenly approach out of the snow perhaps a hundred feet above the garret and slow as a child's kite. Big and blackish-brown with streaks of ice across the nose, which was beginning to rise while the tail sank behind in the snow, it was simply there, enormous and without a trace of smoke, the engines dead and one aileron flapping in the wind. And ceasing to climb, ceasing to move, a vast and ugly shape stalled against the snow up there, the nose dropped and beneath the pilot's window I saw the figure of a naked woman painted against the bomber's pebbly surface. Her face was snow, something back of her thigh had sprung

a leak and the thigh was sunk in oil. But her hair, her long white head of hair was shrieking in the wind as if the inboard engine was sucking the strands of it.

In addition to describing its objects, the many images in this passage—especially the surprising ones, like the "humps of dead geraniums" and the destroyed painting of the woman against the bomber's "pebbly surface"—contribute to the scene's essential *mood of despair and futility.

Implied Author A kind of "second self" the writer creates in the minds of the readers as they read a story.

There is always a distinction between the person who actually sat down and wrote the story and the story's narrator, although sometimes even the author is not aware of it. This implied author usually is an improved version of the author: smarter, more sensitive, and more observant than any real person could be. The author will not allow her worst character traits and moods to show up in a story. Practically speaking, the difference between the real author and the "implied" author usually is most important in the case of a third-person narrator, since in a story with a dramatized *first-person narrator most people take for granted that the character is not the novelist.

Even though the implied author strives to remain invisible, her values are likely to seep into the work and affect the reader's response to it as well: An implied author whose set of values is far from most readers' may well have trouble getting a reader to sympathize closely with her characters.

Implied Reader (*hypothetical reader, ideal reader, intended reader, narratee*) The reader who, in a perfect world, would be the one the writer would choose to read his work, and whom he has in his mind as he writes it.

While Gertrude Stein once said, "I write for myself and strangers," most writers do have an ideal reader in mind—either a real person or an imaginary one. For example, a writer planning to make a literary allusion likely will take for granted that his reader has the educational background necessary to understand it.

A writer also will often implicitly expect that his reader feels the same way about the characters and situations as he does—that the reader appreciates the writer's tone.

About the idea of the ideal reader, Isaac Babel says in *Mes premiers honoraires*:

> My reader is intelligent and cultivated, with hearty and de-manding tastes. . . . He exists within me, but has been there for so long that I have managed to fashion him in my image and semblance. He may have ended up confusing himself with me.

Often it is possible to intuit what kind of reader the author's ideal is from the language, just as it is possible to understand what kind of readers a magazine wants to attract by looking at the advertising it runs. In some works the intended reader is even mentioned in the story itself, as in Charlotte Brontë's *Jane Eyre*, when she tells of her decision to marry Rochester:

> Reader, I married him. A quiet wedding we had: he and I, the parson and clerk, were alone present. When we got back from church, I went into the kitchen of the manor-house, where Mary was cooking the dinner, and John cleaning the knives, and I said:—
> "Mary, I have been married to Mr. Rochester this morning."

Impressionism   A term used to describe a type of writing, especially prevalent in the late nineteenth and early twentieth centuries, in which the writer presents her perceptions of plot, character, and especially descriptive details as they appear to a specific character at a specific time and place, rather than objectively, as the details would seem to a disinterested observer.

The term "impressionism" comes from a style of painting that arose in France during the mid-nineteenth century and included painters Edouard Manet, Claude Monet, Edgar Degas, and Pierre Auguste Renoir among its practitioners. These painters felt it was more mean-ingful to present the impression something makes than to try to describe the thing objectively. They put particular emphasis on the effects of light on objects.

Impressionistic fiction, like its counterpart in painting, was a reaction against what many writers saw as a trend toward a cold, *objective style on the part of those *naturalist writers whose desire was to portray the experience of typical members of a society rather than subjective, individual experience.

Here is Mrs. Dalloway in Virginia Woolf's *Mrs. Dalloway*, at the florist's, preparing for a party:

> There were flowers: delphiniums, sweet peas, bunches of lilac; and carnations, masses of carnations. There were roses; there were irises. Ah yes—so she breathed in the earthy garden sweet smell as she stood talking to Miss Pym who owed her help, and thought her kind, for kind she had been years ago; very kind, but she looked older, this year, turning her head from side to side among the irises and roses and nodding tufts of lilac with her eyes half closed, snuffing in, after the street uproar, the delicious scent, the exquisite coolness. And then, opening her eyes, how fresh like frilled linen clean from a laundry laid in wicker trays the roses looked; and dark and prim the red carnations, holding their heads up; and all the sweet peas spreading in their bowls, tinged violet, snow white, pale—as if it were the evening and girls in muslin frocks came out to pick sweet peas and roses after the superb summer's day, with its almost blue-black sky, its delphiniums, its carnations, its arum lilies was over; and it was the moment between six and seven when every flower—roses, carnations, irises, lilac—glows; white, violet, red, deep orange; every flower seems to burn by itself, softly, purely in the misty beds; and how she loved the grey-white moths spinning in and out, over the cherry pie, over the evening primroses!

In impressionistic fiction, the accent is on the selection of descriptive details that will suggest something about the psychological make-up of the character through whose eyes the impression is given, as well as on whatever object or scene is being described. Writers known for their use of impressionistic techniques include Joseph Conrad, Ford Madox Ford, Henry James, James Joyce and Virginia Woolf.

Improvisation   The creation of a work in which the writer sits down to write without a particular plan in mind as to what will happen, without a structure guiding him to his conclusion. Improvisation is fraught both with rewards and with pitfalls, as John Gardner put it:

> When a writer is jazzing around, he may not feel a powerful need to create consistent, profound, well-rounded characters. In fact, he might start with an elderly Jew crying on a bus and transform him without notice to a boy of eleven, then to a sparrow, then to the Queen of Poland. All the ordinary, decent-hearted reader will ask is that the transformation be astonishing and interesting and that the story in some way appear to make sense, keep us reading.

Improvising successfully requires both a playful imagination and the ability to realize when the improvisation is working and when it is not. Sometimes it is only the appearance of improvisation that counts, especially since it is hard to know whether a work has been improvised without asking the author.

Here, Stanley Elkin, who said in an interview that the creation of *The Dick Gibson Show* was not at all based on improvisation, gives us the demo tape of a radio announcer looking for a job. The tape certainly gives the impression of having been improvised, which is necessary as a way to help characterize the *protagonist:

> "And that's why I'm such a good radio man. Because there are standards, grounds of taste. Because I would rid myself of all dialect and speak only Midwest American Standard, and have a sense of bond, and eschew the private and wild and unacceptable. Because I would throw myself into the melting pot while it's at the very boil and would, if I had the power, pass a law to protect the typical. Because I honor the mass. Because I revere the regular. Because I consent to consensus. Because I would be decent, and decently blind to the differences between appearances and realities, and

daily pray to keep down those qualities in myself that are suspect or insufficiently public-spirited or divergent from the ideal. Because I would have life like it is on the radio—all comfy and clean and everyone heavily brothered and rich as a Credenza. This is KROP, the Voice of Wheat. Your announcer is Marshall Maine, the Voice of Wheat's Voice, staff announcer for the staff of life. Give us this day our daily bread. Amen."

As charming as improvisation can be, however, it is not without risks, as Henry James points out in his introduction to *The Aspern Papers*:

Nothing is so easy as improvisation, the running on and on of invention; it is sadly compromised, however, from the moment its stream breaks bounds and gets into flood. Then the waters may spread indeed, gathering houses and herds and crops and cities into their arms and wrenching off, for our amusement, the whole face of the land—only violating, by the same stroke, our sense of the course and the channel, which is our sense of the uses of a stream and the virtue of a story.... To improvise with extreme freedom and yet at the same time without the possibility of ravage, without the hint of a flood; to keep the stream, in a word, on something like ideal terms with itself: that was here my definite business.

Here, in Eudora Welty's "Powerhouse," the improvisatory character of the writing mirrors the character of the music that Powerhouse, a jazz musician, is playing, making it easier for the reader to hear Powerhouse's music, an important aspect of the story:

Powerhouse is playing!
    He's here on tour from the city—"Powerhouse and His Keyboard—Powerhouse and His Tasmanians"—think of the things he calls himself! There's no one in the world like him....
    Powerhouse has as much as possible done by signals.

Everybody, laughing as if to hide a weakness, will sooner or later hand him up a written request. Powerhouse reads each one, studying with a secret face: that is the face which looks like a mask—anybody's; there is a moment when he makes a decision. Then a light slides under his eyelids, and he says, "92!" or some combination of figures—never a name. Before a number the band is all frantic, misbehaving, pushing, like children in a classroom, and he is the teacher getting silence. His hands over the keys, he says sternly. "You-all ready? You-all ready to do some serious walking?"—waits—then, STAMP. Quit. STAMP, for the second time. This is absolute.

In Medias Res   Latin, for "in the middle of things"; the method of beginning a story in the midst of the action. The more common practice is to begin, with exposition, at some point before the action begins, before the narrator says, "And then one day something unusual happened. . . ."

Starting in medias res allows the author to distribute the exposition and action throughout the work, moving back and forth in time and space without being bound to tell the story chronologically. The author has the option to begin in the middle of the story, then break off and tell what happened before, and finally to continue telling the story from the middle to the end.

In William Faulkner's "A Rose for Emily," the narrator starts the action in medias res, just after the death of Miss Emily, and then skips around, revealing details from different times in Emily's life, moving back to the present only at the end of the story. At the end, the narrator reveals that after Miss Emily's death, the townspeople have learned about a room in her house whose door will have to be forced open. When the door finally is opened, the people find the corpse of a lover Emily poisoned thirty years earlier, but apparently had been sleeping with until the time of her death.

This ending would not be so deliciously shocking if Faulkner had been compelled to tell the story in chronological order: The reader would have become immediately suspicious about the juxtaposition of Emily's purchase of arsenic, her lover's disappearance, and the bad smell coming from her cellar.

Intentional Fallacy   A problem with the reading of fiction, in which the reader judges the quality of a work by the quality of the writer's intended message, or by how it relates to the writer's biography, rather than on the literary merit of the work itself. Some writers, including Philip Roth and John Irving, for example, particularly resent readers reading biographical details into their stories.

The intentional fallacy also becomes a problem for a writer of *thesis fiction, when the writer feels that having a good message is enough; even Karl Marx asserted that the creation of compelling characters and scenes is absolutely vital. *(See: passive characterization, thesis novel.)*

Interior Monologue   An extended passage relating the thoughts inside a character's head.

Interior monologue usually makes more literal sense than *stream-of-consciousness writing, which includes more random thoughts or images; it tends to be coherent and organized, almost as much so as spoken monologue might be. Because it is more rational, however, interior monologue probably is less like the random thoughts of real people than stream of consciousness is.

Here is Granny Weatherall in a lucid moment of interior monologue, on her dying bed in Katherine Anne Porter's "The Jilting of Granny Weatherall." Her thoughts range from subject to subject, but the narrator always is careful to provide enough information so that it is not difficult to follow her train of thought:

> Well, she could just hear Cornelia telling her husband that Mother was getting a little childish and they'd have to humor her. The thing that most annoyed her was that Cornelia thought she was deaf, dumb, and blind. Little hasty glances and tiny gestures tossed around her and over her head saying, "Don't cross her, let her have her way, she's eighty years old," and she sitting there as if she lived in a thin glass cage. Sometimes Granny almost made up her mind to pack up and move back to her own house where nobody could remind her every minute that she was old. Wait, wait, Cornelia, till your own children whisper behind your back!

Interpretive Fiction *(literary fiction)* Fiction in which the writer wants the reader to read not simply to escape from the real world, but to deepen his understanding of life in general.

Writers of interpretive fiction would assert that more goes on in the story than simply the amusing aspects of a good yarn. In interpretive fiction, symbols abound, and there will be one or more *themes relating to big subjects and ideas.

While combing a work for symbols can, of course, deteriorate into reading with the hope of unlocking a secret code, interpretive fiction invites the reader to think about the work's parts, including its structure as well as its content, and demands that the attentive reader take it seriously—that he discover and ponder whatever it is in the work that relates to the world itself. *(See: theme.)*

Intertextuality A term variously attributed to French critics Julia Kristeva and Mikhail Bakhtin, used widely by critics in the last twenty years to refer to the presence of aspects of one or more texts within some other work. The idea of intertextuality suggests, in fact, that every piece of written work in some way is related to other texts that already have been written.

Types of intertextuality include overt literary *allusion, actual quotation from other works, and even plagiarism and *parody. For example, in Stanley Elkin's *The Dick Gibson Show*, local city leaders on a radio talk show apparently are hypnotized into publicly admitting embarrassingly perverse things about themselves, one at a time, in a way that recalls Chaucer's *Canterbury Tales*.

Intertextuality sometimes is used much more broadly, however. Often, the "intertext" of a story will be defined as the wider group of plots, characters and conventions that it calls forth for a given reader, and some critics would include even those influences outside the literary tradition.

While reading Flannery O'Connor's "Everything That Rises Must Converge," for example, a reader may have in her mind not only that particular story but also others by Flannery O'Connor, other religious fiction, and other stories involving *grotesque characters that take place in the South. Since "Everything That Rises Must Converge" takes place on a recently desegregated bus in the South, the reader also will have in her mind newspaper accounts she has read about real-life, non-literary events regarding segregation and busing.

Invented Words *(coined words)*   Words invented by the writer, which are used in a different manner—or not at all—in conventional English.

This example is from Anthony Burgess' "nadsat," an argot spoken by the vicious teenagers in his novel *A Clockwork Orange*. The vocabulary comprises about 250 words, many of which seem to be of Russian origin.

> The Korova Milkbar was a milk-plus mesto, and you may, O my brothers, have forgotten what these mestos were like, things changing so skorry these days and everybody very quick to forget, newspapers not being read much neither. Wel, what they sold there was milk plus something else. They had no licence for selling liquor, but there was no law yet against prodding some of the new veshches which they used to put into the old moloko, so you could peet it with vellocet or synthemesc or drencrom or one or two other veshches which would give you a nice quiet horrorshow fifteen minutes admiring Bog and All His Holy Angels And Saints in your left shoe with lights bursting all over your mozg.

Actually inventing words, rather than just inventing a *dialect, takes the reader one step further away from the real world, yet the invention of a new language also makes the false world the writer has invented seem more real, in the same way that the addition of details to any lie, as long as the details seem plausible, strengthens the lie. *(See: dialect, invented worlds.)*

Invented Worlds   Worlds, created by contemporary non-science-fiction writers, that differ significantly from Earth. Such worlds, when outside the sphere of science fiction, often are created by *meta-fictionists, who do not want readers to forget that they are reading fiction.

The effect sometimes is simple delight, as in the case of Jorge Luis Borges' "Tlön, Uqbar, Orbis Tertius," about an imaginary country near Armenia called Tlön, in which physical objects sometimes can be imagined into existence, but that also is different from what goes on in Earth in other ways:

> In literary matters too, the dominant notion is that every-thing is the work of one single author. Books are rarely signed. The concept of plagiarism does not exist; it has been established that all books are the work of one single writer, who is timeless and anonymous. Criticism is prone to invent authors. A critic will choose two dissimilar works—the *Tao Tê Ching* and *The Thousand and One Nights*, let us say—and attribute them to the same writer, and then with all probity explore the psychology of this interesting homme de letters. . . .
>
> The books themselves are also odd. Works are based on a single plot, which runs through every imaginable permuta-tion. Works of natural philosophy invariably include thesis and antithesis, the strict pro and con of a theory. A book which does not include its opposite, or "counter-book," is considered incomplete.

Sometimes the world is not described; instead, the narrator takes for granted that the reader lives in the alternate universe, too—that the strange universe is the real universe. In Vladimir Nabokov's *Ada*, the narrator, Van Veen, who lives on Antiterra and can only posit the concept of a universe (our world) called Terra, which the insane sometimes bring forth in their dreams, takes for granted that the reader knows that due to an unnamed catastrophe, even mentioning the word "electricity" is illegal:

> Van regretted that because Lettrocalamity (Vanvitelli's old joke!) was banned all over the world, its very name having become a "dirty word" among upper-upper-class families (in the British and Brazilian sense) to which the Veens and Durmanovs happened to belong, and had been replaced by elaborate surrogates only in those very important "utili-ties"—telephones, motors—what else?—well a number of gadgets for which plain folks hanker with lolling tongues,

breathing faster than gundogs (for it's quite a long sentence), such trifles as tape recorders, the favorite toys of his and Ada's grandsires (Prince Zemski had one for every bed of his harem of schoolgirls) were not manufactured any more, except in Tartary where they had evolved "minirechi" ("talking minarets") of a secret make.

(See: fabulation, metafiction.)

Irony   A discrepancy between what seems to be going on—or what, given the rules of nature, societal standards or common sense, *should* be going on in fiction—and what really is going on.

While irony often is divided into subcategories such as tragic irony, irony of fate, irony of events, irony of nature, pure irony and cosmic irony, all of these are somewhat overlapping subcategories of what is called situational (or circumstantial) irony, in which the discrepancy is between what the reader or a character expects—or hopes—will occur, and what does happen.

An example can be found in William Faulkner's "Barn Burning," in which a ten-year-old betrays his father to the owner of the plantation on which the family sharecrops, because the father plans to burn down the man's barn. The boy is not successful in saving the barn, but at the end of the story the plantation owner rides after the boy's father and, though it is not clear, may have killed him. The boy thinks:

Father. My father, he thought. "He was brave!" he cried suddenly, aloud but not loud, no more than a whisper. "He was! He was in the war! He was in Colonel Sartoris' cav'ry!" not knowing that his father had gone to that war a private in the fine old European sense, wearing no uniform, admitting the authority of and giving fidelity to no man or army or flag, going to war as Malbrouck himself did: for booty— it meant nothing and less than nothing to him if it were enemy boots or his own.

The irony here is that the boy's desperately held belief, that his father was a hero, is completely false; his vocation during the war was to sell stolen horses to both armies.

Another main type of irony in fiction, verbal irony, occurs when a character sarcastically says the opposite of what he really means, like "I'm so glad you got mad and bashed in the car with your baseball bat. It's much healthier to walk." Verbal irony also is the use of statements by the author or a character that are contradicted by actual events.

A third type of irony, dramatic irony, occurs most frequently in theatrical works, as in *Oedipus the King*, in which Oedipus, having been told by a prophet that the presence of the murderer of the previous king of Thebes in the city is causing a plague, calls for the murderer to be exiled, not realizing that it is he himself who killed Laius.

J

Jamesian Sentence   Sentences characteristic of the writing of Henry James: long, complex, full of nuances and qualifications of the sentence's main point.

This sentence comes from James' short story, "Pandora":

> For Count Vogelstein was official, as I think you would have seen from the straightness of his back, the lustre of his light elegant spectacles, and something discreet and diplomatic in the curve of his mustache, which looked as if it might well contribute to the principal function, as cynics say, of the lips—the active concealment of thought.

The Jamesian sentence's complexity is most appealing when it is at its most precise, concentrating on the narrowest and most meticulous of description, as here in the description of Count Vogelstein's elegantly furtive demeanor. The danger of the Jamesian sentence, of course, is that the reader will lose the thought at the beginning of the sentence before reaching its end.

Juvenilia   Works written during a writer's childhood, before she has developed a mature style and understanding.

Juvenilia usually is marked either by the way it shows the writer's lack of early promise, as Ernest Hemingway's articles in his high school newspaper appear no more well written than any other high school reports; or in the way it anticipates the writer's later, more developed work.

This example, from "Frederic and Elfrida," a twelve-page novel written when Jane Austen was an adolescent, shows the writer's characteristic subject matter and wit already well on their way to formation. Here, the character Charlotte has just drowned herself, after recollecting with shame that she became simultaneously engaged to two different men the day before:

> She floated to Crankhumdunberry where she was picked up & buried; the following epitaph, composed by Frederic Elfrida & Rebecca, was placed on her tomb.
>
> *Epitaph*
> Here lies our friend who having promis-ed
> That unto two she would be marrie-ed
> Threw her sweet Body & her lovely face
> Into the Stream that runs thro' Portland Place.
>
> These sweet lines, as pathetic and beautifull were never read by any one who passed that way, without a shower of tears, which if they should fail of exciting in you, Reader, your mind must be unworthy to peruse them.

A term sometimes used synonymously with juvenilia is "apprenticeship novel." The apprenticeship novel, however, generally is a published first novel by a writer who still is in the learning stages of her craft. Juvenilia, on the other hand, often remains unpublished until after the writer has achieved acclaim with more mature works.

K

Kmart fiction Fiction that makes a serious point by using icons of popular culture, usually images from lower-class popular culture (hence "Kmart fiction" rather than "Saks fiction"), especially brand names. The technique is used to make the characters and scenes seem real and immediate. Kmart fiction is not the type of fabulous fiction that takes place in an imaginary, unnamed country.

Bobbie Ann Mason is a master of this technique. This conversation takes place in Bobbie Ann Mason's "Graveyard Day," while four friends, the narrator notes, are watching the TV show "The Waltons." The serious promulgation of spurious information—in this case that Colonel Sanders is trying to grow three- (or four-) legged chickens— is another technique of this type of fiction. The characters are of course wrong about the four-legged chickens, and the allusion to these may provoke a chuckle. Although the characters' names veer into the comic variety, their concerns, although pathetic, are not at all comic:

> "Guess who we saw at the Louisville airport?" Betty says.
>
> "I give up," says Waldeen.
>
> "Colonel Sanders!"
>
> "He's eighty-four if he's a day," C.W. adds.
>
> "You couldn't miss him in that white suit," Betty says. "I'm sure it was him. Oh, Joe! He had a walking stick. He went strutting along—"
>
> "No kidding!"

"He probably beats chickens to death with it," says Holly, who is standing around.

"That would be something to have," says Joe. "Wow, one of the Colonel's walking sticks."

"Do you know what I read in a magazine?" says Betty. "That the Colonel Sanders outfit is trying to grow a three-legged chicken."

"No, a four-legged chicken," says C.W.

"Well, whatever."

Detractors of Kmart fiction note that the brand names themselves sometimes are used simply as a kind of shorthand to describe the social class to which the characters belong, that nothing particularly meaningful seems to come from them, and that the interest in lower-class brand names is no more meaningful than the preoccupation with expensive brands found among the sometimes reviled *minimalists. *(See: minimalism.)*

Künstlerroman A type of *bildungsroman about a protagonist who is an artist, which generally follows the protagonist from childhood through adulthood and deals with themes relating to his development as an artist.

In life, there are nearly as many different kinds of artists as there are human beings, but in fiction there usually are two basic types of artists depicted. The first is the isolated, eccentric, often arrogant and rebellious artist who follows a different moral code and sees himself as totally separate from the average person. This type is exemplified by Anne Tyler's mysterious Jeremy Pauling in *Celestial Navigation*. Jeremy has not left his block in many years, is generally untouched by the goings-on of people around him, and is immersed in the world of his own art. Here's the narrator describing the way Jeremy's mind works:

> Jeremy Pauling saw life in a series of flashes, startling moments so brief that they could arrest a motion in mid-air. Like photographs, they were handed to him at unexpected times, introduced by a neutral voice: Here is where you are now. Take a look. Between flashes, he sank into darkness.

He drifted in a daze, studying what he had seen. Wondering if he had seen it. Forgetting, finally, what it was that he was wondering about, and floating off into numbness again.

The second type of artist who typically appears in fiction is the artist who sees his art as an outgrowth of his relations with other people and does not consider himself more important or even very different from other people simply because he is an artist. This type of artist-protagonist is, in fact, a more popular model at the moment, perhaps coinciding with a general decrease in the public's respect for the artist as a visionary. Such artists even realize that they could not create at all without recognizing their common humanity with nonartists.

Here is the protagonist of Margaret Atwood's *Cat's Eye*, visiting Toronto for an exhibit of her art, talking about her relationship to her work:

Alongside my real life I have a career, which may not qualify as exactly real. I am a painter. I even put that on my passport, in a moment of bravado, since the other choice would have been *housewife*. It's an unlikely thing for me to have become; on some days it still makes me cringe. Respectable people do not become painters: only overblown, pretentious, theatrical people. The word artist embarrasses me; I prefer painter, because it's more like a valid job. An artist is a tawdry, lazy sort of thing to be, as most people in this country will tell you. If you say you are a painter, you will be looked at strangely. Unless you paint wildlife, or make a lot of money at it, of course. But I only make enough to generate envy, among other painters, not enough so I can tell everyone else to stuff it.

A combination of the two types can lead to wonderful tensions in a work: a story of an artist pulled between the desire to be alone and create and the desire to fulfill social responsibilities. This type of tension appears in Alison Lurie's *The Truth About Lorin Jones* and in Ann Beattie's *Picturing Will*, in which the artist tries, fairly unsuccessfully, to combine art and motherhood.

L

Lampoon *(pasquinade)* A malicious attack, intended to be humorous, on a famous person or piece of literature.

In his second book, *The Torrents of Spring*, Ernest Hemingway set out to reveal what he felt were the falseness of Sherwood Anderson's ideas in *Dark Laughter*, in particular the concept that poor, uneducated people are closer to nature than more sophisticated types. The main interest now in *The Torrents of Spring*, for many readers, lies in the way the book shows the early development of Hemingway's work and his desire to throw off the influence of Anderson.

Here is the beginning of Anderson's novel:

> Bruce Dudley stood near a window that was covered with flecks of paint and through which could be faintly seen, first a pile of empty boxes, then a more or less littered factory yard running down a steep bluff, and beyond the brown waters of the Ohio River. Time very soon now to push the windows up. Spring would be coming soon now. Near Bruce at the next window, stood Sponge Martin, a thin wiry little old man with a heavy black mustache. Sponge chewed tobacco and had a wife who got drunk with him sometimes on pay-days. Several times a year, on the evening of such a day, the two did not dine at home but went to a restaurant on the side of the hill in the business part of the city of Old Harbor and there had dinner in style. . . .
>
> When he spoke of the other child, a girl playfully called Bugs Martin, Sponge got a little upset and chewed tobacco

more vigorously than usual. She had been a rip-terror right from the start. No doing anything with her. You couldn't keep her away from the boys. Sponge tried and his wife tried but what good did it do?

The first section of Hemingway's work, called "Red and Black Laughter," includes this passage about the protagonist, Scripps O'Neil, who has left his wife and daughter, like the character in *Dark Laughter*:

Scripps had a daughter whom he playfully called Lousy O'Neil. Her real name was Lucy O'Neil. One night, after Scripps and his old woman had been out drinking on the railroad line for three or four days, he lost his wife. He didn't know where she was. When he came to himself everything was dark. He walked along the railroad track towards town. The ties were stiff and hard under his feet. He tried walking on the rails. He couldn't do it. He had the dope on that all right. He went back to walking along the ties. It was a long way into town. Finally he came to where he could see the lights of the switchyard. He cut away from the tracks and passed the Mancelona High School. It was a yellow-brick building. There was nothing rococo about it, like the buildings he had seen in Paris. No, he had never been in Paris. That was not he. That was his friend Yogi Johnson.

A lampoon differs from a *burlesque, *satire or *parody in that there is definite malicious intent.

Legend   A traditional story, often told and changed over time by many storytellers, to illustrate and celebrate illustrious events or to explain the unexplainable.

Legends often began as recountings of real events (Paul Bunyan really may have existed, for example), but the stories have been changed and stylized over the years as they have been passed along. The "legend" category includes *tall tales, but a tall tale is a specialized term used to describe legends that contain so much exaggerated information that they are not believable at all. Even legends that don't come under the category of tall tales, however, often include some supernatural elements.

In the United States, legends often involve the settlement of the West; some traditional American legends include the story of Johnny Appleseed, who walked throughout Pennsylvania and Ohio planting apple trees; Casey Jones, who gave his life to warn crew members on another train that there was going to be a collision; and various stories involving characters like Mike Fink, Davy Crockett, Buffalo Bill and Daniel Boone.

The legends category also includes what Jan Harold Brunvand calls "urban legends"—"modern American folk narratives, stories that most people have heard as true accounts of real-life experiences, and few except scholars recognize as an authentic and characteristic part of our contemporary folklore." An example is the legend that if you send in forty dollars, the U.S. Army will send you a disassembled surplus military jeep packed in motor oil. Another popular urban legend is the story of the teenage couple whose car breaks down on a lonely road. The boy goes for help and warns the girl to stay in the car, since a psychotic murderer with a hook for a right hand is on the loose. This urban legend is recounted once again in Jayne Anne Phillips' "Black Tickets":

> It got darker and the stories got scarier. Finally she told their favorite, the one about the girl and her boyfriend parked on a country road. On a night like this with the wind blowing and then rain, the whole sky sobbing potato juice. Please let's leave, pleads girlie, It sounds like something scratching at the car. For God's sake, grumbles boyfriend, and takes off squealing. At home they find the hook of the crazed amputee caught in the door.

Note that while readers generally are not receptive to fake folksiness, a reference to a legend that everyone has heard can help bring the reader, writer and characters together in the enjoyment of the shared memory of the first time they heard and believed this contemporary legend. *(See: myth, tall tale.)*

Le Mot Juste A French phrase meaning "the appropriate word," used by Gustave Flaubert to describe the importance of choosing the right word at any given place in a story rather than a word that is close to being the right one. *Le mot juste* also refers to the assurance a writer must be able to give that she has chosen every single word carefully, not being satisfied with the nearly right word or phrase that will not succeed in saying exactly what she means to say.

Life Imitating Art A comment on the surprise that is created when something happens in real life that appears oddly like something that has already taken place in fiction.

The opposite concept, that of art imitating life, is very common; many, if not most, fiction writers base their fiction on real-life events. One reason why the imitation of fiction by real-life events, however, is startling is because we do not expect real-life events to have the order and rationality of fiction, and it is surprising when they do. Perhaps this is why the fictional events mirrored by later real-life ones often are bizarre or grotesque—although of course more ordinary bits of real life closely follow fictional plots all the time and are not even noticed.

Here is Truman Capote's description of two real-life killers, described in *In Cold Blood* (first published in 1965), and the philosophy of Ronnie and Latham, the killers:

> "It's a rotten world," Latham said. "There's no answer to it but meanness. That's all anybody understands—meanness. Burn down the man's barn—he'll understand that. Poison his dog. Kill him." Ronnie said Latham was "one hundred percent correct," adding, "Anyway, anybody you kill, you're doing them a favor."
>
> The first person they chose to so favor were two Georgia women, respectable housewives who had the misfortune to encounter York and Latham not long after the murderous pair escaped from the Fort Hood stockade, stole a pickup truck, and drove to Jacksonville, Florida, York's home town. . . . Alas, they [the victims] had lost their way. . . . But the road to which he led them was very wrong indeed: a narrow side-turning that petered off into swamp. . . . the helpful young men approaching them on foot, and they saw, but too late, that each was armed with a black bullwhip.

Here is a passage from Flannery O'Connor's "A Good Man Is Hard to Find," which was published ten years before the murders:

> "... it's nothing for you to do but enjoy the few minutes you got left the best way you can—by killing somebody or burning down his house or doing some other meanness to him. No pleasure but meanness," he said and his voice had become almost a snarl.

Note the similarities between these two works: the killers have escaped from custody (O'Connor's "Misfit" is "aloose from the Federal Pen"); the Georgia-Florida setting; the murders occur on narrow roads and the victims lost their way while traveling. Even the Misfit's fictional comments about "meanness" parallel Latham's real ones. *(See: archetype, intertextuality.)*

Limited Omniscience *(third-person limited point of view; third-person subjective point of view)* A term identifying a third-person point of view in which the narrator can see into the minds of fewer than 100 percent of the characters. Most commonly, a limited-omniscient narrator can see into the mind of just one character. Such a narrator is, in fact, probably the most common type of narrator we can find.

Here's an example from Bruce Jay Friedman's *A Mother's Kisses*, in which the limited-omniscient narrator can see into the mind of Joseph, a college student relieved that his mother is leaving his college town and returning home at last. We learn only Joseph's thoughts "that he had hoped for a bleak day to fit his mood," that the sun was "spinning him around in a nauseated circle," that he found his mother's kiss "mint fresh" and her hair "combed in a subdued style"; we see the other characters only through his eyes and the eyes of the narrator (who seems to be making the judgment that the cab driver was a "petulant, womanish fellow"):

> Joseph had hoped for a bleak day to fit his mood, but the early sun was bright and cool, catching him upon the forehead and spinning him around in a nauseated circle. His mother's mouth was mint-fresh, her hair combed in a subdued style. Tapping her foot on the pavement, as they waited

for a cab, she hummed quietly and said, "Dad will faint when he sees me. He'll think I had an accident." The cabdriver was a petulant, womanish fellow who wore an apron. He put the valises in the trunk and when Joseph and his mother had gotten in and closed the door, he said, "Hey, easy on that, will you? You want to break it?"

Lipogram   A work in which one or more letters of the alphabet has been omitted, as, for example, George Perec's 1969 *La Disparition*, which does not use the letter "e."

Lipograms generally are attempted either as a kind of intellectual *exercise or for the same reasons that *aleatory fiction—fiction that relies on chance or random methods—in general is: as an attempt on the writer's part to penetrate below the conscious level of thought, to make psychological connections that transcend mundane logic.

The concept sounds like a contemporary one, but the lipogram can be traced back to the sixth century B.C. The omission of letters offers different degrees of difficulty in different languages. Omitting the letter "e" is much easier in French than it would be in English (although a 267-page "e"-less novel in English, *Gadsby*, was published in 1939 by Ernest Vincent Wright); German and Italian lipogrammists often choose to leave out the "r."

In a complicated variation on the lipogram, Walter Abish uses only words beginning with "a" in the first chapter of *Alphabetical Africa*; in the second chapter he uses words beginning with "a" and "b"; in the third, "a," "b" and "c," and so on, until he has all the letters in the twenty-sixth chapter. (Obviously life gets much simpler after the "t" chapter, when "the" is allowed.) Then he begins subtracting letters again, with the twenty-seventh chapter omitting the letter "z." Here's a part of a paragraph from the first "p" chapter, in which there are no words that begin with "q," "r," "s," "t," "u," "v," "w," "x," "y" or "z.":

> Paper made books possible. It also helped prevent illiteracy. I have an interest in books and in paper. An overwhelming interest, an interest exceeding my interest in Alva and Alex and Allen. Paper is porous. I freely admit, paper has its defects, its drawbacks. Dipped in a lake it may disintegrate. I'm on a paper chase. A lovely old English paper chase, only

it's in darkest Africa. Paper is essential for me. But Africa has existed for centuries independent of paper. It makes one ponder. Africa also makes me perspire. I had hoped I could avoid Africa because I perspire easily.

A concept related to lipogram is "liponymy," in which a writer is forbidden to use a certain word or words in her book. Stephen Crane once set himself the task of writing a book about love, for example, which did not use the word "love." *(See:* Oulipo.*)*

List Fiction Fiction that is a compilation of details or facts that form a long list. While it is possible to write a story that consists only of a list (see the entry for the short-short story), generally the technique forms only part of a longer work.

This example comes from a six-page paragraph in Philip Roth's *The Anatomy Lesson*, describing protagonist Nathan Zuckerman's activities as a college student at the University of Chicago, capturing both his pretentiousness and his genuine excitement for learning:

> He phoned home that night in ecstasy from all the erudition, but nobody in New Jersey knew who Thomas Mann was, or even Nelson Algren. "Sorry," he said aloud, after hanging up, "sorry it wasn't Sam Levenson." He learned German. He read Galileo, St. Augustine, Freud. He protested the underpaying of the Negroes who worked at the university hospital. The Korean War began and he and his closest friend declared themselves enemies of Syngman Rhee. He read Croce, he ordered onion soup, he put a candle in a Chianti bottle and threw a party. He discovered Charlie Chaplin and W.C. Fields and documentary films and the dirtiest shows in Calumet City. He went up to the Near North Side to look down his nose at the advertising types and the tourists. He swam off the Point with a logical positivist, he savagely reviewed beat novels for *The Maroon*, he bought his first classical records—the Budapest String Quartet—from a homosexual salesman at the co-op whom he called by his first name. He began in conversation to call himself "one." Oh, everything was wonderful, as big and exciting a life as could

be imagined, and then he made his first mistake. He published a short story while still an undergraduate, an "Atlantic
First" . . .

The tone shifts after the mention of the "Atlantic First," which the
narrator represents as a terrible mistake on his part, for it began his
life as a writer.

Literature of Exhaustion   A phrase coined by John Barth in a 1967
Atlantic Monthly article to describe his concept that the attempts of
*modernist novelists to imitate reality no longer are relevant to writers
of the contemporary world; that the modern novel is, in fact, a "used-
up," depleted from.

In his article, Barth wrote that the best writers now were turning
to other concepts and to more "technically contemporary" techniques
in the writing of fiction, including James Joyce, Franz Kafka, Samuel
Beckett and Jorge Luis Borges. Barth suggests that an appropriate
way to deal with the obsoleteness of the form of the contemporary
novel is to write a novel in which this obsoleteness is pointed out,
played with, as it is in *metafiction, a kind of "imitation of a novel."

Twelve years later, in "The Literature of Replenishment," also published in *The Atlantic Monthly*, Barth reiterated his assertion that it
was not the end of all literature he was talking about in the earlier
argument, simply the realistic techniques of *modernism, and that he
held great hope for the literature of *postmodernism, which he called
"The Literature of Replenishment."

Local Color   Fiction whose main concentration is on showing unusual
customs, dress, habits and speech patterns of ordinary people from a
particular region of the United States—generally an isolated, rural
region, although the concept can be expanded to include the exotic
vocabularies and lifestyles of other subcultures as well: groups of people with interesting jobs or hobbies or followers of unusual philoso-
phies.

Writers of local-color fiction include Bret Harte, Joel Chandler
Harris, Hamlin Garland, Mark Twain, Sarah Orne Jewett and Kate
Chopin. In "The Town Poor," by Sarah Orne Jewett, the characters'
milieu—and certainly the rural Maine dialects of Mrs. William

Trimble and Miss Rebecca Wright—comes through even in this bit of dialogue that appears early in the story.

> "There must be a good deal o'snow to the nor'ard of us yet," said weather-wise Mrs. Trimble. "I feel it in the air; 't is more than the ground-damp. We ain't goin' to have real nice weather till the upcountry snow's all gone."
>
> "I heard say yesterday that there was good sleddin' yet, all up through Parsley," responded Miss Wright. "I should n't like to live in them northern places. My cousin Ellen's husband was a Parsley man, an' he was obliged, as you may have heard, to go up north to his father's second wife's funeral; got back day before yesterday. 'T was about twenty-one miles, an' they started on wheels; but when they'd gone nine or ten miles, they found 't was no sort o' use, an' left their wagon an' took a sleigh. The man that owned it charged 'em four an' six, too. I should n't have thought he would; they told him they was goin' to a funeral; an' they had their own buffloes an' everything."

Local-color fiction became a trend toward the end of the nineteenth century, when Americans became curious about regional differences and began writing fiction describing daily life and local customs, focusing especially on quaint and unusual customs and on creating a mood. The writing was either carefully researched, or, more likely, based on the personal observation and first-hand experience of the writers.

Local-color fiction is different from other kinds of regional fiction—all of which depict the customs, speech characteristics and mannerisms of people of a particular geographical region—in that in local-color fiction the accent is on description of habit and custom rather than on character development, *plot or *theme. Indeed, in local-color fiction, characters often become *caricatures, amalgamations of all the clichés and quirks that come together to make, say, a southern granny a particular *type. *(See: Kmart fiction, naturalism.)*

Loose Sentence *(cumulative sentence)* A sentence whose subject and predicate come at its beginning but that continues on after the first independent clause and is followed by one or more prepositional phrases and/or other dependent clauses. The loose sentence is the opposite of the *periodic sentence, whose subject and predicate do not appear until the end.

Most long sentences are loose; the loose sentence's less common opposite, the periodic sentence, usually is brought out on special occasions, for emphasis or to create a sense of anticipation. This example of a loose sentence takes place during an important party in Marcel Proust's *Swann's Way* (*Du côté de chez Swann*); the sentence is grammatically complete after just the first four words, but it meanders on for one hundred and seventy-five:

> Swann had gone forward into the room at Mme de Saint-Euverte's insistence, and in order to listen to an air from Orfeo which was being rendered on the flute, had taken up a position in a corner from which, unfortunately, his horizon was bounded by two ladies of mature years seated side by side, the Marquise de Cambremer and the Vicomtesse de Franquetot, who, because they were cousins, spent their time at parties wandering through the room each clutching her bag and followed by her daughter, hunting for one another like people at a railway station, and could never be at rest until they had reserved two adjacent chairs by marking them with their fans or handkerchiefs—Mme de Cambremer, since she knew scarcely anyone, being all the more glad of a companion, while Mme de Franquetot, who, on the contrary, was extremely well-connected, thought it elegant and original to show all her fine friends that she preferred to their company that of an obscure country cousin with whom she had childhood memories in common.

Despite its length, the sentence does not become bulky and cumbersome; on the contrary, the reader is encouraged to read it quickly and easily, and to appreciate the smoothness and fluency that the lack of full-stop punctuation provides it.

The loose sentence is similar to the Jamesian sentence in that it is generally long; the loose sentence is less restrictive than the Jamesian sentence, however, in which every phrase and clause must specifically amplify and clarify the sentence's topic. *(See: Jamesian sentence, periodic sentence.)*

Lyrical Novel   A novel that combines the features of most conventional novels and those of lyric poetry. Lyric poetry, in general, seeks to show the feelings of the writer at a particular time and place about a particular subject through imagery and patterns of imagery. In a lyrical novel, the plot becomes less important than the revelation of the *protagonist's thoughts and psychological and emotional character.

An example is Virginia Woolf's *The Waves*, which follows the lives of six friends from childhood to old age. In each chapter, we learn about the characters primarily from what they say about themselves; in between each chapter is an interchapter that describes the effects of light and weather on the landscape, and especially the waves as they reach the shore. These descriptive interchapters mirror the passage of the characters through life and help create the rhythm of the novel. Here are three passages about the waves from the novel:

> As they neared the shore each bar rose, heaped itself, broke and swept a thin veil of white water across the sand. The wave paused, and then drew out again, sighing like a sleeper whose breath comes and goes unconsciously.

Then, about seventy pages later:

> The wind rose. The waves drummed on the shore, like turbaned warriors, like turbaned men with poisoned assegais who, whirling their arms on high, advance upon the feeding flocks, the white sheep.

And on page 150:

> The waves broke and spread their waters swiftly over the shore. One after another they massed themselves and fell; the spray tossed itself back with the energy of their fall. The waves were steeped deep-blue save for a pattern of diamond-pointed light on their backs which rippled as the backs of great horses ripple with muscles as they

move. The waves fell; withdrew and fell again, like the thud
of a great beast stamping.

These *repetitions of important images mark the lyric novel form.
Ideally, on each repetition, the image changes somewhat, deepening
and redefining itself in meaning.

While lyrical fiction does not necessarily have a *poetic style, the
form often seems particularly appropriate for showing the character's
psychological state rather than his physical states, and the repetition
often creates dreamlike effects. *(See: motif, subjective style.)*

M

Magic Realism *(magical realism)* A term introduced by Cuban novelist Alejo Carpentier in 1949 to describe a style of writing that combines both the reasonable, logical events of everyday life—told by an *implied author who herself is obviously sophisticated—and aspects of the supernatural, often based on native religions and myths of Latin-American peoples. The goal of magic realism is to expand the definition of reality to include supernatural aspects like religion and myth.

Probably the most celebrated recent example of magic realism is Gabriel García-Márquez's *One Hundred Years of Solitude*. In the following example, much is unusual and imaginative, but everything seems plausible except the reason why the "Guajiro Indian woman" and her brother have left their village. Yet the epidemic of insomnia is presented as matter-of-factly as every other aspect of the paragraph:

> At that time there was so much activity in the town and so much bustle in the house that the care of the children was relegated to a secondary level. They were put in the care of Visitacion, a Guajiro Indian woman who had arrived in town with a brother in flight from a plague of insomnia that had been scourging their tribe for several years. They were both so docile and willing to help that Ursula took them on to help her with her household chores. That was how Arcadio and Amaranta came to speak the Guajiro language before Spanish, and they learned to drink lizard broth and eat spider eggs without Ursula's knowing it, for she was too busy with a promising business in candy animals.

The term "magic realism" usually is used to describe Latin-American work—although certainly work from other cultures, like Mikhail Bulgakov's *The Master and Margarita*, in which the Devil appears in twentieth-century Moscow, fulfill the magic-realism criteria.

Magic realism is different from some other types of fantasy fiction in that the illogical elements generally are presented in magic realism as being just as reasonable and real as the logical ones. Magic realism also is different from surrealism in that in surrealism the juxtapositions often are much more illogical and free-associative, much more obviously there to jolt the reader. In magic realism, there is a system to the madness, although it certainly is an illogical system.

Mainstream Fiction   Fiction that appeals to a wide range of readers because it depicts situations and explores themes of broad interest, and because it portrays characters with whom many people can empathize.

An example of mainstream fiction is Anne Tyler's *The Accidental Tourist*. The novel, which was later made into a movie, concerns the relationships of the Leary family, Macon and Sarah, a couple whose child has been killed in a robbery at a fast-food restaurant. The couple separates, gets back together, and then separates for good. Macon Leary finally seems to find lasting love with a much younger woman of a different social class and background.

While no one, of course, lives a life with the exact circumstances of the *protagonist, many people can relate closely to Macon Leary's feelings of grief, of being disapproved of by family members because of his behavior, and of breaking up and reforming love relationships.

Malapropism   The humorous accidental substitution of one word for another, similar-sounding word.

The term is taken from the name of a character, Mrs. Malaprop, from Richard Sheridan's *The Rivals*, who at one point refers to "an allegory on the banks of the Nile," meaning, of course, an alligator.

The purpose of malapropisms, beyond a little laughter at the expense of a character, is to express the character's ignorance or naïveté, as when the child detective in Dorothy Sayers' *Murder Must Advertise* repeatedly says "constickate" rather than "confiscate."

Mannerism   Writing in a style characterized by eccentricity, exaggeration and odd word choice. In mannered writing, the author seems to intrude on himself not only at certain moments, as an editorially omniscient narrator might, but constantly, through a writing style that seems unnatural for no reason that relates to the kind of story being told. Mannered writing may be used to create some special effect.

In mannered prose, each word reminds us that it has been created by a living person outside the story. When the effect of this is pleasing, the reader praises rather than calls it mannered; the word "mannered" generally is used when the intrusive style is distracting rather than appealing.

Sometimes mannered writing indicates some worse fault lurking below the surface; other times—as in this passage from the beginning of Ronald Firbank's short novel *The Flower Beneath the Foot*—it simply is a matter of style:

> Neither her Gaudiness the Mistress of the Robes nor her Dreaminess the Queen were feeling quite themselves. In the Palace all was speculation. Would they be able to attend the Fêtes in honour of King Jotifa, and Queen Thleeanouhee of the Land of Dates?—Court opinion seemed largely divided. Countess Medusa Rappa, a woman easily disturbable, was prepared to wager what the Countess of Tolga "liked" (she knew), that another week would find the Court shivering beneath the vaulted domes of the summer Palace.
>
> "I fear I've no time (or desire) now, Medusa," the Countess answered, moving towards the Royal apartments, "for making bets"; though, turning before the ante-room door, she nodded: "Done!"

(See: camp fiction, decadence.)

Maxim   A short, terse statement that provides a common-sense recommendation on how life should be lived, or that offers a general truth about human nature. Some examples—these come from Finnish culture—are:

He who gets angry without reason is conciliated without a gift.

One cannot ski so softly that the traces cannot be seen.

Cold days in summer are also warm.

Like *epigrams, maxims can be thought of as a very short form of fiction, embodying as they do the *theme of a story while omitting *plot, perhaps carrying the idea of the *short-short story to its minimum limit.

Maximal Fiction   A term coined by John Barth to describe long, multiplotted works—mostly longer than five hundred pages—that encompass what critic Tom LeClair calls "huge ecological and cultural wholes." Like much *postmodern fiction, maximal fiction plays with the idea of realism and reality by portraying characters in a world somewhat different from our own, in which characters deal with a different kind of culture and assumptions about what can and might happen. The term mainly refers to works written in the 1970s, by authors including William Gaddis, Thomas Pynchon, Joseph McElroy, Don DeLillo and Barth himself.

Maximal fiction differs from science fiction in the extent of its imagining of new kinds of technology and life forms. Maximal fiction portrays situations closer to those of our world, in general, than science fiction does. It also differs from science fiction in the intent of its authors: Speculation about the future is much less important in maximal fiction than in science fiction; the objective is more to show the behavior of real people in a differently imagined world.

An example of maximal fiction is Thomas Pynchon's *Gravity's Rainbow*, which details the development during World War II of a U.S. rocket that would carry nuclear armaments. The work also details the difficulties of a soldier named Tyrone Slothrop, who becomes sexually excited when he visits the areas in London in which the rocket ultimately hits. The novel encompasses a number of other *subplots as well, many of which seem to sprawl absurdly out of control, mirroring the tragic absurdity of the creation of weapons that could annihilate humanity.

The term "maximal fiction" sometimes is used synonymously with *systems novel, and the writers of each overlap. The difference lies mainly in the works' length, rather than in a particular philosophical outlook. *(See: systems novel.)*

Melodrama   A generally derogatory term, traditionally used to describe drama that involves a sensational, sentimental plot full of events designed to thrill. Melodrama appeals to the reader's emotions rather than striving to portray realistic motivation; its characters tend to be either all good or all bad.

Typically, a melodrama ends happily, with the villain getting what he deserves and the rest of the characters ending up better off than before. *(See: bathos, sentimentality.)*

Metafiction   *(self-conscious fiction, self-depicting fiction, self-reflexive fiction)*   Fiction that deals with the subject and writing of fiction.

Metafiction does what conventional fiction tries not to do: It calls attention to the fact that the story is not real. Metafiction, generally an intellectual device rather than an emotional one, strives to show the reader the techniques the writer uses to achieve a desired fictional effect—techniques that writers of conventional fiction usually try to mask.

In *The French Lieutenant's Woman*, John Fowles has been describing the growing infatuation of Charles Smithson with Sarah, a young woman also known locally as "Tragedy," who claims to have been seduced and abandoned by a French lieutenant and who spends hours at a time staring out into the sea, apparently in wait of his return. Despite frequent *anachronistic devices, the story has been told through the end of the twelfth chapter in a realistic style, with the kind of language one would expect in a book written in 1867, when the story takes place, rather than in 1969, when the book was written.

Chapter twelve ends with Sarah standing in her window, contemplating jumping to her death. The narrator assures us that Sarah will not jump:

> I will not make her teeter on the windowsill; or sway forward, and then collapse sobbing back onto the worn carpet of her room. We know she was alive a fortnight after this incident, and therefore she did not jump. Nor were hers the sobbing,

hysterical sort of tears that presage violent action; but those produced by a profound conditional, rather than emotional misery—slow-welling, unstoppable, creeping like blood through a bandage.

Who is Sarah?

Out of what shadows do I come?

Reasonably, the reader expects an answer to this question. Why on earth *is* Sarah ruining her life, waiting for her former lover against all odds that he will come back. But Fowles surprises us here, pulling the reader abruptly out of what John Gardner calls "the fictional dream" at the beginning of the thirteenth chapter:

> I do not know. This story I am telling is all imagination. These characters I create never existed outside my own mind. If I have pretended until now to know my characters' minds and innermost thoughts, it is because I am writing in (just as I have assumed some of the vocabulary and "voice" of) a convention universally accepted at the time of my story: that the novelist stands next to God. He may not know all, yet he tries to pretend that he does. But I live in the age of Alain Robbe-Grillet and Roland Barthes; if this is a novel, it cannot be a novel in the modern sense of the word.

One reason that it is useful to pull the reader away from the literal story from time to time is to maintain the reader's appropriate *aesthetic distance from the material—to remind her that the deeply neurotic and, it turns out, rather manipulative Sarah, for example, is not someone she should admire.

Metafiction generally announces itself in some way by incorporating a spirit of self-parody or at least playfulness ("ludism" in contemporary critical theory), emphasizing the idea that it should not be taken too seriously. There is something playful, for example, in that the last two hundred pages of Julio Cortàzar's *Hopscotch* are announced as "expendable chapters."

At the same time, metafiction also is influenced by what seem to be the opposite values from those of simple playfulness—the idea that artistic values are more important than any other. This kind of paradox is one of the key tenets of metafiction: It is both about real things happening in the real world and about fiction itself.

Metaphor A figure of speech that describes the qualities of one object by saying that it is something else, without, as is the case with a simile, the use of "like" or "as."

Here are two examples: the first from *Main Street* by Sinclair Lewis, the second from *The French Lieutenant's Woman* by John Fowles:

> Ezra Stowbody was a troglodyte. He had come to Gopher Prairie in 1865. He was a distinguished bird of prey—swooping thin nose, turtle mouth, thick brows, port-wine cheeks, floss of white hair, contemptuous eye.

> She was one of those pudgy-faced Victorian children with little black beads for eyes; an endearing little turnip with black hair.

Metaphors and similes, like other figures of speech, tend to bring the reader out of total involvement with the text and make them concentrate more on surface features of the writing—which is sometimes desirable and sometimes not. *(See: simile.)*

Mimesis *(imitation)* The literary process of attempting to create a convincing and uninterrupted illusion of real life.

The term originally was used by Plato and Aristotle in a slightly different sense: as a description of the copying of eternal forms, accessible only to intellect and reason, to reveal universal truths. Mimesis is now often used in exactly the way that "imitation" might be.

In this passage from "A Sense of Shelter," John Updike imitates the smells, sights and sounds of the old high school so richly that the millions of readers who have attended similar schools get a clear image of what he means:

> The warmth inside the door felt heavy, like a steamed towel laid against his face. William picked up his books and ran his pencil along the black ribs of the radiator before going down the stairs to his locker in the annex basement. The

shadows were thick at the foot of the steps; suddenly it felt late, he must hurry and get home. He had the irrational fear they were going to lock him in. The cloistered odors of paper, sweat, and, from the woodshop at the far end of the basement hall, sawdust were no longer delightful to him. The tall green lockers appeared to study him through the three air slits near their tops.

At the same time, the vivid description of the high school at the end of the day echoes something in William's own life; that he suddenly desires to leave his beloved school mirrors his grief at being gently rejected by a girl he's loved for years from a distance. The story continues:

When he opened his locker, and put his books on his shelf, below Marvin Wolf's, and removed his coat from his hook, his self seemed to crawl into the long dark space thus made vacant, the ugly, humiliated, educable self.

It is useful to think of mimesis as the concept of trying to recreate reality for the purpose of showing something universal about life— that there is a goal in trying to recreate this reality beyond creating a simple snapshotlike view.

Erich Auerbach, whose work *Mimesis* has been influential in contemporary criticism, suggests that the attempts of contemporary *metafiction to retreat from mimesis are "a symptom of the confusion and helplessness" of the age and "a mirror of the decline of the world."

Minimalism *(dirty realism, super-realism)*   A method of writing characterized by a spare, often subdued or even numb style; a greater than usual reliance on dramatic action, scene and dialogue instead of narration or summary; an obsession with apparently random details, especially brand names of consumer products that indicate an upper-middle-or-above social class; and an ending that often seems inconclusive. Although the term relates more to a style than a subject, minimal stories often revolve around minor changes in the quietly desperate lives of upper-middle-class characters.

At its best, minimalism can tell stories that are "small, concise, precise," according to Amy Hempel, who prefers the term "miniaturist." As with many styles of writing whose time recently has passed, however, minimalism is much criticized nowadays and sometimes is seen as merely a 1980s reaction against the *metafiction of the 1970s. Editors of *Granta*, in England, have characterized most of the American minimalists as "dirty realists."

Minimalism has its roots in the spare styles of Hemingway and, later, Raymond Carver, and also has been influenced by the subtle epiphanies in James Joyce's fiction—endings in which the characters receive some small revelation. Minimalists, however, often bury the *epiphanies to a degree that they're hard to recover.

Here is an example from Ann Beattie's *Falling in Place* that shows how fiction in the minimalist style tends to use the accumulation of detail to characterize:

> She pulled off into the breakdown lane and sat there, staring straight ahead. The windshield was dirty. Blondie was singing "Heart of Glass." There was no real introduction to that song; it just started, sounding like music from outer space, seeming to be pulsed out instead of played. Cars whizzed by. Monday. Always a difficult day. A lot of people got depressed on Monday. In order to keep her job, it was necessary to get back onto the highway and drive to school and listen to teenagers recite lines memorized from Macbeth as they circled a wastebasket. To watch Karin Larsen hold out a hand, her wrist loaded with thin gold chains, to hear her say that there was no way the hand would ever be clean.

(See: epiphany.)

Mise en Abîme   A French term taken from heraldry and used more commonly in film than in fiction writing, where in one corner of a coat of arms a miniature version of the entire coat of arms appears, which in turn contains its own miniature version of the coat of arms, and so on. This relates to the idea of a story within a story within a story ad infinitum.

An example is André Gide's *The Counterfeiters*, in which the novel's protagonist is in the process of writing a novel called *The*

Counterfeiters, whose protagonist is writing a novel called *The Counterfeiters*, and so on. The effect is similar to the process of holding a mirror in front of you as you look into another mirror so you see an unlimited number of reflections of yourself.

Marcel Proust's *A la recherche du temps perdu*, translated as *Remembrance of Things Past* or *In Search of Lost Time*, works in the same way: In the last section of the book the narrator, who has spent much of his life unsuccessfully searching for meaning outside of himself, realizes that the time has come to begin writing—and presumably the work he writes is the one we have nearly finished reading.

Mock-Epic Fiction *(mock-heroic fiction)*   A kind of fiction that makes fun of the sometimes elevated style of the conventional epic novel. The mock-epic novel often has a rather trivial subject, so that the subject and/or the style of the novel are the subject of parody.

In Henry Fielding's *Joseph Andrews*, which concerns a young footman who is dismissed from his job for resisting the advances of his employer, Lady Booby, some of the events seem intrinsically improbable yet are told in the dignified, high style of many fictional epics. In this scene, Parson Adams, who ultimately rescues Joseph Andrews and his fiancée from robbers, is set upon by a pack of wild dogs:

> The hare was caught within a yard or two of Adams, who lay asleep at some distance from the lovers; and the hounds in devouring it, and pulling it backwards and forwards, had drawn it so close to him, that some of them (by mistake perhaps for the hare's skin) laid hold of the skirts of his cassock; others at the same time applying their teeth to his wig, which he had with a handkerchief fastened to his head, began to pull him about; and had not the motion of his body had more effect on him than seemed to be wrought by the noise, they must certainly have tasted his flesh, which delicious flavour might have been fatal to him; but being roused by these tuggings, he instantly awaked and with a jerk delivering his head from his wig, he with most admirable dexterity recovered his legs, which now seemed the only members he could entrust his safety to. Having, therefore, escaped likewise from at least a third part of his cassock, which he

willingly left as his exuviae or spoils to the enemy, he fled with the utmost speed he could summon to his assistance. Nor let this be any detraction from the bravery of his character: let the number of the enemies, and the surprise in which he was taken, be considered; and if there be any modern so outrageously brave that he cannot admit of flight in any circumstance whatever, I say (but I whisper that softly, and, I solemnly declare, without any intention of giving offence to any brave man in the nation), I say, or rather I whisper, that he is an ignorant fellow, and hath never read Homer nor Virgil, nor knows he anything of Hector or Turnus; nay, he is unacquainted with the history of some great men living, who, though as brave as lions, ay, as tigers, have run away, the Lord knows how far, and the Lord knows why, to the surprise of their friends, and the entertainment of their enemies.

Here, the reader's attention is drawn away from the events themselves, in part because of the narrator's participation in the story, and in part because of the intrinsic ridiculousness of the way that the parson's clothes and wig are torn off by the dogs. *(See: epic.)*

Modernism A period of literature covering, roughly, the beginning of World War I until about 1965.

Although the style of modernist fiction generally is realistic, it sometimes is marked by experimental techniques like *stream-of-consciousness writing and *opaque language. Common themes of modernist fiction involve a close look at the psychological nature of the characters and some kind of protest against the nature of modern society.

The experimental techniques of the modernists can be difficult to penetrate, but their impulse generally was toward the creation of a verisimilar reality—both physical reality and a kind of psychological reality. Often realistic writers desired to immerse the reader so strongly in the story that he would become unconscious not only that he was reading fiction, but also unconscious that a specific author is telling the story.

Some modernist writers are Dorothy Richardson, Virginia Woolf,

Evelyn Waugh, Aldous Huxley, Marcel Proust, William Faulkner, James Joyce and Ford Madox Ford. (*See: mimesis, realism.*)

Monologue A longish speech by a single character. A monologue is different from a soliloquy—although both terms are taken from drama—in that a monologue usually is perceived as having listeners, while a soliloquy has no listeners but the reader.

In life, long speeches by a single person can become dull, but in fiction, even if the other characters perceive a monologue to be dull, it must provide information necessary to the plot, at the very least. This excerpt is from Miss Bates' monologue (one of many) in *Emma*, by Jane Austen:

"I declare I cannot recollect what I was thinking of.—Oh! my mother's spectacles. So very obliging of Mr. Frank Churchill! 'Oh!' said he, 'I do think I can fasten the rivet; I like a job of this kind excessively.'—Which you know shewed him to be so very . . . Indeed, I must say that, much as I have heard of him before and much as I had expected, he very far exceeds any thing . . . I do congratulate you, Mrs. Weston, most warmly. He seems every thing the fondest parent could . . . 'Oh!' said he, 'I can fasten the rivet. I like a job of that sort excessively.' I shall never forget his manner. And when I brought out the baked apples from the closet, and hoped our friends would be so very obliging as to take some, 'Oh!' said he directly, 'there is nothing in the way of fruit half so good, and these are the finest looking home-baked apples I ever saw in my life.' That, you know, was so very . . . And I am sure, by his manner, it was no compliment. Indeed they are very delightful apples, and Mrs. Wallis does them full justice—only we do not have them baked more than twice, and Mr. Woodhouse made us promise to have them done three times—but Miss Woodhouse will be so good as not to mention it. The apples themselves are the very finest sort for baking, beyond a doubt; all from Donwell—some of Mr. Knightley's most liberal supply. He sends us a sack every year; and certainly there never was

such a keeping apple any where as one of his trees—I believe there is two of them. My mother says the orchard was
always famous in her younger days. . . .

This monologue continues for another page and certainly establishes Miss Bates as a dull chatterbox, but the information she provides about Frank Churchill's and Mr. Knightley's kindness to the
Bates household is important to the plot.

Other monologues are allowed to continue uninterrupted for variety or dramatic effect, such as the three-page monologue at the end of
Walter Abish's 1979 novel *How German Is It*, in which the protagonist,
Ulrich von Hargenau, who has been avoiding many important facts
about his own life, opens up to a psychiatrist. He reveals that he must
face that the man he has identified throughout the novel as his father,
a celebrated anti-Nazi hero, could not have been his father at all:

But then, I must also confess, at the age of seven or eight,
I can't exactly remember when, I came to realize that I
wasn't, that I couldn't be, a Hargenau. It might have been
something my brother had told me. Or perhaps it was Franz.
Certainly not my mother. The information was easily con-
firmed . . . I had been born too long after my father's impris-
onment and execution for me to be his son. I pretended that
it wasn't true. I practiced a sort of self-deception. I still don't
have the slightest clue as to who my father could be . . . and
I almost prefer it that way, prefer it to discovering that my
father was someone in the Einsatzkommando.

Allowing Ulrich to tell his story without interruption either by other
characters or by an authorial voice adds to its dramatic effect; we hear
only the words of Ulrich; everything else is a dramatic silence.

Montage *(impingement)* A word from filmmaking to describe the
effect of many quick scenes or pieces of descriptive language linked
seemingly without relation to order or plot to create a desired
*atmosphere.

Here are two short scenes juxtaposed at the beginning of John Dos

Passos' *Manhattan Transfer*, which seem unrelated at this point in the book but that somehow combine to form a single memorable image:

> Three gulls wheel above the broken bones, orangerinds, spoiled cabbage heads that heave between the splintered plank walls, the green waves spume under the round bow as the ferry, skidding on the tide, crashes, gulps the broken water, slides, settles slowly into the slip. Handwinches whirl with jingle of chains. Gates fold upwards, feet step out across the crack, men and women press through the manuresmelling wooden tunnel of the ferryhouse, crushed and jostling like apples fed down a chute into a press.
>
> *
>
> The nurse, holding the basket at arm's length as if it were a bedpan, opened the door to the big dry hot room with greenish distempered walls where in the air tinctured with smells of alcohol and iodoform hung writhing a faint sourish squalling of other baskets along the wall. As she set her basket down she glanced into it with pursed-up lips. The newborn baby squirmed in the cottonwool feebly like a knot of earthworms.

One effect of the combining of these different scenes will be a lack of flow and continuity in the plot. Often this discontinuity is important to show discord in the emotional or psychological lives of the characters—or in the world in which the characters live. When two radically separate images are combined, the result often will be a new image that is more evocative and interesting than each would be separately.

The definition of montage fiction sometimes is expanded to include *narrative collage—the merging of different points of view and times, as well as physical settings. *(See: crot, narrative collage.)*

Mood A word generally used as a synonym with *atmosphere, to describe the story's prevailing ambiance. Mood also includes the idea of *tone, the attitude of the author toward the subject of the work.

The word "mood" differs slightly from atmosphere in that atmosphere usually includes the concept of *setting, whereas mood does not. A mood can be composed of many different emotions; the term, however, like atmosphere, usually is reserved for dark, dour or otherwise unhappy emotions, although there is no reason the mood of a work cannot be cheerful.

This passage from Ivan Turgenev's "The Country Doctor" creates a confused, surreal, rather nightmarish mood, and not only because of the subject matter. The mood is created through the author's *style, his use of long sentences broken by ellipses and dashes, and the fact that the doctor's story does not break into paragraphs at expected intervals. The speaker is, as the story's title implies, a country doctor, called out to visit a patient. The mood of the story makes it clear even at this early stage in the story that the patient is unlikely to recover:

> "I say: 'Pray calm yourself. . . . where is the patient?' 'Here, please come this way.' I see a small, clean room, an oil-lamp in the corner, on the bed a girl of about twenty, unconscious, heat fairly blazing from her, breathing heavily: a high fever. There are two other girls there, too, her sisters—badly scared, and in tears. 'Yesterday,' they say, 'she was perfectly well and had a good appetite; this morning she complained of a headache, then suddenly in the evening she became like this.' I repeat again, 'Pray calm yourselves'—it's part of the doctor's job, you know—and I set to work. I bleed her, I order mustard-plasters, I prescribe a mixture. Meanwhile I look at her. I look and look; my goodness, never have I seen such a face before . . . an absolute beauty!"

Moral Fiction John Gardner's phrase, from his belief that "true art is moral: it seeks to improve life, not debase it." In his 1977 book *On Moral Fiction*, Gardner criticizes writers who seem more interested in fiction's "decorations" than its themes, who try through persuasion to convince readers of things that are not strictly true, who oversimplify, who waste time on the trivial, especially including the *metafiction writers of the 1960s and 1970s.

In his controversial book, Gardner praises Henry James, Leo Tolstoy and John Fowles for producing work that aspires to show the reader a higher moral truth, exploring and clarifying human values.

Gardner criticizes writers he feels are too concerned with the surface of fiction.

Gardner makes the point that moral fiction is not simply *didactic fiction, using the example of *Mein Kampf* to point out that just because something tries to teach you something does not mean it is moral. *(See: didactic fiction.)*

Motif *(leitmotif)* A theme, idea, image or subject that recurs in a work and that, ideally, will become more important each time it re-appears.

In Stephen Crane's "The Open Boat," four men are trapped in a lifeboat, the only survivors of a shipwreck. Three times, the character whose thoughts we see asks himself why nature has picked him to be drowned, using the same general images:

> "If I am going to be drowned—if I am going to be drowned—
> if I am going to be drowned, why, in the name of the seven
> mad gods who rule the sea, was I allowed to come thus far
> and contemplate sand and trees? Was I brought here merely
> to have my nose dragged away as I was about to nibble the
> sacred cheese of life?"

The phrase is repeated about seventy paragraphs later, and then, in slightly different form, about thirty paragraphs after that:

> "If I am going to be drowned—if I am going to be drowned—
> if I am going to be drowned, why, in the name of the seven
> mad gods who rule the sea, was I allowed to come thus far
> and contemplate sand and trees?"

This is not symbolism: the "sand and trees" are literally "sand and trees," not standing for any other particular thing. The sand and trees in these passages is a motif, showing the character's gradual awareness that nature is indifferent to him, and to the plight of the individual in general. *(See: lyrical novel, symbol.)*

Motivation The reason(s) why a character does something.

Motivation must arise from a combination of the character's personality, physical and psychological characteristics, past experiences, and moral nature, as well as from the specific situation in which he happens to find himself. When the character's motivation seems real or plausible, his action seems convincing; otherwise, the plot may seem phony or arbitrary.

Even improbable actions can seem believable if the character's motivation is strong enough: Jay Gatsby's decision in F. Scott Fitzgerald's *The Great Gatsby* to take the blame for Daisy's hit-and-run killing of her husband's mistress seems real because previous details have established the extent of Gatsby's love for Daisy: that he bought a house just because it was across the sound from Daisy's; that he gives parties simply on the chance that Daisy will attend. His motivation is convincing.

Multiple Narrators *(shifting point of view)* A technique in which a story is told from the point of view of more than one narrator. Usually, this will be a range of first-person narrators, although there are exceptions: in Sherwood Anderson's *Winesburg, Ohio*, the reader sees into the minds of twenty-three third-person narrators.

The narrators in a story told by multiple narrators can either divulge the same events, or each can tell of different events. In the first type, interest springs from the variations in their versions of the story, as occurs when different witnesses to crimes in real-life court trials (and novels describing them) give conflicting testimony. Examples of the second type of story, in which each character tells a different part of the plot in a linear fashion, include William Faulkner's *As I Lay Dying* and *The Sound and the Fury*, and Alice Walker's *The Color Purple*. *(See: Rashomon effect.)*

Myth A story that does not have a specific author but that comes from the collective primitive beliefs of an entire culture. Generally, myths involve the use of supernatural events and heroes to explain the mysterious forces whose causes are unknown to primitive peoples, including the creation of the world and the meaning of life and death.

Before the twentieth century, Greek, Roman and Norse myths were the main ones known by English speakers; increasingly, however, scholars have begun to look at Asian and other myths.

Myths are different from *legends in that they do not involve a recognizable historical background and are more likely than legends to be concerned with supernatural events. Myths are different from *fables as well, in that they often end with no recognizable moral. Many myths do not seem to offer concrete explanations for cosmic events, but seem to exist for some other, mysterious reason, like this short myth of Melampus, taken from Edith Hamilton's *Mythology*:

> He saved and reared two little snakes when his servants killed the parent snakes, and as pets they repaid him well. Once when he was asleep they crept upon his couch and licked his ears. He started up in a great fright, but he found that he understood what two birds on his window sill were saying to each other. The snakes had made him able to understand the language of all flying and all creeping creatures. He learned in this way the art of divination as no one ever had, and he became a famous soothsayer. He saved himself, too, by his knowledge. His enemies once captured him and kept him a prisoner in a little cell. While there, he heard the worms saying that the roof-beam had been almost gnawed through so that it would soon fall and crush all beneath it. At once he told his captors and asked to be moved elsewhere. They did as he said and directly afterward the roof fell in. Then they saw how great a diviner he was and they freed and rewarded him.

Some modern writers have been influenced by the idea of mythology and work with mythology in various ways, either by altering old ones or creating new ones, sometimes to give meaning to their own perceptions and questions about the world, other times simply to express the largeness and mysteriousness of the world. *(See: archetype, mythic method.)*

Mythic Method *(mythopoeic method)* Fiction created either through using ancient myths as subject matter, as does John Gardner's *Grendel*, which retells the story of Beowulf from the monster's point of view, or through an attempt to create new stories that have the same ambitions as the old myths did—to give order to life and show the reasons for the seemingly illogical ways of nature.

Writers of this second type of mythic fiction attempt to fill their works with *archetypes and cause the reader to feel something that is both exotic and deeply familiar.

The term "mythic method" was first used by T.S. Eliot to describe the way in which James Joyce's *Ulysses*, which takes place in the course of a single day, follows the general structure of Homer's *Odyssey*, which describes Ulysses's ten-year journey back to Ithaca after the Trojan War.

Another example of fiction using the mythic method is Henry Fielding's 1751 *Amelia*, which follows some of the same structures as Virgil's *The Aeneid*. Here, Fielding is not particularly commenting on the myth in *Amelia* but is using *The Aeneid* as a kind of guide to assist the imagination. The reader does not need a familiarity with *The Aeneid*, however, to appreciate the novel.

John Updike's *The Centaur* retells the myth of Chiron, a centaur who, although painfully wounded by an arrow in his heel, is for a long time unable to find peace in death due to his "gift" of immortality. In Updike's version, Olympus becomes Olinger High School, and Chiron a science teacher who has been shot in the heel by a rowdy student. In *The Centaur*, Updike alternates chapters about the ancient mythical figures with chapters about the science teacher's actions in Pennsylvania in 1947. Updike includes an index at the end of the book that helps relate the mythic characters with their fictional counterparts. *(See: archetype.)*

N

Naïve Narrator   A first-person narrator who usually is either a child or mentally handicapped person and who is unable to understand all of the subtleties and/or implications of the story she tells. Often, a story with a naïve narrator will give the illusion that the story is being told orally to the reader; if the narrator is naïve enough, after all, she will not be literate enough to write it down. Probably the most well-known example of a naïve narrator is Huckleberry Finn.

In a generally upbeat story, the result of using a naïve narrator often is humor and irony; with a darker story a naïve narrator often creates a feeling of pathos, as when a child tells a story whose horrible implications she cannot understand.

Here is the naïve teenage narrator of Sherwood Anderson's "I'm a Fool," who is upset when the girl he met at a race track and was romancing asks for his address so they can write letters, because he knows he must give her a false address so she will not find out he's not the "swell" he has pretended to be:

> When Wilbur come back from being alone with his girl, and she saw him coming, Lucy she says, "We got to go to the train now," and she was most crying too, but she never knew nothing I knew, and she couldn't be so all busted up. And then, before Wilbur and Miss Woodbury got up to where we was, she put her face up and kissed me quick and put her head up against me and she was all quivering and—Gee whizz.
>
> Sometimes I hope I have cancer and die. I guess you

know what I mean. We went in the launch across the bay to the train like that, and it was dark, too. She whispered and said it was like she and I could get out of the boat and walk on water, and it sounded foolish, but I knew what she meant.

And then quick we were right at the depot, and there was a big gang of yaps, the kind that goes to the fairs, and crowded and milling around like cattle, and how could I tell her? "It won't be long because you'll write and I'll write to you." That's all she said.

The language tells us that this is a naïve narrator; in fact, he turns out to be a foolish narrator, too, giving up the chance for love with a girl who likes him and probably would have forgiven him for misrepresenting his income.

The naïve narrator is a close cousin to the *unreliable narrator; the two often overlap. Unlike an unreliable narrator, however, the naïve narrator is not capable of consciously trying to mislead the reader. The term "naïve narrator" generally is not used to describe mentally ill narrators who do not know the difference between right and wrong.

Narration *(narrative, storytelling)*   The part of the story that tells the reader what happened, the physical details of what is going on. The term also is sometimes used as a synonym for *"summary."

This example comes from a passage near the beginning of Mark Helprin's novella *Ellis Island*. Although a character is recounting what he saw, there is no dialogue: The narrator speaks straight to the reader rather than to another character.

As if by magic, a procession of launches came from the fog. The water was calm enough for our ship to unload by lighter. After we had stepped onto the smaller vessels, our suitcases in our hands, we moved into the low-lying clouds, engines echoing off the water as if we were moving in between the walls of a high canyon. Because the Americans on the launch were about twice our size, most of us thought that we had come into a country of giants, but I guessed that it was a measure taken to impress us. Indeed, we were impressed by these red-faced, uniformed Goliaths who spoke over our heads in a strange and difficult language.

(See: summary.)

Narrative Collage *(fictional pointillism)* A term coined by Annie Dillard in her book on fiction writing, *Living by Fiction*, to describe fiction created from a compilation of small, independent segments, sometimes called *crots. Although these independent crots do not follow each other logically or even sequentially, they come together to form a story in which something does happen, although the action is more likely to be on a psychological or emotional level than on the level of the traditional story, with its orderly *exposition, *rising action, *climax and *denouement.

While the individual sections of a piece of narrative collage may be juxtaposed in a jarring fashion, the writer, by repeating images from section to section, is able to build *symbols and *motifs.

One striking example of the technique is William Gass' "In the Heart of the Heart of the Country," in which the individual sections are descriptions of the narrator's life in a small town in Indiana and the rather sad, defeated characters who inhabit it with him. It is only through the recapitulation of various images about the dreariness of life in the town, and the narrator's desperate attempt to record those details accurately, that the reader eventually perceives the full force of the narrator's personal sorrow and his desire to forget about his own life by writing about others. Here are some sections from this long story:

The Church
The church has a steeple like the hat of a witch, and five birds, all doves, perch in its gutters.

My House
Leaves move in the windows. I cannot tell you yet how beautiful it is, what it means. But they do move. They move in the glass.

Politics
. . . for all those not in love.

I've heard Batista described as a Mason. A farmer who'd
seen him in Miami made this claim. He's as nice a fellow as
you'd ever want to meet. Of Castro, of course, no one speaks.

For all those not in love there's law: to rule . . . to regu-
late . . . to rectify. I cannot write the poetry of such proposals,
the poetry of politics, though sometimes—often—always
now—I am in that uneasy peace of equal powers which
makes a State; then I communicate by passing papers, proc-
lamations, orders, through my bowels. Yet I was not a State
with you, nor were we both together any Indiana . . .

At one point, trying to describe the town's schoolteacher, the narrator breaks off and writes: "I must concentrate. I must stop making up
things. I must give myself to life: let it mold me."

Often the technique of narrative collage, shattering as it does the
reader's sense of continuity, serves as an attempt to recreate the idea
that the world, like the fiction, is shattered—that senseless, strange
things happen for no particular reason at random times. *(See: crot.)*

Narrative Hook   A seldom-used term describing the common method
of beginning a story in such a way that the reader's interest is immediately captured.

Since all good fiction should create interest right from the start,
the term "narrative hook" usually is associated with stories that begin
in some way other than with description of character or scene or any
other general exposition, such as a shocking or otherwise arresting
statement—sometimes a piece of dialogue.

This opening paragraph from David Foster's *Testostero* is a hook
because it begins with such a bizarre assertion about the character's
initial reaction to Venice. The reader immediately must realize that
he is in the company of a narrator with a skewed, arresting view of
the world:

The most astounding feature of Venice to Noel Horniman,
who at age forty is seeing it for the first time, is not the
architecture—which seems shabby and run down—but the
fact one can walk from Campo de Gheto Novo to Piazza San
Marco and vice versa without seeing anyone pushing anyone

into a canal, which would be the easiest thing in the world
to do, given there are no railings.

This hook, from Grace Paley's "Gloomy Tune," also is a hook because of the unusual assertion with which it begins (that nearly everybody knows this family), as well as because of the children's unusual
names:

There is a family nearly everybody knows. The children of
this family are named Bobo, Bibi, Doody, Dodo, Neddy,
Yoyo, Butch, Put Put, and Beep.

Narrator The consciousness that tells the story.

Narrators may speak in the first person ("I can't believe you're
letting her wear makeup!"); rarely, the second person ("You get up
and do your business; you think everything's going to be fine—but
no!"); and, most commonly, especially in novels, the third person
("Frank did not want to get violent with the man from the golf course,
but he knew it might come to that.").

*First-person narrators may be major or minor characters in the
story they tell. Third-person narrators may be omniscient, able to see
into the minds of more than one character; *limited omniscient, able
to see into the minds of one character; or *objective, in which case
they can report only what they see, not what anyone thinks.

Narrators may be reliable—telling a story in such a way that a
reasonable reader will have no reason to disbelieve what they say; or
*unreliable—either too young or too sneaky to tell the story in a way
that is likely to lead the reader to understand the truth—in which case
the reader will be left to gather whatever the truth is from sources
outside of the narrator's words.

Narrators may tell their stories so that the reader always is aware
that she is reading a work of fiction; or the narrator may seem almost
to disappear, so the reader may almost forget that she has not stepped
into a window leading to the story. *(See: point of view.)*

Naturalism *(social realism)* A category of fiction, primarily written
during the late nineteenth and early twentieth centuries, that

emphasized the ways human beings respond to forces in their social environment.

In naturalist fiction, humans typically are unable to understand or change much of what goes on in their lives. Control of the characters' destinies is in the hands of indifferent—or actively hostile—outside forces. Human beings usually are portrayed as being without the necessary willpower to change their situations for the better.

A great accomplishment of the naturalists was to help fiction move away from the depiction of members of the upper and middle classes, and also from mere romance and escapism, by striving to show the dark, seamy side of the lives of characters from the lower strata of society. Naturalist writers stressed the importance of first-hand observation, and they were careful to show with accuracy details of the characters' historical and sociological background.

An example of naturalist fiction is James T. Farrell's *Young Lonigan: A Boyhood in Chicago Streets*, which tells the story of Studs, a recent eighth-grade graduate whose father, proud of his family, wants him to become a printer while his mother wants him to become a priest. Studs, however, wants to become tough like a friend who he has seen passionately kissing a girl at a graduation party.

Later in the summer, Studs fights with this tough friend, beats him, and becomes the "champ fighter of the block." Although his father wants him to find a job, Studs spends most of his time playing and fighting.

After breaking up with his girlfriend, Lucy, Studs seems increasingly unhappy, drifting into more and more fights and becoming more and more remote from his parents. The book is a record of Studs' disillusionment and moral deterioration. Studs is presented, however, as a victim of a kind of spiritual deficiency, as living in a society that left him no chance to avoid the troubles in which he finds himself.

The first naturalistic novel was Stephen Crane's *Maggie: A Girl of the Streets*, about a young prostitute; other naturalist writers include Frank Norris, Jack London, Gustave Flaubert, Honoré de Balzac and Theodore Dreiser. Naturalism also is known as "social realism"; note that "social realism" and "socialist realism" are *not* synonyms.

New Journalism A type of writing originating after World War II, different from conventional journalism mostly in its rejection of the traditional concept of the impersonality of the reporter. Instead, in new journalism, the reporter makes it clear that he, as well as his subject, is a character in the action he covers. Often the goal of new journalism is, as Tom Wolfe put it, "to create in one form both the kind of objective reality of journalism and the subjective reality that people have always gone to the novel for."

New journalism is especially related to fiction in that it uses many of the techniques—*dialogue and *interior monologue, for example— associated with fiction writing. Indeed, interior monologue perhaps is the most controversial of the new journalist's techniques, since no writer can really know the thoughts of his subject.

The most vocal and visible contemporary practitioners of new journalism have been Tom Wolfe, Norman Mailer, Hunter S. Thompson, Joan Didion, Mark Harris, John McPhee, and Truman Capote; Ernest Hemingway's *Death in the Afternoon* is an especially notable early inspiration. Here, in his long essay "Los Angeles Against the Mountains," John McPhee describes his decision to talk to a geologist about the mud slides that Los Angeles experiences from time to time:

> I went to Caltech one day and, in a very impromptu manner, asked to see a geologist. Any geologist. It had not been my purpose, in pursuing the present theme, to get into the deep geology. I meant to roam the mountains and the mountain front with foresters and engineers, to talk to people living on the urban edge, to interview people who sell the edge—a foreign correspondent covering the battle from behind both lines. But not beneath them. This was a planned vacation from projects in geology—the continuation of a holiday that had begun with stream capture in the lower Mississippi and had spread forth into such innocent milieus as eruptions in Iceland and flowing red lava in Hawaii. Now, in Los Angeles, I had been avoiding geologists in the way that one tries to avoid visits to medical doctors. All had gone well for a matter of weeks, but then, one morning, I just happened to be in Pasadena looking up into the veiled chimeric mountains, and severe symptoms began to develop. Right off the street—in much the way that a needful patient would seek out a Doc-in-the-Box—I walked into the geology department of

the California Institute of Technology, found the departmental office, and asked for professional help.

The term "new journalism" often is used synonymously with *"nonfiction novel"; indeed, both categories sometimes claim Truman Capote's *In Cold Blood* as their ancestor. The main difference is that in new journalism, the "I" of the writer always will be present, while the focus in the nonfiction novel is on giving real events the shape and structure of a novel without necessarily including the authorial "I." *(See: faction, nonfiction novel.)*

Noble Savage   A *stock character created as the ideal "primitive" man, living a simple life, uncorrupted by civilization, with uninhibited, warm and generous emotions, living in an unsophisticated but just and moral society.

While the concept of primitive people who have attained a kind of serene Utopia despite (or because of) a lack of education and technology has existed since the ancient Greeks, the notion became particularly popular with the discovery of the New World, and many novels idealizing the noble savage appeared between the sixteenth and nineteenth centuries—the novels of James Fenimore Cooper, for example. *(See: lampoon, Utopian novel.)*

Nonfiction Novel *(docufiction)*   A term coined by Truman Capote to describe a long work that reports on real events and, at the same time, employs the devices of conventional fiction, including *flashbacks, *flashforwards and *interior monologue. In general, the goal of the nonfiction novel is to give to real-life events a kind of *plotted, *thematic coherence that they might not have had in real life. Capote used the term to describe *In Cold Blood*, his book about the murder of a Kansas family.

Here, Truman Capote describes one of the murder victims, the day before the murder, in *In Cold Blood*:

> Now, upstairs, she changed into faded Levis and a green sweater, and fastened round her wrist her third-most-valued belonging, a gold watch; her closest cat friend, Evinrude, ranked above it, and surmounting even Evinrude was

Bobby's signet ring, the cumbersome proof of her "going-steady" status, which she wore (*when* she wore it; the least flare-up and off it came) on a thumb, for even with the use of adhesive tape its man-size girth could not be made to fit a more suitable finger. Nancy was a pretty girl, lean and boyishly agile, and the prettiest things about her were her short-bobbed, shining chestnut hair (brushed a hundred strokes each morning, the same number at night) and her soap-polished complexion, still faintly freckled and rose-brown from last summer's sun.

The nonfiction novel differs from *new journalism, technically, although the terms sometimes are used synonymously. In new journalism the reporter inserts herself into the story as a character in the work; the nonfiction novel is defined as one in which real events are shaped into novel form—the author is not necessarily a character in the book. The nonfiction novel also differs from *faction in that in faction, the writer incorporates in her novel the results of research and interviewing but invents the plot. *(See: new journalism.)*

Nouveau Roman *(antinovel, new novel)* Literally meaning "new novel," this is the product of a French literary movement, begun in the 1950s, which concerns itself with various forms of innovative novelistic techniques. Although not a tightly knit "school," with a single set of aesthetics and doctrine, the new novelists—Alain Robbe-Grillet, Michel Butor, Nathalie Sarraute, Claude Simon, Marguerite Duras and Claude Mauriac—share some common views and interests. In general, they all desire, as Robbe-Grillet asserts in *For a New Novel*, to "abandon outworn forms" and do away with the reader's preconceptions about what a novel should be.

Robbe-Grillet in particular strives to concentrate on the physical objects that exist and the natural events that occur in a novel, rather than on conventional concepts of characterization and plot. By focusing on these objects and events, the goal is somehow to evoke realistically the psychological realities of the characters.

Here, in Robbe-Grillet's *Jealousy*, we see the deterioration of a husband who fears his wife has been unfaithful. We feel the husband's anguish not by sharing his thoughts but by observing the way in which he sees the inanimate objects that surround him as he looks out the window:

> All that remains is a large black spot contrasting with the dusty surface of the courtyard. This is a little oil which has dripped out of the motor, always in the same place.
>
> It is easy to make this spot disappear, thanks to the flaws in the rough glass of the window: the blackened surface has merely to be brought into proximity with one of the flaws of the window-pane, by successive experiments.
>
> The spot begins by growing larger, one of its sides bulging to form a rounded protuberance, itself larger than the initial object. But a few fractions of an inch farther, this bulge is transformed into a series of tiny concentric crescents which diminish until they are only lines, while the other side of the spot shrinks, leaving behind it a stalk-shaped appendage which bulges in its turn for a second; then suddenly everything disappears.
>
> Behind the glass, now, in the angle determined by the central vertical frame and the horizontal cross-piece, there is only the greyish-beige color of the dusty gravel that constitutes the surface of the courtyard.
>
> On the opposite wall, the centipede is there, in its tell-tale spot, right in the middle of the panel.

By observing the obsessive way the husband concentrates on these trivial objects, described by a completely unjudging narrator, we see his disturbed state of mind better than we might by more conventional narrative. In some ways the effect is the same as with lyric poetry, which expresses the thoughts and feelings of an individual without telling a story.

Novel   Often defined as any piece of fiction longer than 60,000 words or so; the novel generally includes a *plot, carefully controlled by the writer, comprising a number of *episodes. Because of its greater length, a novel will have more characters, take place over a longer period of time, and involve more movement among *settings than a *novella or *short story.

Some critics narrow the definition to include only those works concerned with real people in the real world. Henry James, referring to the novels of Leo Tolstoy, called the novel a "loose, baggy monster," although, as John Gardner points out, it cannot be *too* loose or *too* baggy. Still, part of the pleasure of a novel is the luxury it has of not saying things in the shortest possible way, of sometimes going off on apparent *digressions, of letting the reader know a lot when the writer could conceivably get away with telling only a little.

Early novels were *picaresque, comprising a set of adventures that could be reordered or ended anywhere without trouble to a plot. Nowadays novels usually are more tightly plotted—events generally cannot be rearranged without seriously affecting the story.

Some contemporary writers say that the novel is dead, that conventions of plot and character have led to a lack of exploration of new forms. Ronald Sukenick, for example, notes:

> The form of fiction that comes down to us through Jane Austen, George Eliot and Hemingway is no longer adequate to capture our experience. Either the novel will change, or it will die. Today's money-making novels are those that sell to the movies—in other words, they are essentially written for another medium.

Still, the novel written with *verisimilitude as a goal has remained the most popular form of fiction for more than 125 years, re-emerging even since the 1960s and 1970s.

Novel of Character   A novel whose main concern is with the development or revelation of character, rather than with plot or other concerns.

Other times, the term is used more specifically, to describe a work that shows how the protagonist's character (as opposed to her personality) is formed or changed—generally for the better. The aim of this kind of novel has often been *didactic—to instruct the reader as well as the character.

Most often, however, the term simply is used to differentiate novels that are more concerned with people than with incident, such as those of Jane Austen or Barbara Pym—and, indeed, of most contemporary literary novels.

Novel of Incident   A novel in which character development and plot built on cause and effect are subordinated to exciting episodes and action; often, as in a *picaresque novel, the episodes are not placed in an order that leads to a particular climax; the character simply travels to adventure after adventure.

Lewis Carroll's *Alice's Adventures in Wonderland* is an example of a novel of incident. *(See: action plot, picaresque novel.)*

Novel of Manners   A novel that concerns itself with the customs and mores of a specific, well-defined group of people. Although members of a poor social class could be described in a novel of manners, it usually is a relatively upper class whose behavior is depicted.

In a novel of manners, the strictures and restraints on the members of this class usually come to control the protagonist's life to an uncomfortable degree. Often a novel of manners is a *thesis novel in disguise: The purpose often is to criticize the conventions of the society being depicted. Some well-known novelists of manners include Jane Austen, Henry James, Anthony Trollope and Edith Wharton.

Here, in *Persuasion*, Jane Austen describes the values of her protagonist's sister; this description also serves to clarify the mores of the 1814 aristocracy described in the novel:

> Elizabeth did not quite equal her father in personal contentment. Thirteen years had seen her mistress of Kellynch Hall, presiding and directing with a self-possession and decision which could never have given the idea of her being younger than she was. For thirteen years had she been doing the honours, and leading the way to the chaise and four, and walking immediately after Lady Russell out of all the drawing-rooms and dining-rooms in the country. Thirteen winters' revolving frosts had seen her opening every ball of credit which a scanty neighborhood afforded; and thirteen springs shown their blossoms, as she travelled up to London with her father, for a few weeks annual enjoyment of the great world.

Novel of Sensibility A novel dealing with characters who are portrayed in terms of their emotional responses to the events that take place in their lives; the protagonist of a novel of sensibility generally will be a person of higher-than-average emotional responses.

The danger is that the "sensibility" ultimately will become *"sentimentality." The term "novel of sensibility" is occasionally, in fact, used synonymously with the "sentimental novel," a more pejorative term. However, the character with "sensibility" rather than "sentimentality" will show an emotional response when one is in order, while a sentimental person will show emotion where none can reasonably be expected.

An example of a novel of sensibility is Virginia Woolf's *To the Lighthouse*, in which the protagonist, Mrs. Ramsey, is characterized as a good person because she has the ability to feel deeply, whereas her husband is less esteemed, by the author and by the reader, because he is insensitive.

Novel of the Soil *(rural novel)* A novel portraying people struggling to survive on farms in isolated rural areas, often in the American Midwest before those parts of the country had been fully settled. The style of a true novel of the soil often is starkly realistic. With the country becoming less and less rural, though, the genre has become less and less common.

O.E. Rolvaag's *Giants in the Earth*, originally written in Norwegian, is a good example of a novel of the soil. It is the story of a Norwegian immigrant family of the 1870s who moves to a Norwegian settlement in the Dakota territory. Per and his sons build a house for the family. Per is a successful farmer and fisherman, but his wife, Beret, becomes increasingly despondent, feeling lonely and unhappy by the lack of religious fervor among the other settlers.

After giving birth to a fourth child, Beret becomes more unhappy—even insane with despair at her isolated life. Life becomes increasingly bleak when the settlement is plagued with locusts and bad weather. Then one of Per and Beret's sons becomes mortally ill after almost freezing to death, and Per is distraught when Beret asks him to bring a minister rather than a doctor. Still, he sets out into the blizzard; however, the son dies and Per never returns to the family. In a sort of *epilogue, Per's frozen body is found, facing west.

Novel-Within-a-Novel *(synchronous narrative)* A novel that contains another novel within it, often one written by a character in the outer *frame story.

In John Gardner's *Freddy's Book*, a writer/professor on a lecture tour visits a colleague whose physically disabled and mentally disturbed teenaged son has written a novel based on his fantasies about supernatural events and characters in sixteenth-century Lappland. The first part of *Freddy's Book* is realistic and engrossing; the reader comes to care deeply about the professor character and to worry about the fate of the son. The novel of the teenage son involves horror and fantasy and is written in a very different style.

Freddy's Book is not a frame novel like *Wuthering Heights*, because the book ends as we reach the end of the teenager's manuscript; we never return to the life of the professor, which we would certainly do in a frame novel.

Another novel-within-a novel, Austin Wright's *Tony and Susan*, includes an entire novel written by Edward, the ex-husband of Susan, who has mailed her a copy of his completed manuscript. As Susan reads chapters of Edward's novel—which become as interesting as the "real" lives of the characters—she reflects on her life with her ex-husband.

In *The World According to Garp*, John Irving includes a short story and part of a novel by his protagonist and talks in detail about the writing process of the character's supposedly acclaimed story, "The Pension Grillpartzer."

Novels-within-novels (or stories-within-stories) are not always the supposed product of fictional writer-characters. In Muriel Spark's first novel, *The Comforters*, a character in the process of having a nervous breakdown begins to hear the sound of typing in her head and imagines she is a character in a novel being written by someone else; lines from the novel in her head also appear in the novel.

Novella *(nouvelle, novelette)* The most popular name for a short novel (or long story) of approximately 30,000 to 50,000 words.

A novella is longer than a short story, contains more episodes, and, unlike a short story, usually builds to several crises before reaching a climax. The final climax of a novella usually is much more conclusive than that of a contemporary short story.

A novella generally differs from a novel, however, in the spareness of its language and in the fact that it contains only a single plot line, into which there is little room for digression.

A well-known example of a novella is Ernest Hemingway's *The Old Man and the Sea*, which contains only two human characters: Santiago, a Cuban fisherman and a minor character, Manolin, who was once apprenticed to Santiago.

At the beginning of the story, Santiago has gone for eighty-four days without catching a fish when he feels a gentle tug on his line, which he knows must be a huge marlin, hundreds of feet below the surface.

The struggle with the huge fish lasts all night, all the next day, and into a second night; Santiago prays that he'll be able to catch the fish. On the third morning, the fish leaps, the line almost tears through Santiago's hand; increasingly, he feels love for the fish and is sorry that he must kill it. Finally, though, his pride prevails, and he kills the huge fish and ties it to the side of his boat.

As Santiago is returning to Cuba, however, a shark attacks the marlin; then several sharks devour it. Left with only the fish's head and tail, the old man returns home to rest and dream.

The Old Man and the Sea can be read as an adventure story and also as a religious *allegory; the basic plot has the shape of a typical novella, however: very linear, taking place over a short time, and following few characters in a limited number of actions.

O

Objective Correlative A phrase invented by T.S. Eliot to describe the use of specific, concrete images or patterns of images to express an abstract idea, so that a certain emotion is immediately evoked without that emotion ever having to be named. The idea of the objective correlative always has been a difficult one, as Eliot never truly defined it and critics have disagreed about what it means.

In the first chapter of Ralph Ellison's *Invisible Man*, the black narrator in 1930s Harlem squats in the walled-off basement of a building "rented strictly to whites," apparently convinced that he is invisible, especially to whites:

> That is why I fight my battle with Monopolated Light & Power. The deeper reason, I mean: It allows me to feel my vital aliveness. I also fight them for taking so much of my money before I learned to protect myself. In my hole in the basement there are exactly 1,359 lights. I've wired the entire ceiling, every inch of it. And not with fluorescent bulbs, but with the older, more-expensive-to-operate kind, the filament type. An act of sabotage, you know. I've already begun to wire the wall. A junk man I know, a man of vision, has supplied me with wire and sockets. Nothing, storm or flood, must get in the way of our need for light and ever more and brighter light. The truth is the light and the light is the truth. When I finish all four walls, then I'll start on the floor.

Here, the narrator's feelings of bitterness, rage and resignation are made apparent through the image of the illegally wired basement—much more vividly and memorably than if they were simply described. *(See: showing versus telling.)*

Objective Narrator *(camera-eye narrator, fly-on-the-wall narrator)*   A third-person narrator who cannot see into the minds of the characters, who can see and report only what a camera, mounted on the wall where the *story occurs, might see, leaving the reader to interpret what the characters feel.

This example comes from Dashiell Hammett's *The Maltese Falcon*:

> In the girl's apartment he switched on all the lights. He searched the place from wall to wall. His eyes and thick fingers moved without apparent haste, and without ever lingering or fumbling or going back, from one inch of their fields to the next, probing, scrutinizing, testing with expert certainty. Every drawer, cupboard, cubbyholer, box, bag, trunk—locked or unlocked—was opened and its contents subjected to examination by eyes and fingers. Every piece of clothing was tested by hands that felt for telltale bulges and ears that listened for the crinkle of paper between pressing fingers.

This type of narrator obviously must report enough to make it clear, to the extent that it is necessary for the reader to know, just what the character feels and thinks.

Objective Style   A *style in which things are expressed dispassionately and precisely, revealing as little as possible about the feelings and thoughts of the writer or narrator. In general, a story told in the objective style will not reveal any particular *atmosphere or prevailing *mood; the *tone will be noncommittal, even colorless.

Objective writing focuses on external elements and events, presenting reality as it is—or as it appears to be—unaffected by the personal reflections, sentiments or emotions of the writer.

This passage of objective writing comes from Ernest Hemingway's *For Whom the Bell Tolls:*

> It was three o'clock in the afternoon before the planes came.
> The snow had all been gone by noon and the rocks were

hot now in the sun. There were no clouds in the sky and Robert Jordan sat in the rocks with his shirt off browning his back in the sun and reading the letters that had been in the pockets of the dead cavalryman. From time to time he would stop reading to look across the open slope to the line of the timber, look over the high country above and then return to the letters. No more cavalry had appeared. At intervals there would be the sound of a shot from the direction of El Sordo's camp. But the firing was desultory.

Obligatory Scene A scene that has been foreshadowed so completely and that seems likely to be so interesting and relevant to the plot that the writer is compelled to include it in the narrative.

This scene, from Gloria Naylor's *Linden Hills*, deals with two young men, Willie and Lester, who have been doing odd jobs in the wealthy neighborhood of Linden Hills during the week before Christmas. They finally have been invited to the home of the richest and most evil man in Linden Hills, to help trim his Christmas tree, where they have this conversation:

"No, not there, Mr. Mason." Luther stopped him from hanging a crocheted stocking. "We have to leave sufficient space for the candles, and I prefer to have the metal trinkets near them."

"You mean there's gonna be candles on this tree?" Lester asked.

"There have always been candles on our trees. I couldn't imagine Christmas without them. And just wait until you see what that type of light does to some of these ornaments." He spun a mirrored diamond on its string.

Willie frowned. "But isn't that dangerous, Mr. Nedeed?"

"Not if you know what you're doing. And I plan to position them all myself."

Such foreshadowing inevitably must be followed by this obligatory scene that appears later in the novel.

The front door burned through, sending flames fed by the relentless wind curling all the way up to the third-floor windows. With his chest forced against the ice, his chin jammed into the air, Willie listened as the roar of hot and cold blasts caved in the porch roof. It fell as if moving through solidified air, charred ashes fanning out on the snow in loops and curves that matched the arc of red embers against the smoke. The air kept beating in a dull hum, a deliberate rhythm and pattern that branded itself on his mind. Something inside of him ended there, but the nightmare was still to begin.

Omniscient Narrator *(all-knowing narrator)*   A narrator who can see into the minds and hearts of any character she chooses, rather than just one, as does a *limited-omniscient narrator. This type of narrator is much more common in the novel than in the short story, which often does not offer enough room for the reader to get to know more than a single character well. Here in Gail Godwin's short story "interstices," however, we do see into the minds of four separate characters, starting with a couple that has spent the night in a house after a party:

> Esther thinks of seasons. She can't get back to sleep since Sidney half killed her that second time, so she lies with her back against the sleeping man, and tries to make autumnal metaphors to fit her life. Her personality, she decides, has always had the sorrowful colors of autumn.

Later, Sidney, in bed with Esther, thinks:

> God, she's made him sore. He puts on his socks, his pants, his T-shirt, and the V-necked cinnamon sweater that Lucy bought him. Then he sees the stream trickling across the cement floor. It leads him into the adjoining room.

Meanwhile, one of the owners of the house, a former lover of Sidney, has gone quietly insane:

A smile brushes the corners of her mouth and wings its way up as she plans the dinner party she will give with all the rotten meat. Let it freeze again. Then, in a couple of days, she will lose herself in a flurry of roasting and baking and boiling. A gala affair, just for the family. The ruby cut glass and the Royal Worcester she'd made him give her for agreeing to be his laundress. She sees them gathered at that sumptuous last supper, little Davie, napkin tucked beneath his chin, serious Mark, happy Taylor. She herself will propose the toast.

With a narrator who can see into the minds of more than one character, the reader does not simply have to guess how various characters feel; she has the ability, often, to know things that other characters do not (as in this story, that Lucy plans to poison her family).

The idea of the omniscient narrator should not be confused with a phrase that sounds similar, *editorial omniscience, in which the voice of the author seems to intrude into the narration, giving her own thoughts and opinions about what is going on in the story. *(See: multiple narrators.)*

Opaque Language *(willful obscurity)* Language that is so difficult, idiosyncratic or obscure that the meaning behind it is difficult to understand, forcing the reader's attention to remain on the language itself, rather than on the "reality" of the story.

Today, opaque language is an approach of *metafictionists, who want to keep the reader's attention on the language of the story rather than allowing him to slip into the lull of the story and become, as the *modernists would prefer, deeply involved in the characters and the plot. The hope is that opaque language will help the imaginative reader explore possibilities outside the context of story and plot.

Some modernists, however—notably James Joyce in *Finnegans Wake*—have used opaque language in an unconventional attempt to get at a deeper kind of reality than more transparent language might; their goals are very different from those of the metafictionists, although the means may seem similar. Here is an example from the first page of *Finnegans Wake*:

The fall (bababadalgharaghtakamminarronnkonnbronnton-
nerronntuonnthunntrovarrhounawnskawntoohoordenenth-
urnuk!) of a once wallstrait oldparr is retaled early in bed
and later on life down through all christian minstrelsy. The
great fall of the offwall entailed at such short notice the
pftjschute of Finnegan, erse solid man, that the humptyhill-
head of humself prumptly sends an unquiring one well to
the west in quest of his tumptytumtoes: and their upturn-
pikepointandplace is at the knack out in the park where
oranges have been laid to rust upon the green since devlins-
first loved livvy.

Oulipo A French experimentalist movement founded in 1960, characterized by its use of arbitrary methods and techniques, many based
on invented mathematical formulas, to create literature. *Oulipo* is a
French term, an abbreviation of *Ouvroir de Littérature Potentielle*,
translated as "Workshop of Potential Literature." One example is Jean
Lescure's "S + 7 method," which, as the handbook, *Oulipo: A Primer
of Potential Literature*, explains, "consists in taking a text and replacing each substantive word with the seventh following it in a given
dictionary."

Founder Raymond Queneau defines *Oulipo*'s goal as "the search
for new forms and structures that may be used by writers in any way
they see fit." The group asserts that it is a grave mistake to think
that constraining structures—such as the acrostic, spoonerisms, the
*lipogram, the palindrome or the holorhyme—are "mere examples of
acrobatics and deserve nothing more than a wry grin, since they could
never help to engender truly valid works of art."

Harry Mathews, an American writer who has lived in France for
many years, suggests that no matter how good a text written in the
conventional way (without word substitution) may seem, by dissecting
it through a method like "S + 7," the author will see that his choice of
the obvious word rather than a more surprising one may not have
been wise or appropriate after all. Other members of the group, while
admitting that it is difficult to maintain literary quality while following
so-called artificial constraints, point out that much poetry, for more
than four centuries, has been governed by the laws of prosody. *(See:
aleatory fiction, algorithmic fiction.)*

Outsider Fiction   Work that does not get published and seldom gets read because its writers have no idea what processes likely will lead to publication, do not try to get published, are not good enough to be published, or are so misunderstood by those in the publishing field that their genius is missed.

Often writers of outsider fiction really are outsiders—mental patients for example, whose illness has fostered the kind of obsession that can, in an artist, lead to accomplishment.

True outsider fiction is hard to find, since it seldom is published. Here is a paragraph from Zelda Fitzgerald's unpublished *Caesar's Things*, much of which was written while its author was confined to a North Carolina mental institution. This passage takes place right after the protagonist, Janno, a young married woman, has kissed a young French officer, about which she feels guilty:

> The trouble was she should never have kissed him. First, she should never have kissed Jacques; then she shouldn't have kissed her husband; then after the kissing had become a spiritual vivisection and half-masochistic there should not have been any more. Life in those darkened days behind the blinds with unidentified purposes humming outside and poitesses hanging abeyant and reproachful over the inside, was venemous and poisoned. There wasn't much in calling the doctor; though she did. He prescribed champagne.

Certainly there are some wonderful images here—of the doctor who, confronted with mental illness, prescribes champagne—but the general effect is chaotic, structureless. Had it not been found and printed in the appendix of Nancy Milford's biography, *Zelda*, *Caesar's Things* certainly would have taken its place among other examples of unpublished outsider fiction.

Overwriting   Prose marked by excess description and detail, far more than is interesting or necessary for the reader.

Overwritten fiction occurs especially often in the first few paragraphs of stories that strive to show the effects of nature at their most beautiful. Stella Gibbons explains at the beginning of *Cold Comfort*

Farm that she is going to mark her finest passages with three asterisks; these passages always turn out to be comically overwritten. Here
is Gibbons' purposely overwritten description of dawn at the decrepit
farm to which her young protagonist has come to live:

> ***Dawn crept over the Downs like a sinister white animal,
> followed by the snarling cries of a wind eating its way be-
> tween the black boughs of the thorns. The wind was the
> furious voice of this sluggish animal light that was baring
> the dormers and mullions and scullions of Cold Comfort
> Farm.
>
> The farm was crouched on a bleak hillside, whence its
> fields, fanged with flints, dropped steeply to the village of
> Howling, a mile away.

Oxymoron   A word or phrase made of two words that seemingly contradict each other. The word comes from Greek words meaning
"sharp" and "dull." Some examples are "bittersweet," "jumbo shrimp,"
"guest host," "pianoforte" (which means loud-soft), and Shakespeare's
examples from *Romeo and Juliet*, "O loving hate!" and "O heavy
lightness!"

P-Q

Pace *(tempo)*   The speed and rhythm at which a story moves. Clearly, parts of any work will move at different rates, depending not only on what is going on but also on the *mood the writer wishes to produce.

A fast pace can be created through using short phrases with abrupt transitions, short snippets of dialogue, and a number of actions following each other in quick succession. In this excerpt from George P. Elliot's "Among the Dangs," the pace speeds up as the protagonist, an anthropologist who has joined a remote South American tribe to study it, falls into a prophetic trance. Although his slipping into the trance must have taken a long time, the excitement and fear he feels— if he does not fall into a trance and give a good prophesy, he could be killed by the Dangs; if he does not stay alert enough to remember the trance afterward, he will not be able to write about it and get his Ph.D.—make this frenetic, nervous pace appropriate:

> Two moon slaves seized my arms, took off my mask, and wrapped and bound me, arms at my sides and legs pressed together, in a deer hide, and then laid me on my back in the channel under The Stone with my head only half out, so that I was staring up the sheer side of rock. The dancers continued, though the master prophets had disappeared. My excitement; the new, unused position; being mummied tightly; the weakness of the drug; my will to observe; all kept me conscious for a long time. Gradually, however, my eyes began to roll up into my head, I strained less powerfully against the thongs that bound me, and I felt my breathing

approach the vatic rhythm. At this point, I seemed to break out in a new sweat, on my forehead, my throat, in my hair; I could hear a splash; groggily I licked my chin; an odd taste; I wondered if I was bleeding.

On the other hand, a writer might slow the pace to excite tension or suspense, usually through long passages of description or digressions from the subject at hand. Here, in John Cheever's "The Country Husband," the pace of this emergency landing, which must have happened quickly, is kept slow by the writer's deliberate descriptions of some of the random events that take place in the plane as it goes down:

> The plane had begun to drop and flounder wildly. A child was crying. The air in the cabin was overheated and stale, and Francis' left foot went to sleep. He read a little from a paper book that he had bought at the airport, but the violence of the storm divided his attention. It was black outside the ports. The exhaust fires blazed and shed sparks in the dark, and, inside, the shaded lights, the stuffiness, and the window curtains gave the cabin an atmosphere of intense and misplaced domesticity. Then the lights flickered and went out. "You know what I've always wanted to do?" the man beside Francis said suddenly. "I've always wanted to buy a farm in New Hampshire and raise beef cattle." The stewardess announced that they were going to make an emergency landing. All but the child saw in their minds the spreading wings of the Angel of Death. The pilot could be heard singing faintly, "I've got sixpence, jolly, jolly sixpence. I've got sixpence to last me all my life."

The pace of this passage speeds up after the man in the seat next to Francis looks away, but remains slow, in comparison to the first passage, throughout; the incidental details and dialogue make the plane's descent seem to last much longer than it would in real life.

Painterly Prose *(high style)* A style of writing that includes a great deal of *imagery, including *metaphors, *similes, literary *allusions, colorful adjectives and adverbs, long sentences, a wide vocabulary, and complex sentence structure.

Painterly prose is appreciated for elaborate imagery, as well as for its rhythms, complexity and beauty. Writers noted for their painterly prose include William Faulkner, Henry James, Franz Kafka, Marcel Proust and Virginia Woolf.

This example of painterly prose is from Proust's *Swann's Way*. The much-admired Princesse des Laumes is quite proud of herself for attending this party, even though it is being given by people she considers—as everyone indeed is—of a lower social class than she. Here, she shows her uncertainty at how to react to an intermezzo by Liszt for which the people around her are ostentatiously showing their appreciation:

> She began to ask herself whether these gesticulations might not, perhaps, be a necessary concomitant of the piece of music that was being played—a piece which did not quite come within the scope of the music she was used to hearing—whether to abstain from them might not be evidence of incomprehension as regards the music and of discourtesy towards the lady of the house; with the result that, in order to express by a compromise both of her contradictory inclinations in turn, at one moment she would confine herself to straightening her shoulder-straps or feeling in her golden hair for the little balls of coral or of pink enamel, frosted with tiny diamonds, which formed its simple but charming ornament, scrutinizing her impassioned neighbour with cold curiosity the while, but at the next would beat time for a few bars with her fan, but, so as not to forfeit her independence, against the rhythm.

The opposite of a painterly style is *plain prose, used by Hemingway and Chekhov and many contemporary writers, which prizes instead of flowery language the kind of precision in which each word is chosen as carefully as possible to create a scene, with the caveat that no word be wasted. *(See: Jamesian sentence, le mot juste, plain prose, style.)*

Panoramic Method *(deep focus)*   A style of writing in which, rather than developing a specific scene, a narrator presents information by briefly "panning" from a distance an imaginary camera over a wide collection of objects or people.

The panoramic method keeps the narrator at a distance from her characters and scene; the reader, too, is unlikely to develop immediate empathy with the characters whose actions are being described, since so little is said about them. Indeed, the panoramic method is useful when the characters are not behaving in a completely sympathetic manner, and the writer desires that the reader keep a certain ironic detachment from what is going on.

The panoramic method most often is used to open a chapter, giving the writer the opportunity to present a wide overview of a scene and then choose which particular element to zero in on and highlight.

This example is from E.M. Forster's *A Room With a View*:

> The sun rose higher on its journey, guided, not by Phaethon, but by Apollo, competent, unswerving, divine. Its rays fell on the ladies whenever they advanced towards the bedroom windows; on Mr. Beebe down in Summer Street as he smiled over a letter from Miss Catharine Alan; on George Emerson cleaning his father's boots; and lastly, to complete the catalogue of memorable things, on the red book mentioned previously. The ladies move, Mr. Beebe moves, George moves, and movement may engender shadow. But this book lies motionless, to be caressed all the morning by the sun and to raise its covers slightly, as though acknowledging the caress.

Parable   A story that offers a vivid narrative as well as teaches a lesson, often without ever overtly expressing that lesson.

In the Western world, the most well-known parables are Christ's parables from the Bible, including the parable of the ten virgins from the Book of Matthew:

> Then shall the kingdom of heaven be likened unto ten virgins, which took their lamps, and went forth to meet the bridegroom.

And five of them were wise, and five were foolish.

They that were foolish took their lamps, and took no oil with them:

But the wise took oil in their vessels with their lamps.

While the bridegroom tarried, they all slumbered and slept.

And at midnight, there was a cry made, Behold, the bridegroom cometh; go ye out to meet him.

Then all those virgins arose, and trimmed their lamps.

And the foolish said unto the wise, Give us of your oil: for our lamps are gone out.

But the wise answered, saying, Not so; let there be not enough for us and you: but go ye rather to them that sell, and buy for yourselves.

And while they went to buy, the bridegroom came; and they that were ready, went in with him to the marriage: and the door was shut.

Afterward came also the other virgins, saying, Lord, Lord, open to us.

But he answered and said, Verily I say unto you, I know you not.

Watch therefore, for ye know neither the day nor the hour wherein the Son of man cometh.

A parable is different from a *fable in that a fable usually includes an obvious moral, which makes it impossible for a careful reader to misunderstand the point. The *theme of a parable is more likely to be misunderstood, and parables often are the object of several different interpretations.

A contemporary parable, which usually is short—a few pages at most—must both tell an interesting story and incorporate some meaningful message, creating tension between the brevity of the story and the depth and substance of the philosophical theme.

Herman Hesse's "The Poet" tells, in simple language, the story of a young man, Han Fook, who wants to learn everything there is to know about poetry. He is engaged to be married and one night attends a festival:

He leaned against the trunk of a tree which grew over the water, and saw reflected in the river thousands of lights swimming and shimmering. He saw men and women and young girls greeting each other on the boats and floats, all glowing like beautiful flowers in their festive dress. He heard the soft murmur of the shining water, the songs of the girls, the humming of the zithers, the sweet tones of the flutes, and over the whole scene the blue night hovered like the vaulting of a temple.

He is overcome by the beauty of the scene and realizes that he will truly be happy only if he can write poetry that will be a perfect mirror image of the world, just as the reflection in the river is a perfect mirror image of the festival of lanterns. Then he meets an old man who speaks a few words of poetry; Han Fook desires that this man become his master, and asks his father for two years' time before his wedding to study with him. Eventually, Han Fook spends his whole life studying with this master, returning only many years later as an old man. There is another festival at the same spot, but his family is gone. Han Fook takes out his lute and plays; the people are bewitched by the playing:

But Han Fook smiled. He looked into the river, where the reflected images of a thousand lanterns were swimming. Just as he no longer knew how to distinguish the reflected images from the real ones, so he found no difference in his soul between this festival and the first one, where he had stood here as a young man and heard the words of the strange master.

This parable says something about the relationship between time and art, as well as questioning the role of art in a society where its presence can cause every human thing in the world (like Han Fook's fiancée) to disappear. But the meaning can be expressed in other ways by different readers. *(See: allegory.)*

Paradox A statement that contains elements that at first seem to contradict each other but that, over time, begin to make sense—to seem potentially true—at least on some interior level.

An example is Oscar Wilde's "Life is far too important a thing ever to talk seriously about." Another is a truism like "The longest way 'round is the shortest way home."

The point of a paradox generally is to surprise the reader into reflection about the subject—or sometimes a paradox will remain obscure. (*See: epigram, maxim, oxymoron.*)

Parody A work created in conscious imitation of another piece, generally for the purpose of ridiculing either the other piece itself or the subjects of the piece. A parody is distinguished from a *satire in that a parody generally does not have the motive of inspiring the reader to change or to reform some aspect of society.

The parodist has the option of sticking close to the original, changing a word here and there for comic effect; or he may parody only the style of the other work, as James Thurber does in his *Fables for Our Time*, which includes the story of "The Birds and the Foxes," in which a pack of foxes attacks and kills a group of Baltimore orioles in a bird sanctuary. After the slaughter of the orioles, the foxes' leader, "a fox from whom God was receiving daily guidance," announces that the foxes have in fact "liberated all the birds." The moral of the fable is:

> Government of the orioles, by the boxes, and for the foxes, must perish from the earth.

Judith Roscoe's "A Lot of Cowboys" is a story that parodies the concept of the tough, macho cowboy rather than a particular literary form:

> When it began to snow all the cowboys came into town and rented motel rooms with free TV. One of the cowboys said his favorite program was "Bonanza." "It's pretty authentic."
>
> "Aw shit, what do you know about authentic?"
>
> "Well, I know. I'm a cowboy, aint I?"
>
> "Well, so am I, and I think 'Bonanza' is a bunch of bull-pucky. Now if you want authentic stuff you ought to watch 'Gunsmoke.' "
>
> "Well, you old cuss, I will show you what's authentic." So

the cowboy hit the other cowboy with his fist.

"No fighting in here, so you cut that out," said the motel manager.

(See: burlesque, lampoon, mock-epic fiction, pastiche novel, pekoral, satire.)

Passive Characterization   A term, used by critic Jonathan Wilson in a *Literary Review* article, to describe characters the reader comes to understand fully only through observing similarities between the writer herself and her characters—and ascribing personality traits of the writer to the character.

The difference between a work that uses passive characterization and a *roman á clef is in the intent of the writer: A writer using passive characterization often will reject the idea that, despite appearances to the contrary, the work is autobiographical, while the writer of a roman á clef generally will not. In addition, the writer of a work using passive characterization must be a prominent figure, or no one would even notice the similarities between the character and the writer.

The clear resemblance between the writer's life and the character's in works using passive characterization, coupled with the author's angry denial that there are any similarities, actually serves to create a rather lively tension in the work, not only between the writer and the protagonist, but between the writer and the reader, inviting the reader into a kind of implied dialogue with the writer. *(See: author-as-character, autobiographical fiction, roman à clef.)*

Pastiche Novel   An uncommon type of novel in which a writer creates his work from pieces of other published novels and "found" documents.

These excerpts may be combined to form a plot of some kind; since it is difficult to do this, the appeal of a pastiche novel often is in the reader's delight in recognizing the bits from other works and enjoying the novelty of their juxtaposition. The term is sometimes also used as a synonym for *narrative collage or for the *documentary novel.

In many ways this is an unrealized type, but Kathy Acker probably has come closest to exploiting it with her works *Don Quixote*, *Great Expectations*, and *Hello, I'm Erica Jong*, in which she uses passages from Shakespeare, the Marquis de Sade, Jean Genêt, *Cosmopolitan*, Harlequin romances, Cervantes, graffiti, bathroom walls, the Koran, "Dick and Jane" primers and Charles Dickens. The first chapter of Acker's *Great Expectations*, for example, is called "Plagiarism" and begins with the first couple of paragraphs from Charles Dickens' more famous *Great Expectations*.

In the pastiche novel, the documents that make up the narrative are actual published texts, written by real people, whereas in the documentary novel the documents can be either real or ones invented by the writer.

The intent—and usually the effect—of the pastiche should not be seen as mere *plagiarism, since no attempt is made to pass off the work as the writer's own; the intent is to jar the reader through the unusual juxtaposition of relatively familiar works. Clearly, of course, it is important that the originator of the work, if it is not in the public domain, be consulted, or trouble could erupt, as it did in a lawsuit against artist Jeff Koons, who got in trouble for painting a picture from a photograph without the permission of the photographer. *(See: documentary novel, narrative collage, plagiarism.)*

Pataphysics A "pseudoscience" proposed by writer Alfred Jarry, which he defined in his *Gestes et opinions du docteur Faustroll* as "the science of imaginary solutions."

Pataphysics is relevant to fiction writers because of its allure to a group of editors and readers of small literary magazines—"fanzines"—from time to time. The primary appeal of pataphysics is in its denial of conventional scientific wisdom, and through the possibilities it opens for the creation of a new kind of world dependent on new kinds of natural laws.

Pataphysics, which Jarry describes as "the science of the Possible, not the Probable," is the study of bizarre phenomena, things that exist only in a "supplementary universe." The "science" has two important principles: the equivalency of all objects and the equal likelihood of any events taking place; and the concept that what seem to be polar opposites (night and day, zero and infinity) periodically switch, making nothing in the world really knowable. Not surprisingly, prose about the pataphysical universe tends to be somewhat dreamlike and hallucinatory.

In *Gestes et Opinions du docteur Faustroll*, the protagonist, Dr. Faustroll, seeking to escape paying his overdue rent, shrinks to the size of an insect and sails from Paris to Paris in a sieve, wearing a shirt made of woven quartz.

Pathetic Fallacy A term first used by nineteenth-century writer and critic John Ruskin to describe what happens when writers ascribe human emotions to nonhumans. The term also is used to describe a more general kind of sentimentality that results from overdescribing some act of nature, especially one that happens frequently, like a sunrise or a thunderstorm.

It is possible to describe nature in a way that compares naturally occurring phenomena with real things done by real people in a new and original way and not be accused of using the pathetic fallacy; the term is only used if the resulting writing is melodramatic or seems clichéd. Here is a delightful, nonclichéd example from Katherine Mansfield's "Miss Brill," in which the pathetically lonely protagonist sees love in the eyes of her fur collar:

> Dear little thing! It was nice to feel it again. She had taken it out of its box that afternoon, shaken out the moth-powder, given it a good brush, and rubbed the life back into the dim little eyes. "What has been happening to me?" said the sad little eyes. Oh, how sweet it was to see them snap at her again from the red eiderdown! . . . But the nose, which was of some black composition, wasn't at all firm. It must have had a knock, somehow. Never mind—a little dab of black sealing-wax when the time came—when it was absolutely necessary. . . . Little rogue! Yes, she really felt like that about it. Little rogue biting its tail just by her left ear.

Probably what keeps this passage from falling into the pathetic fallacy trap is the irony that is so clear in it: Miss Brill may think the fur is communicating with her, but it is obvious that the writer of the story does not think so. *(See: overwriting.)*

Pathetic Plot A plot recognized in Norman Friedman's "Forms of the Plot," describing a novel in which a sympathetic but naïve, weak-willed or otherwise imperfect protagonist suffers misfortune in part because of innate character flaws but mostly through no fault of her own.

An example is Stephen Crane's *Maggie: A Girl of the Streets*, the story of a girl from the slums of New York whose father is harsh and cruel, and whose mother is an alcoholic. Maggie grows up, gets a factory job, and falls in love with a boy named Pete, which at first provides the story a hopeful note. But hope disappears when Pete seduces her, her mother abandons her, she is forced to become a prostitute and finally commits suicide.

Although occasional hopeful moments arise in the pathetic plot, its general trend is downward; at the end, the reader is left with a feeling of pity for the suffering, broken protagonist. The pathetic plot often is found in the work of *naturalist writers; Crane found the material for *Maggie: A Girl of the Streets* while living in a New York slum. *(See: naturalism.)*

Pathos   The aspect of a story that makes its reader feel pity or sorrow for the fates of the various characters.

Taken from a Greek word for "feeling," pathos now is generally used as a negative term to describe the kind of gratuitous pity a reader feels upon reading *sentimental fiction, rather than the more honest sorrow he experiences for a character he has grown to care about in a more serious, literary work. *(See: bathos.)*

Pedantry   The flaunting of education simply to show off, rather than to instruct.

A pompous character often will appear as a pedant for the sake of humor, as the professor of history in Kingsley Amis's *Lucky Jim* does, pointing out to the protagonist a trivial mistake in a newspaper article as they walk through the campus:

> "Anyway, there it was in the *Post* as large as life: Dowland, yes, they'd got him right; Messrs Welch and Johns, yes; but what do you think they said then?"
>
> Dixon shook his head. "I don't know, Professor," he said in sober veracity. No other professor in Great Britain, he thought, set such store by being called Professor.

"Flute and piano."

"Oh?"

"Flute and piano; not recorder and piano." Welch laughed briefly. "Now a recorder, you know, isn't like a flute, though it's the flute's immediate ancestry, of course. To begin with, it's played, that's the recorder, what they call *à bec*, that's to say you blow into a shaped mouthpiece like that of an oboe or a clarinet, you see. A present-day flute's played what's known as traverso, in other words you blow across a hole instead of . . ."

Different effects of pedantry can be created by letting the pedant spout learned information of varying degrees of difficulty: a character showing off by imparting truly abstruse information might seem genuinely learned, while a pedant offering information that is common knowledge or incorrect will seem like even more of a buffoon. *(See: academic fiction, allusion, didactic fiction.)*

Pekoral A Swedish term introduced by critic Hans Kuhn to define the kind of poor writing by ungifted writers who try to imitate some specific, generally unpromising genre: the romantic love novel, for example, or poetic doggerel. A variation on this definition of the pekoral, which is not a frequently used term, is the parody of bad writing that sometimes is done by characters in a novel and recreated in the novel's text.

This example comes from Elizabeth Jolley's comic novel *Foxybaby*, the story of Alma Porch, a novelist and an English instructor at a girls' school, who is employed for the summer at a combination writers' workshop and weight-reducing camp for women.

Miss Porch decides to have her students produce a play called *Foxybaby*, which she is in the process of writing. It is the story of a young drug-addicted woman, her child, and her father's attempts to rescue her. The style of the play that Miss Porch has her students try to put on—with surprisingly good results—is different from the style of the novel as a whole—much more *melodramatic and serious:

The sound of screaming rouses Steadman. He gropes toward the cradle. He picks up the frantic baby. Everything is all right, he tells Sandy. She is standing huddled in a corner of the room. Terrified. He tries to approach her with the crying baby. She holds up both hands as if to scratch his face. Her face, smeared with melting make-up, is like the face of a frightened animal.

As quickly as he can, using one hand, Steadman fills the kettle and takes the baby's bottle from the refrigerator. He tries to talk softly to the child who is trembling against his chest. He tries to comfort Sandy. His voice shakes and he blunders about in the small spaces between the fixed furniture. He thinks he will make tea.

In his mind he goes back to the previous night, a scene of horror, during which the girl had torn up her clothes and defaced the walls of the pretty nursery at home. She had smashed cups and plates and mirrors and pictures and bitten her own arms and fingers till everything was bloodstained.

A pekoral is different from a *parody in that the pekoral may not be comic, while a parody usually is. As with a parody, however, appreciation of a pekoral rests on the reader's knowing both the work being parodied and understanding why the work is deserving of parody. (*See: parody.*)

Periodic Sentence *(suspended sentence)* A sentence created through the use of a string of dependent clauses and prepositional phrases before the end of the sentence, when the main subject and verb appear. In a periodic sentence, the main point is not obvious before its conclusion. Usually a periodic sentence is long, and sometimes it creates frustration rather than a sense of anticipation. Its purpose is to capture the reader's interest and create a sense of anticipation and suspense before the point of the sentence is revealed. Here is an example:

Angry, humiliated, desperate as usual when Jessica had gone after a visitation day with the children, returning to the tasteless house she now shared with her friend Tricia, who, Frank suspected, didn't like him at all and even scorned him for not finding out on his own that his wife had been conducting a full-blown affair with her six boyfriends for nearly three months (he thought—it was really over two years!), for learning the truth only after one of the wives had called him anonymously from a downtown bar, Frank opened the bag of lentils that would be his children's supper.

(See: loose sentence.)

Peripety *(peripeteia)*   A term originating with Aristotle to describe an action that turns out to have the opposite effect from the one the doer originally intended.

In Herman Wouk's *The Caine Mutiny*, the mutineers celebrate after having been found innocent of relieving Captain Queeg from his duties during a typhoon, claiming that he had lost his mind and the ability to steer the ship. The primary mutineer's drunken lawyer, however, sobers the group by explaining that the mutiny and its aftermath were not the sort of heroic gestures they seemed at the time:

> "Steve, the thing is, this dinner is a phony. You're guilty. I told you at the start that you were. Course you're only half guilty. F' that matter, you've only been half acquitted. You're a dead duck. You have no more chance now of transferring to the regular Navy than for running for President. The reviewing authorities'll call it a miscarriage of justice, which it is, and a nice fat letter of reprimand will show up in your promotion jacket—and maybe in mine—and it's back to the fishing business for Steve Maryk. I got you off by phony legal tricks—by making clowns out of Queeg and a Freudian psychiatrist—which was like shooting two tuna fish in a barrel— . . .

(See: reversal.)

Persona   A term widely used to refer to the *implied author or "second self" created by an author and through whom a story is told.

The term also is used more broadly to include all *first-person narrators, as well as undramatized third-person narrators—especially those narrators who obviously are quite distant from the author.

Here is an example, from the second paragraph of Doris Lessing's "An Unposted Love Letter":

> If I said, "I don't need a husband, I have so many lovers," then of course everyone at the dinner table would have laughed in just such a way: it would have been the rather banal "outrageousness" expected of me. An aging star, the fading beauty ... "I have so many lovers"—pathetic, and brave too. Yes, that remark would have been too apt, too smooth, right for just any "beautiful but fading" actress. But not right for me, no, because after all, I am not just any actress, I am Victoria Carrington, and I know exactly what is due to me and from me. I know what is fitting (not for me, that is not important) but for what I stand for.

In *Huckleberry Finn*, the use of the persona of the irrepressible but ignorant Huckleberry serves the function of allowing Mark Twain to talk about slavery in a way he might not have dared to in his own voice.

Note that in the 1990s the word *"voice" is used frequently as a synonym for the older word "persona." *(See: implied author, voice.)*

Personification A figure of speech in which inanimate objects or abstract concepts are represented as having the ability to think and feel in the same way that human beings do. Personification also includes *anthropomorphism, in that it comprehends the endowing of animals with human feelings.

This example comes from a passage of Edwin Abott's *Flatland: A Romance of Many Dimensions*. It describes the subjugation of women in the book's two-dimensional society in which males come in a variety of geometric shapes while females are only straight lines. The narrator announces himself proudly on the title page as "A SQUARE":

> If our highly pointed Triangles of the Soldier class are formidable, it may be readily inferred that far more formidable are our Women. For if a Soldier is a wedge, a Woman is a needle; being so to speak, *all* point, at least at the two

extremities. Add to this the power of making herself practically invisible at will, and you will perceive that a Female, in Flatland, is a creature by no means to be trifled with.

Note, of course, that in many places in the book the observations concerning the personified geometric shapes are relevant to human society as well. *(See: anthropomorphism, symbol.)*

Philosophical Novel   A novel whose purpose is to present an intellectual proposition, or one that exhibits a philosophical approach to life, in which ideas generally are more significant than *characterization, *plot and incident.

In John Barth's *The End of the Road*—which begins with the narrator, Jacob Horner, announcing, "In a sense, I am Jacob Horner"—dialogue that moves the plot along explores philosophical ideas as well. Jacob has just commented that the children of his new colleague Joseph Morgan and his wife Rennie are remarkably self-sufficient for their ages:

> "Don't think we drive them," Rennie said. "We don't really give a damn. But I guess we demand a lot tacitly."
>
> Joe listened to this remark with casual interest.
>
> "Why do you say you don't give a damn?" he asked her.
>
> Rennie was a little startled at the question, which she had not expected.
>
> "Well—I mean ultimately. Ultimately it wouldn't matter one way or the other, would it? But immediately it matters because if they weren't independent we'd have to go through the same rigamarole most people go through, and the kids would be depending on all kinds of crutches."
>
> "Nothing matters one way or the other ultimately," Joe pointed out. "The other importance is all there is to anything."
>
> "That's what I meant, Joe."
>
> "What I'm trying to say is that you shouldn't consider a value less real just because it isn't absolute, since less-than-absolutes are all we've got. That's what's implied when you say you don't really give a damn."

Picaresque Novel   A novel that presents the life of a rascally, amoral character, usually from a low social class, who goes through life taking part in various adventures. Usually told in the first person by the "picaro" herself, this cheerful, raffish character gets through life on her wits, often cheating (or nearly cheating) the gullible, the pompous and the rich.

An example of a picaresque novel is William Makepeace Thackeray's *Barry Lyndon*, told in the form of the autobiography of an Irishman who serves in both the English and Prussian armies, becomes a successful gambler and marries a wealthy countess, whom he treats cruelly and whose fortune he squanders. Eventually he dies in prison, of delirium tremens.

The picaro's adventures usually follow no particular order, and one episode in her life does not lead logically into the next. Although a picaresque novel often has no recognizable climax or resolution, its author generally strives for a realistic style, especially in the creation of characters who are *not* "too good to be true."

Other picaresque novels have included Daniel Defoe's *Moll Flanders*, Erica Jong's *Fanny: Being the True History of the Adventures of Fanny Hackabout-Jones*, Saul Bellow's *The Adventures of Augie March*, and Mark Twain's *Huckleberry Finn*.

Picaro *(picaroon)*   The likeable-in-spite-of-himself protagonist in a picaresque novel, who experiences various adventures while trying to improve his own lot in life (and often succeeds—at least temporarily). In his attempt to attain wealth, he often shows up the weaknesses of characters who on the surface may appear more respectable and praiseworthy than he—but ultimately are much less so. *(See: picaresque novel.)*

Plagiarism   The unauthorized use of someone else's material, which is then presented as being the result of the plagiarist's own primary research, creative impulse or insight.

Plagiarism technically encompasses the borrowing of the ideas of others, as well as their exact words, but in fiction many writers have created variations on universal themes without being accused of stealing. Samuel Butler's *The Way of All Flesh* and Charles Dickens' *Great Expectations*, for example, both concern the coming of age of sensitive, idealistic boys under less-than-ideal circumstances, but the *styles of writing, as well as the individual adventures of the *protagonists, are so different that the novels remain worlds apart.

Thomas Mallon's *Stolen Words: Forays Into the Origins and Ravages of Plagiarism* describes recent controversies regarding the fiction of a young writer, Jacob Epstein, whose novel bore a striking similarity to a novel by Martin Amis; of Alex Haley, the author of *Roots*, who had to pay a settlement to another writer for information that appeared in his book; and of D.M. Thomas' best-selling *The White Hotel*, which bore striking similarity to Anatolii Kuznetsov's memoirs of Babi Yar.

Certainly, however, it is possible to manipulate the work of other writers in ways that are not necessarily plagiarism, as Jorge Luis Borges does in his story, "Pierre Menard, Author of the Quixote," about a writer whose great work is actually Cervantes' *Don Quixote*. In Vladimir Nabokov's *Ada* (which takes place on Antiterra, a planet different in some ways from Earth) a character is presented as the author of works that sound exactly like Guy de Maupassant's. *(See: pastiche novel.)*

Plain Prose *(simple style)*   A style of writing that began with Gustave Flaubert in the mid-1800s, in which elaborate sentences are eschewed in favor of simple but precise language that strives not to call attention to itself.

Plain prose, which is much the opposite of *painterly prose, is noteworthy for its simple sentences with few adjectives and adverbs, little figurative language and few literary allusions. Instead, the intent is extreme precision, so that the image or scene being created is clear, with every word being as near to the perfect one as possible.

Writers noted for the masterly use of plain prose include Anton Chekhov, Gustave Flaubert, Ernest Hemingway and Ivan Turgenev. This paragraph comes from Hemingway's *The Sun Also Rises*:

> I lit the lamp beside the bed, turned off the gas, and opened the wide windows. The bed was far back from the windows, and I sat with the windows open and undressed by the bed. Outside a night train, running on the street-car tracks, went by carrying vegetables to the markets. They were noisy at night when you could not sleep. Undressing, I looked at

myself in the mirror of the big armoire beside the bed. That was a typically French way to furnish a room. Practical, too, I suppose. Of all the ways to be wounded. I suppose it was funny. I put on my pajamas and got into bed. I had the two bull-fight papers, and I took their wrappers off. One was orange. The other yellow. They would both have the same news, so whichever I read first would spoil the other. *Le Toril* was the better paper, so I started to read it. I read it all the way through, including the Petite Correspondance and the Cornigrams. I blew out the lamp. Perhaps I would be able to sleep.

(See: le mot juste, *objective style, painterly prose)*

Plant Information included early in a work of fiction for the sole purpose of making later events in the story, which could otherwise seem improbable and inappropriately coincidental, seem likely and believable.

In Joyce Carol Oates' "Where are You Going, Where Have You Been," a fifteen-year-old girl, her mind "filled with trashy daydreams," is taken out of her house to a field at the end of a story to be raped by a psychotic—perhaps even a demonic—stranger. The stranger is planted at the beginning of the story in a seemingly innocent phrase when the girl notices him while driving with a different boy she has picked up:

> It was a boy with shaggy black hair, in a convertible jalopy painted gold. He stared at her and his lips widened into a grin. Connie slit her eyes at him and turned away, but she couldn't help glancing back and there he was still watching her. He wagged a finger and laughed and said, "Gonna get you, baby," and Connie turned away again without Eddie noticing anything.

The shaggy-haired boy's words seem innocent at first; it is only later, when he appears at her house, that they take on a new and ominous meaning.

The idea of a "plant" is closely related to *foreshadowing but the focus is a bit narrower: foreshadowing can be related to *mood, *atmosphere and other abstract ideas; a plant is a physical, tangible thing that has definitely been included to avoid the appearance of unnatural coincidence. *(See: foreshadowing.)*

Plot *(récit)*   A term first used by Aristotle in the fourth century B.C. to describe the arrangement of a story's events, including the actions of the protagonist and how these actions affect other characters.

In a story or novel said to be heavily plotted, each incident that occurs is closely related to the next one; one incident, in fact, usually leads to the next. The events could not be rearranged in a heavily plotted novel, because the chain of cause and effect would be broken. Eventually, in a novel with a strong plot, the tension will build to a climax. A heavily plotted novel's opposite is the episodic novel, whose *episodes are not interrelated, and in which one incident does not lead logically into the next.

Real life does not always divide itself into episodes in which one event leads directly into or causes the next; yet writers whose goal is to write fiction that closely mimics the effects of real life often find themselves seeking a definite shape or structure to the events. The challenge is to make such a structure seem real without appearing contrived. *(See: story.)*

Poetic Style   Prose in a style that uses the techniques and devices of poetry, including rhythm and imagery, to create its effects.

While there is little imagery in this passage from Gertrude Stein's *Melanctha*, the *novella uses a poetic style in its incorporation of a repetitive rhythm, with the many sentences beginning with "he"; the consistently unconventional word order of the sentences, meant to show the speech and thought patterns of Jeff Campbell; and the recurrence of individual words, like "always" and "now":

> These months had been an uncertain time for Jeff Campbell.
> He never knew how much he really knew about Melanctha.
> He saw her now for long times and very often. He was beginning always more and more to like her. But he did not seem to himself to know very much about her. He was beginning to feel he could almost trust the goodness in her. But then,

always, really, he was not very sure about her. Melanctha always had ways that made him feel uncertain with her, and yet he was so near, in his feeling for her. He now never thought about all this in real words any more. He was always letting it fight itself out in him. He was now never taking any part in this fighting that was always going on inside him.

Poetry-as-Fiction   A genre of fiction utilizing the techniques of formal poetry, including line breaks and, sometimes, rhyme and meter, to create a work of fiction that also incorporates traditional elements such as *plot and character development. Poetry-as-fiction is the opposite of *prose poetry, which uses the techniques of prose to create poetry.

Poetry-as-fiction is much less common than the prose poem, partly because it is difficult to keep a narrative poem going, in terms of word length, as long as is necessary to tell a short story.

This is the way Vikram Seth's verse novel *The Golden Gate*, whose general meter is iambic tetrameter, begins:

> To make a start more swift than weighty,
> Hail Muse. Dear Reader, once upon
> A Time, say, circa 1980,
> There lived a man. His name was John.
> Successful in his field though only
> Twenty-six, respected, lonely,
> One evening as he walked across
> Golden Gate Park, the ill-judged toss
> Of a red frisbee almost brained him.
> He thought, "If I died, who'd be sad?
> Who'd weep? Who'd gloat? Who would be glad?
> Would anybody?" As it pained him,
> He turned from this dispiriting theme
> To ruminations less extreme.

Peter Taylor's story "The Hand of Emmagene" does not rhyme and has no metrical pattern, yet the odd line breaks add a sense of bizarreness and mystery to a story that becomes bizarre and mysterious only toward the end (at which point Emmagene cuts off one of her hands, angry and upset at being pressured into dating a young man from her hometown to whom she is attracted but whom she believes to be an immoral influence):

> More than once the phone rang while we are at the supper table
> On Sunday night. Emmagene always prepared that meal
> And did up the dishes afterward since the servants were off
> On Sunday night. And ate with us too, of course.
> I suppose it goes without saying
> She always sat at the table with us.
> She rather made a point of that from the start.
> Thought it never would have occurred to us
> For it to be otherwise.
> You see, up in Hortonsburg
> Her family and my wife's had been kin, of course,
> But quite different sorts of people really.
> Her folks had belonged to a hard-bitten fundamentalist sect
> And Nancy's tended to be Cumberland Presbyterians
> Or Congregationalists or Methodists, at worst
> (Or Episcopalians, I suppose I might say "at best").
> The fact was, Nancy's family—like my own—
> Went usually to the nearest church, whatever it was.

Point of View *(center of vision, viewpoint)* The vantage point from which a story is presented.

The choice of a point of view is one of the most important a writer makes over the course of a work, and each point of view presents advantages and pitfalls. In the *first-person point of view, a view with great potential for expressing a sense of immediacy, the *narrator will be the "I" (or occasionally the "we," as in the case of William Faulkner's "A Rose for Emily") who tells the story. This first-person narrator is the *protagonist in Tess Gallagher's "The Lover of Horses":

> I did not learn, until I traveled to where my family originated
> at Collenamore in the west of Ireland, that my great-grand-
> father had most likely been a "whisperer," a breed of men
> among the gypsies who were said to possess the power of
> talking sense into horses.

But it is also possible for the first-person narrator to be only a minor character in the story, as is the case in "A Rose for Emily."

The third-person point of view is the most widely used, especially in the novel. Here, the narrator will be some person, closely or distantly affiliated with the author, who identifies the characters as "he" or "she" or "they" (or perhaps "it," in science fiction).

In this example, from Anton Chekhov's "The Man in a Case" the narrator seems to have the ability to make judgments about the characters (his comment that Ivan Ivanitch's surname does not suit him at all), an ability that most third-person narrators enjoy to a greater or lesser degree:

> On the outskirts of the village of Moronitski, in a shed belonging to the bailiff Prokofi, some belated huntsmen were encamped for the night. There were two of them: the veterinary surgeon Ivan Ivanitch and the schoolteacher Burkin. Ivan Ivanitch had a rather strange, hyphenated surname, Tchimsha-Himalaiski, which did not suit him at all, and so he was known all over the province simply by his two Christian names. He lived on a stud farm near the town and had now come out hunting to get a breath of fresh air.

This narrator also seems to have the ability to see into Ivan Ivanitch's mind (the narrator knows the reason he has gone out hunting—to get a breath of fresh air, rather than, say, killing anything in particular), which is another of the choices the author makes in selecting a point of view. The writer may choose to see into one character's mind (*limited omniscience), or into the mind of more than one character (*omniscience), as occurs in William March's short novel, *Company K*, in which the author uses 113 different points of view.

The writer also has the option of choosing a narrator who cannot see into the minds of any characters, as in the *objective narrator.

It also is possible to combine points of view; William Faulkner's *The Sound and the Fury*, for example, consists of first-person narratives by three different characters and then ends with a passage told from the author's *omniscient point of view. *(See: first-person point of view, narrator.)*

Political Novel   A novel whose plot deals with politicians and life in the political arena.

As with the *Hollywood novel, the point of the political novel often is to expose the differences between what appears to be happening—generally something honorable and above-board—and what is really happening—generally something not at all honorable.

Robert Penn Warren's *All the King's Men* is a famous example: both the story of the dictatorial governor of a southern state (apparently based on Huey Long), and the story of a young journalist's unmasking of his former hero, an apparently incorruptible judge, whom he reveals to have once accepted a bribe. *(See: Hollywood novel, thesis novel.)*

Polyphonic Prose   A term taken from music, used in contemporary criticism to describe fiction in which a number of characters, in dialogue, speak in voices that represent a variety of ideological positions. The narrator allows them to express themselves differently depending on who they're talking to, and they often get into discussions where no one single point of view is dominant.

This term comes from Mikhail Bakhtin's 1929 *Problems of Dostoevsky's Poetics*, in which Bakhtin describes these characteristics as he finds them in the novels of Fyodor Dostoevsky. In addition to the works of Dostoyevsky, the novels of James Joyce and D.H. Lawrence often are presented as examples of polyphony.

In this example, from D.H. Lawrence's *Women in Love*, while the narrator can see into the minds of various characters, he does not comment on what they are saying, nor does he take a particular point of view as to the rightness of either side of this argument. Here, the first speaker is Gerald; the scene is a wedding of two of his friends:

> "If I go and take a man's hat from off his head, that hat becomes a symbol of that man's liberty. When he fights me for his hat, he is fighting me for his liberty."
>
> Hermione was nonplussed.
>
> "Yes," she said, irritated. "But that way of arguing by imaginary instances is not supposed to be genuine, is it? A man does not come and take my hat from off my head, does he?"
>
> "Only because the law prevents him," said Gerald.

"Not only," said Birkin. "Ninety-nine men out of a hundred don't want my hat."

"That's a matter of opinion," said Gerald.

"Or the hat," laughed the bridegroom.

"And if he does want my hat, such as it is," said Birkin, "why, surely it is open to me to decide, which is a greater loss to me, my hat, or my liberty as a free indifferent man. If I am compelled to offer fight, I lose the latter. It is a question which is worth more to me, my pleasant liberty of conduct, or my hat."

"Yes," said Hermione, watching Birkin strangely. "Yes."

"But would you let somebody come and snatch your hat off your head?" the bride asked of Hermione.

The face of the tall straight woman turned slowly and as if drugged to this new speaker. "No, I shouldn't let anybody take my hat off my head."

"How would you prevent it?" asked Gerald.

"I don't know," replied Hermione slowly. "Probably I should kill him."

There was a strange chuckle in her tone, a dangerous and convincing humour in her bearing.

"Of course," said Gerald, "I can see Rupert's point. It is a question to him whether his hat or his peace of mind is more important."

"Peace of body," said Birkin.

Each of these voices is allowed to have its say, and no particular point of view ever becomes dominant (although this scene continues for quite a while). The disagreements among the voices are never resolved, and each speaker's feelings are granted equal validity.

"Polyphonic prose" occasionally is used as a synonym for a *prose poem—but this is rare. *(See: philosophical novel.)*

Polysemous Language *(amphibology)* Words with more than one meaning.

The term "polysemous language" includes puns and *double entendres, like this one from *Ulysses*, in which "beaver" has both an innocent and an obscene meaning:

> And childe Leopold did up his beaver for to pleasure him
> and took apertly somewhat in amity for he never drank no
> manner of mead which he then put by and anon fully privily
> he voided the more part in his neighbor glass and his neigh-
> bor wist not of his wile.

Often, as in the *Ulysses* example, the effect of polysemous language
is to call attention to the cleverness of the writer rather than to involve
the reader deeply in the story, as is generally the intent in *realistic
fiction.

In addition, the language of characters possessed of supernatural
abilities—like the witches of *Macbeth*—often is polysemous. One fictional example comes in Herman Melville's *Moby Dick*, when the mysterious harpooner Fedallah, who seems to have psychic powers, de-
clares, among other things, that Captain Ahab can be killed only by
hemp—an enigmatic and seemingly impossible prophecy. Much later,
however, Ahab is killed when he is strangled, in a fluke accident, by
the hemp rope he had attached to the harpoon he was heaving into
the side of Moby Dick, and the double meaning—the polysemous
quality—of Fedallah's words is suddenly clear. *(See: double entendre.)*

Pop Fiction   Fiction incorporating images or characters from popular
culture as important elements.

Two examples are T.C. Boyle's "Greasy Lake," titled for a Bruce
Springsteen song, and "Heart of a Champion," in which the TV dog
Lassie becomes intimate with an attractive male coyote while a horri-
fied Timmy looks on:

> "What was she doing, Dad?" Timmy asks over his milk
> and sandwich.
> "The sky was blue today, son," he says.
> "But she had him trapped, Dad—they were stuck to-
> gether end to end and I thought we had that wicked old
> coyote but then she went and let him go—what's got into
> her, Dad?"
> "The barn was red today, son," he says.

To fall into the category of pop fiction, a large portion of the work
must relate to popular culture; just a title taken from a popular song,

like Madison Smartt Bell's *Waiting for the End of the World,* which in no other way relies on characters or events taken from popular culture, is not enough to place the work in the "pop" category.

The intent of pop fiction often is *parody or *satire, since superheroes and cartoon characters, for example, usually would not hold an adult reader's interest without an extra twist—although certainly simple enjoyment of popular culture *images also are a part of the point of the work. *(See: camp fiction.)*

Popular Fiction *(escape fiction)*   Fiction read purely for entertainment rather than for its educational value.

One requisite for popular fiction is that, to be truly popular, the work must be read by many people. Although literary works do occasionally make the best-seller list, the term "popular fiction" most often is applied to books with wide commercial appeal.

A recent example of a novel praised both by literary critics and by readers looking for an engrossing and entertaining experience is Umberto Eco's *The Name of the Rose,* which functions in part as a murder mystery but also works on a more sophisticated level. The mystery involves seven monks being murdered, and a monk from another abbey, Brother William, is called in to investigate. The novel's literary value comes from the narrator's intricate discussion of various theological and logical arguments that Brother William uses, along with more conventional techniques of detection, to solve the case.

Portmanteau Word   A word formed as a combination of two separate words. An example is "smog," formed as a combination of "smoke" and "fog." Another, from Lewis Carroll's "Jabberwocky," is "chortle," from "chuckle" and "snort."

Poshlost   A Russian word defined in English by Vladimir Nabokov to include "corny trash, vulgar clichés, Philistinism in all its phases, imitations of imitations, bogus profundities, crude, moronic and dishonest pseudo-literature." Nabokov continues:

> Now, if we want to pin down poshlost in contemporary writing we must look for it in Freudian symbolism, moth-eaten

mythologies, social comment, humanistic messages, political allegories, overconcern with class and race, and the journalistic generalities we all know. Poshlost speaks in such concepts as "America is no better than Russia" or "We all share in Germany's guilt." The flowers of poshlost bloom in such phrases and terms as "the moment of truth," "charisma," "existential" (used seriously), "dialogue" (as applied to political talks between nations), and "vocabulary" (as applied to a dauber).

Positive Hero The protagonist created in works of Soviet *socialist realism in the first part of the twentieth century.

Positive heroes were meant to serve as role models for readers, to inspire them to participate actively in the Communist Revolution and accept personal difficulties as a necessary sacrifice for the advancement of society in general. *(See: radical novel, socialist realism.)*

Postmodernist Fiction *(surfiction, postrealist fiction, antifiction, new fiction, parafiction, metafiction, postcontemporary fiction)* A term used to describe fiction written since the mid-1960s that is often ironic and whose real subject is often (although not necessarily) the writing of fiction itself. Postmodernist fiction includes both the traditional conventions and techniques of *modernism and undermines them, frequently pointing out that the work is, in fact, fictional. It often combines aspects of both popular and literary culture.

Postmodernists maintain that fiction is able to say something true about life and even bring about change—and at the same time that fiction is a form of play, which should be fun to read.

An example of postmodernist fiction is Robert Coover's "The Elevator," a short story divided into fifteen parts, each one concerned with the elevator ride of a character named Martin between his building's lobby and his office on the fourteenth floor. Each section is told in a fairly realistic style: We get involved in such traditional elevator-fiction events as Martin's deciding to hit the "B" button instead of the usual "14"; a psychopath's killing of Martin in the darkened elevator after work; the snapping of the cable while Martin and a woman are alone in the elevator; a bullying co-worker's accusation that he is "Old

Farty Marty," after the elevator's passengers detect a suspicious smell.

The reader gets involved in each of these ministories, only to be pulled up short when it ends abruptly and a new story starts, reminding the reader that what she is reading is not the literal truth.

Postmodernism sometimes is seen as a continuation of *modernism, other times, as a clear break from the coherent structure of works of modernism and especially from that part of modernism that strove to find ways of expressing different types of reality. Some well-known postmodernists include Walter Abish, John Barth, Don DeLillo, Grace Paley and Thomas Pynchon. *(See: metafiction.)*

Predictable Plot A negative term applied to fiction in which it is too easy for the reader to guess what will happen next.

Generally, the predictable plot will be based on a *stock or otherwise overly familiar situation (the quiet, dreamy chap, fired from his job at the post office, will eventually return with his gun; the young couple with a flat tire will knock on the door of a vampire's house). Other times, the foreshadowing of some event that is about to occur may be so obvious (Frank, confident that he will be offered the job he desires and deserves, does not even bother to apply for any others, despite a long-standing relationship of animosity with one of the interviewers) that when the inevitable does happen (he doesn't get the job), the surprise that the writer had hoped to create falls flat.

The writer must walk a fine line between making a plot too predictable and making the actions and characters seem motivationally believable. Shirley Jackson's "The Lottery," for example, would be ruined if it were immediately clear from this sentence, buried in the second paragraph, that the stones mentioned would be used at the end of the story to murder one of the villagers:

> Bobby Martin had already stuffed his pockets full of stones, and the other boys soon followed his example, selecting the smoothest and roundest stones; Bobby and Harry Jones and Dickie Delacroix—the villagers pronounced this name "Dellacroy"—eventually made a great pile of stones in one corner of the square and guarded it against the raids of the other boys.

On the other hand, the sentence foreshadows the ending and gives the story, especially on rereading, a satisfying sense of inevitability. *(See: cliché, foreshadowing, stock situation.)*

Preface *(prologue)* An introductory statement, usually written by the author, that explains to the reader anything the writer wants him to know about the work—how it came to be written, for example, or if there is some organizing principle the reader should know.

Here is a passage from Nathaniel Hawthorne's second edition of *The Scarlet Letter*, in which he defends his decision to write and include the introductory sketch "The Custom-House" in the new edition:

> ... the author begs leave to say, that he has carefully read over the introductory pages, with a purpose to alter or expunge whatever might be found amiss, and to make the best reparation in his power for the atrocities of which he has been adjudged guilty. But it appears to him, that the only remarkable features of the sketch are its frank and genuine good-humor, and the general accuracy with which he has conveyed his sincere impressions of the characters therein described.

"Preface" often is used synonymously with *"foreword"; if there is a difference, it is that a foreword more often is written by someone other than the author, while a preface generally is written by the author himself. *(See: foreword.)*

Privileged Narrator A third-person narrator who knows information that none of the characters would have the capacity to know.

All authors, presumably, have information they do not divulge to their characters (where and when the characters are likely to die, for example, and other pleasant and unpleasant surprises that await them). When the narrator relates some or all of this information to the reader, however, the narrator is said to be privileged.

Anton Chekhov's "Vanka" tells the story of an orphaned boy who writes a letter to his grandfather complaining of his new life as a shoemaker's apprentice and begging his grandfather to come and take him away. This passage comes after the boy finishes the letter:

Vanka twice folded the sheet of paper and then he put it in an envelope bought the previous day for a kopeck. He reflected for a while, dipped the pen in ink, and wrote the address:

> To Grandfather in the Village

Then he scratched his head and thought for a while, and added the words: Konstantin Makarich. . . .

. . . When he talked to the clerks in the butcher shop the previous day, they told him that letters were dropped in boxes, and from these boxes they were carried all over the world on mail coaches drawn by three horses and driven by drunken drivers, while the bells jingled. Vanka ran to the nearest mailbox and thrust his precious letter into the slot.

Vanka goes to sleep happy; the writer—and the reader—are privileged to know, however, that the chances of Vanka's grandfather receiving the letter, with no stamp or proper address, are pathetically small.

Profluence A term used in John Gardner's *The Art of Fiction* to describe the concept that, in conventional fiction, there must be a sense that the story is moving toward some satisfying conclusion.

Generally, it is a story's *plot, with its blend of related incidents and scenes, that satisfies this need on the reader's part for forward motion. Profluence, according to Gardner, is most necessary in a long work. "A story of three or four pages," he says. "may still interest though it has practically no movement." *(See: plot.)*

Propaganda Novel *(polemical novel)* A subgenre of the *thesis novel category—often used simply to describe an unsuccessful thesis novel—where, as with the thesis novel, the characters, *plot, and other elements are there solely to present a particular point of view or describe a particular social problem, with no specific attention paid to literary merit. *(See: didactic fiction, thesis novel.)*

Prose Poem A type of poem that differs from other poetry for the most part only in that it lacks line breaks; until you read it, prose poetry looks like prose. While prose poetry has been written by European poets for several centuries, American poets began to explore the form only in the twentieth century.

Prose poets usually see themselves as poets rather than as fiction writers, despite the fictionlike physical appearance of their work. They point out that the great prose poets of France, including Charles Baudelaire, Arthur Rimbaud, Stéphane Mallarmé and Paul Valéry, wrote what is considered to be great poetry, although it has no line breaks.

The rhythm of prose poetry is less obvious than in plain prose, since line breaks are absent. In addition, many prose poems use everyday speech and humor to create their effects.

Prose poems also are generally marked by a special attention paid to the subconscious, to subtle links between images and ideas that might seem less apparent in conventional prose, as the rhythm of this prose poem by Arthur Rimbaud shows:

Bridges
Skies the gray of crystal. A crazy pattern of bridges, these at right angles, those convex, the others descending or slanting at angles over the first ones, and these forms renewing themselves in other illuminated circuits of the canal, but all as long and slow as the dome-crusted banks, dwindle and descend. Some of these bridges are still covered with hovels. Others support masts, signals, frail parapets. Minor chords cross and lengthen, ropes climb the banks. We notice a red jacket, maybe other costumes and musical instruments. Are they popular airs, bits of Godly concerts, the remnants of public hymns? The water is gray and blue, as wide as an arm of the sea. A white ray, falling from the peak of the sky, destroys this comedy.

(See: poetic style, poetry-as-fiction.)

Protagonist *(focal character, hero/heroine)*   A story's or novel's central character. The word usually is used now to replace "hero," because the central character of a work may not have the heroic, positive characteristics the reader associates with a hero or heroine.

Protest Novel   A type of novel, most popular in the United States in the 1930s, that deals with social, economic, and military experiences and the injustices faced by society's underclass.

The purpose of protest fiction often is to reform, but unlike with *satire, the author's main tool is the graphic and angry description of the shameful wrongs and inequities of society.

An example is Dalton Trumbo's 1939 *Johnny Got His Gun*, whose protagonist goes off eagerly to fight in World War I and comes back limbless, deaf and blind. The novel progresses as the narrator ponders his situation and reminisces about the innocence of his earlier years, only near the end making the nurses aware that his mind still is alive inside his body. Ironically, after he finally succeeds in communicating with the outside world through Morse code, his isolation becomes even more complete when authorities, unwilling to listen to his horrible stories, quiet him with drugs. The inevitable conclusion the writer asks the reader to make is that war must always be wrong when it leads to such terrible results.

Sometimes the protest novel ends with suggestions for how society's problems can be rectified—often the implied answer is a violent workers' uprising. Two other examples of protest novels are Richard Wright's *Native Son* and James T. Farrell's *A World I Never Made*. *(See: propaganda novel, thesis novel.)*

Psychic Distance   The intimacy of the relationship between the reader and a story's characters.

Psychic distance sometimes is used synonymously with *aesthetic distance; the difference is that psychic distance relates especially to the relationship between the reader and the characters, while aesthetic distance relates to the relationship between the reader and all aspects of the work.

A writer creates psychic distance (rather than psychic intimacy) through the narrative voice, and through the use of *summary rather than *dialogue. The effect of a greater psychic distance is to make the individual lives of the characters seem less important than they would if the psychic distance were less great.

In John Steinbeck's "The Chrysanthemums," we feel close to the protagonist, Elisa, bored and frustrated by the limitations of her life, because of the care Steinbeck uses to describe her, even though we cannot see into her mind here at all:

> Elisa watched them for a moment and then went back to her work. She was thirty-five. Her face was lean and strong and her eyes were as clear as water. Her figure looked blocked and heavy in her gardening costume, a man's black hat pulled low down over her eyes, clod-hopper shoes, a figured print dress almost completely covered by a big corduroy apron with four big pockets to hold the snips, the trowel and scratcher, the seeds and the knife she worked with. She wore heavy leather gloves to protect her hands while she worked.
>
> She was cutting down the old year's chrysanthemum stalks with a pair of short and powerful scissors. She looked down toward the men by the tractor shed now and then. Her face was eager and mature and handsome; even her work with the scissors was over-eager, over-powerful. The chrysanthemum stems seemed too small and easy for her energy.

The elaborate details of Elisa's gardening make it easy to see and sympathize with her, and when her feelings are hurt at the end of the story, we share her hurt and frustration.

In Joyce Carol Oates' "Where Are You Going, Where Have You Been," however, we feel much less close to Connie, even though we can see some of her thoughts, partly because she is a less likeable character than Elisa and partly because the quick, jumpy style of the writing, and the switches in point of view from Connie to her mother, keep us from getting too close to her:

> Her name was Connie. She was fifteen and she had a quick nervous giggling habit of craning her neck to glance into mirrors, or checking other people's faces to make sure her own was all right. Her mother, who noticed everything and knew everything and who hadn't much reason any longer to look at her own face, always scolded Connie about it. "Stop gawking at yourself, who are you? You think you're

so pretty?" she would say. Connie would raise her eyebrows at these familiar complaints and look right through her mother, into a shadowy vision of herself as she was right at that moment: she knew she was pretty and that was everything.

Often a novelist will establish different levels of psychic distance at different times, perhaps starting with a great deal of psychic distance and then moving closer for emotional or intense scenes. Writers will avoid, however, apparently random and meaningless changes in psychic distance and will not move from a far distance to a close one and then back again, say, in a single paragraph.

Psychological Novel   A novel influenced by the teachings of Freud and Jung that deals with the emotional and mental workings of a unique, usually troubled individual.

Techniques like *stream of consciousness and *interior monologue often are part of the psychological novel, showing as they do the subconscious mind at work. Here, Darl, the protagonist of William Faulkner's *As I Lay Dying*, has gone insane, responding to the horror of his journey with his distraught family to bury his dead mother, followed by buzzards hovering above the coffin. After attempting to burn down the barn in which his mother's body has been stored while waiting for burial, Darl loses his mind completely and is sent to an insane asylum:

> Darl has gone to Jackson. They put him on the train, laughing, down the long car laughing, the heads turning like the heads of owls when he passed. "What are you laughing at?" I said.
>
> "Yes yes yes yes yes."
>
> Two men put him on the train. They wore mismatched coats, bulging behind over their right hip pockets. Their necks were shaved to a hairline, as though the recent and simultaneous barbers had had a chalk-line like Cash's. "Is it the pistols you're laughing at?" I said. "Why do you laugh?" I said. "Is it because you hate the sound of laughing?"
>
> They pulled two seats together so Darl could sit by the

window to laugh. One of them sat beside him, the other sat on the seat facing him, riding backward. One of them had to ride backward because the state's money has a face to each backside and a backside to each face, and they are riding on the state's money which is incest. A nickel has a woman on one side and a buffalo on the other; two faces and no back. I don't know what that is. Darl had a little spy-glass he got in France at the war. In it it had a woman and a pig with two backs and no face. I know what that is. "Is that why you are laughing, Darl?"

"Yes yes yes yes yes yes."

While *As I Lay Dying* uses *multiple narrators, Darl has always seemed the most reaonable member of the Bundren family, and his breakdown comes as a shock. A second reading of the novel, however, reveals a number of indications that Darl's normal level of sensitivity is not likely to allow him to remain sane in his impossible family environment.

Pure Novel   A term used to describe an idealized, probably impossible-to-realize novel type that has as little as possible to do with events in the real world and its values and social problems, and in which all parts of the novel relate only to each other rather than to issues outside the work.

The pure novel, like the general idea of *art for art's sake, is, in some ways, a reaction against the *thesis novel and other forms of *naturalism. The pure novel is not *didactic, in the sense of offering a moral or lesson; nor does it offer any kind of journalistic information about a particular region, for example, or a particular social class. In a pure novel only the story and the characters—and whatever else is pure invention of the writer—are important.

Gustave Flaubert was the initiator of the idea of the pure novel, hoping, perhaps after the completion of *Madame Bovary*, to write "a book about nothing—a book that will have almost no subject, or at least where the subject is almost invisible, if that is possible."

Sometimes the definition of the pure novel becomes even more austere, as in *The Counterfeiters*, when André Gide's protagonist, Edouard, says:

"I should like to strip the novel of every element that does not specifically belong to the novel. Just as photography in the past freed painting from its concern for a certain sort of accuracy, so the phonograph will eventually no doubt rid the novel of the kind of dialogue which is drawn from life and which realists take so much pride in. Outward events, accidents, traumatisms, belong to the cinema. The novel should leave them to it. Even the description of the characters does not seem to me properly to belong to the genre. No; this does not seem to me the business of the pure novel (and in art, as in everything else, purity is the only thing I care about.)"

Fiction as abstract as nonobjective painting, however, with as few relations to real life as possible, may be unachievable, since it is impossible to divorce words from their meanings, in fiction anyway. Annie Dillard points out another objection to the pure novel in *Living By Fiction*:

> Purity seeks to eliminate inessentials. But even if we could agree on the essentials of any art . . . what have we got when we are "down" to them?

(See: art for art's sake.)

Question-Answer Fiction   A technique in which part or all of the plot and characters in a work of fiction are presented as a series of queries and responses.

The questions can be addressed to a character in the work, as they are in Gilbert Sorrentino's *Odd Number*, which takes the form of a pretrial legal deposition in which the questions and responses become ever more bizarre. The questions also can be addressed directly to the reader, as they are at the end of Part One of Donald Barthelme's *Snow White*:

1. Do you like the story so far? Yes ( ) No ( )
2. Does Snow White resemble the Snow White you re-member? Yes ( ) No ( )

3. Have you understood, in reading to this point, that Paul is the prince-figure? Yes ( ) No ( )

4. That Jane is the wicked stepmother-figure? Yes ( ) No ( )

5. In the further development of the story, would you like more emotion ( ) or less emotion ( )?

6. Is there too much *blague* in the narration? ( ) Not enough *blague*? ( )

7. Do you feel that the creation of new modes of hysteria is a viable undertaking for the artist of today? Yes ( ) No ( )

8. Would you like a war? Yes ( ) No ( )

9. Has the work, for you, a metaphysical dimension? Yes ( ) No ( )

10. What is it (twenty-five words or less)? _____

_____

_____

R

Radical Novel *(Marxist novel, proletarian novel, resistance literature)* Work by communists, socialists, anarchists, and other writers with strong, usually left-wing political viewpoints, who are committed to finding revolutionary solutions to social, economic and political problems.

The radical novel, associated until recently with communism, has worked best when it avoids the more formulaic aspects of *socialist realism and creates its characters as individuals—as does the *naturalistic work of James T. Farrell, John Steinbeck and John Dos Passos; and Louis Aragon's Marxist novel, *Les Communistes*, which shows its tenets subtly rather than by overtly preaching morals. *(See: socialist realism, thesis novel.)*

Rap Novel A novel that uses the techniques of rap music, especially a lot of quick cuts, as one might employ in a documentary novel, to represent "sampling"—that is, the musical technique of distorting prerecorded music to create one's own work.

Inner-city African-American street life usually is the subject of the rap novel. So far, the main example of a rap novel is Ricardo Cortez Cruz's *Straight Outta Compton*, whose title is taken from a 1988 album by the rap group NWA.

Although the scene is different, the techniques and desires of rap novels are similar to those desired by the *naturalists of the early twentieth century: a closely observed, authentic look at a kind of life with which many readers are unfamiliar.

Here is a passage from *Straight Outta Compton*:

Imagine the scene set, Billy Bugle and a group of gang-bangers like Boyz in the Hood saying "This Beat is Hot." They're in Compton. Luther is signing "A House is Not a Home" on compact disc. Outside, Hollywood is filming another blaxploitation movie. The producers are looking for garbage cans to make the street scenes appear authentic. Barry Michael Cooper adds the music score. Queen Latifah brings along Troop and Levert to help kick the ballistics. Chris Rock is practicing his lines and doing his make-up to look drugged out. Latifa/Troop/Levert sample "Living for the City." They do a mellow medley by the trash cans. The backdrop is Black buttered soul, Billy Bugle Boy blowing his trumpet.

Rashomon Effect A technique by which different characters in a work tell the same story from different points of view.

An example comes from one of the stories by Ryunosuke Akutagawa, "In a Grove," from which director Akira Kurosawa created his well-known film *Rashomon*, the story of a man who rapes a woman, after which the woman and her husband are both found dead. The conflicting stories of the rapist, the woman and her husband are all told in such a way that we never know for sure who killed the woman and her husband. Here is the rapist's point of view, after he ties up the woman's husband and stuffs his mouth with leaves so he will not talk:

At last I could satisfy my desire for her without taking her husband's life.

... I was about to run away from the grove, leaving the woman behind in tears, when she frantically clung to my arm. In broken fragments of words, she asked that either her husband or I die. She said it was more trying than death to have her shame known to two men. She gasped out that she wanted to be the wife of whichever survived.

The story ends with the husband's point of view, told after his death "through a medium":

After violating my wife, the robber, sitting there, began to speak comforting words to her. Of course I couldn't speak. My whole body was tied fast to the root of a cedar. But meanwhile I winked at her many times, as much as to say, "Don't believe the robber." . . . In the meantime the robber went on with his clever talk, from one subject to another. The robber finally made his brazen proposal. "Once your virtue is stained, you won't get along with your husband, so won't you be my wife instead? It's my love for you that has made me violent toward you."

Realism A type of fiction, still the most popular in the twentieth century, that tries to provide an authentic picture of real life, to give the reader a chance to become deeply involved with the story through identification with its major characters.

Realism began in the nineteenth century as an attempt to show how real, everyday people actually lived, showing their quotidian problems and experiences. The realist movement, like *naturalism, was a reaction against more fanciful writing—stories, for example, of romances among royalty as well as work marked by resolutions full of improbable coincidences.

Even events that seem bizarre, however, may appear realistic, if they are presented in a believable way, and though postmodernists of the 1970s sometimes claimed that realism was dead, writers such as Philip Roth, Anne Tyler and William Kennedy have proven those claims false.

This paragraph comes from Anne Tyler's *Morgan's Passing*. The protagonist of this section of the book is Emily Meredith, who is accompanying her comedian husband and some of his friends on their largely unsuccessful performing tour of the Eastern seaboard. One night Emily skips her husband's performance and takes a long walk through town instead:

In the drugstore, which was the only place still open, she bought a zippered cosmetic kit for traveling, completely fitted with plastic jars and bottles and a tiny tube of Pepsodent. She and Leon were almost penniless at this point. They were having to sleep apart—Emily and the other two women at

the Y, the men in the van. The last thing they could afford
was a $4.98 cosmetic kit. Emily rushed back to her room,
feeling guilty and pleased. She started rearranging her belongings—carefully pouring hand lotion into one of the bottles, fitting her silver hairbrush into a vinyl loop. But she
really didn't wear much make-up; the zippered bag took
more room than her few cosmetics had taken on their own.
It was a mistake. She couldn't even get her money back;
she'd used the bottles. She began to feel sick. She went
through her suitcase throwing things out—her white school
blouses, her jeans, every bit of underwear. (If she wore only
leotards, she wouldn't need underwear.) When she was
done, all that remained in her suitcase were two extra wrap
skirts, two extra leotards, a nightgown, and the cosmetic
bag. The small cardboard wastebasket next to her bed was
overflowing with filmy, crumpled, shoddy non-essentials.

The accumulation of small details makes this passage seem authentic: the fact that the wastebasket is made of cardboard, for example,
and the catalogue of Emily's typical, mid-1960s college-girl wardrobe.
The description of the make-up case seems genuine because most
people have seen similar make-up cases—with their cheap vinyl, their
little tubes of toothpaste. The description remains interesting because
inexpensive make-up cases are seldom described in fiction.

These realistic details form a background that makes the less-
plausible details of the scene seem authentic also—that a young
woman would throw away most of her clothes, for example, and keep
only the belongings that would fit into the suitcase. Even the *mood
of the passage becomes real: despite Emily's initial pleasure at her
purchase, she remains anxious and depressed. Her feelings and motivations seem as complicated as those of living people. *(See: mimesis,
modernism, verisimilar fiction.)*

Religious Fiction The term includes novels about clergy and religion, like much of Anthony Trollope's work, as well as novels of personal salvation, like Herman Hesse's *Siddhartha*.

Contemporary fiction dealing with religion often satirizes it, pointing out hypocrisies and greed among religious leaders. Still, some

fiction deals seriously with religious issues, like Anne Roiphe's *Lovingkindness*, in which the narrator, the feminist mother of an aimless, troubled daughter who has joined a rigid Orthodox Jewish sect and plans to marry another member she's met only a few times, decides eventually to give a sort of qualified blessing to the marriage. The narrator confronts her own religious values—or lack of them—as well, in the book's last chapter:

> I lie down on my bed with a cup of tea and open my mail. Maybe if I am very quiet I will hear God whispering, explaining matters to me or releasing me from the need for explanations. If reason cannot lead to reconciliation, can I abandon reason? Maybe I am not too old for revelation. After all, Sarah was ninety when she conceived a child. If that happens, will I have found my own way to Jerusalem or will I have joined the ladies matted and scabbed who wander on Broadway looking for a doorway that will shelter them from the cold? On the plane I made notes from a monograph on Rabbi Nachman. I would like to open his life and works to rational analysis. There are biographies in the library. His disciples wrote down all he told them. He is the ideal figure for a study on psychosis and God. Without heavenly visitations I will console myself.

Repetition   A device to ensure that the reader will remember important facts and details, and that their importance will be noted. Repetition also unifies the novel, by tying elements of the plot into some kind of a pattern.

This example of repetition, which emphasizes the *atmosphere of the boarding house where a group of young women in post-war London live, comes from Muriel Spark's *The Girls of Slender Means*:

> Anne trod her cigarette-end contemptuously on the floor of the large entrance hall with its pink and grey Victorian tiles. This was pointed to by a thin middle-aged woman, one of the few older, if not exactly the earliest members. She said, "One is not permitted to put cigarette-ends on the floor." The words did not appear to impress themselves on the ears

of the group, more than the ticking of the grandfather clock behind them. But Anne said, "Isn't one permitted to spit on the floor, even?" "One certainly isn't," said the spinster. "Oh, I thought one was," said Anne.

And then, two pages later:

> It was Greggie who had said to Anne by the notice-board:
> "One isn't permitted to put cigarette-ends on the floor."
> "Isn't one permitted to spit on the floor, even?"
> "No, one isn't."
> "Oh, I thought one was."

In the example below, on the other hand, the effect of the repeated language is much the same as that which occurs in poetry, where the repetitions and variations of elements form a rhythmic pattern of sound, in which one looks for and appreciates variations. Gertrude Stein's "Miss Furr and Miss Skeene" begins:

> Helen Furr had quite a pleasant home. Mrs. Furr was quite a pleasant woman. Mr. Furr was quite a pleasant man. Helen Furr had quite a pleasant voice a voice quite worth cultivating. She did not mind working. She worked to cultivate her voice. She did not find it gay living in the same place where she had always been living. She went to a place where some were cultivating something, voices and other things needing cultivating. She met Georgine Skeene there who was cultivating her voice which some thought was quite a pleasant one. Helen Furr and Georgine Skeene lived together then. Georgine Skeene liked travelling. Helen Furr did not care about travelling, she liked to stay in one place and be gay there. They were together then and travelled to another place and stayed there and were gay there.

The piece goes on, several paragraphs later:

> The voice Helen Furr was cultivating was quite a pleasant one. The voice Georgine Skeene was cultivating was, some

said, a better one. The voice Helen Furr was cultivating she cultivated, and it was quite completely a pleasant enough one then, a cultivated enough one then. The voice Georgine Skeene was cultivating she did not cultivate too much. She cultivated it quite some. She cultivated and she would sometimes go on cultivating it and it was not then an unpleasant one, it would not be then an unpleasant one, it would be a quite richly enough cultivated one, it would be quite richly enough to be a pleasant one.

The creation of *motif or *symbol is one main reason for repetition, as in the Spark example above, where the repetition of the anecdote about throwing cigarette ends and spitting on the floor emphasizes the theme of the book: how people of different ages and situations deal with the effects of World War II.

The term also encompasses the idea of using repetition to create rhythmic effects in the prose, as Stein does in the example above. *(See: lyrical novel, motif, symbol.)*

Response Fiction *(imitation)* Fiction written as a conscious response or answer to another work.

Some examples include Jean Rhys' *Wide Sargasso Sea*, a story told from the point of view of Rochester's deranged first wife in Charlotte Brontë's *Jane Eyre*; and Jane Austen's parody of the gothic romances of her day in *Northanger Abbey*. Various writers have written works based on Chaucer's *Canterbury Tales*, including Stanley Elkin (*The Dick Gibson Show*), and Vance Bourjaily (*Now Playing at Canterbury*). Gloria Naylor's *Linden Hills* refers to Dante's *Inferno*.

Writers who refer consciously to other works (as opposed to plagiarists, who hope that no reader makes the connection between the new work and the original) often do so to enrich their own fictional worlds, by making the reader contemplate the older work as well as consider the new creation. Writing a work that harks back to an important earlier work also can simply be satisfying as an intellectual exercise and serve as a grateful nod to a source of inspiration. *(See: allusion, intertextuality, mythic method.)*

Revelation Plot One of Norman Friedman's categories of plot types, which depends on the protagonist's ignorance of what's going on—

the literal facts of her situation—for suspense. The outcome of the plot depends on whether the protagonist figures out the truth of her situation and, if so, what she does.

A good example, described by Friedman, is Roald Dahl's short story, "Beware of the Dog," in which an RAF pilot at first believes he has been brought safely to a British hospital after his crash landing but then comes to believe, correctly, that he really is in the hands of the Germans. He realizes the truth by noticing discrepancies in small details. For example, he knows that the water in the location of the hospital he's been told he is in is very soft, and this water is hard; and that German airplanes, whose engine sounds he recognizes, would not really be flying unchecked over a British hospital.

Finally, the pilot crawls out of his bed to look out the window:

> He was looking at the hedge when he saw the sign. It was just a piece of board nailed to the top of a short pole, and because the hedge had not been trimmed for a long time, the branches had grown out around the sign so that it seemed almost as though it had been placed in the middle of the hedge. There was something written on the board with white paint. He pressed his head against the glass of the window, trying to read what it said. The first letter was a G, he could see that. The second was an A, and the third was an R. One after another he managed to see what the letters were. There were three words, and slowly he spelled the letters out aloud to himself as he managed to read them. G-A-R-D-E A-U C-H-I-E-N, *Garde au chien*. That is what it said.

At the end of the story, the officer, now convinced that he is being held by the German Army in France, gives only his rank and serial number to the officer who comes to debrief him about his experiences.

In the revelation plot, the reader begins with the false sense that everything is fine; then nagging doubts develop. As Friedman says:

> Our short-range fears develop and then are superseded by our long-range hopes—he is in enemy hands all right,

but he has found it out just in time—followed by a final sense of relief and pleasure.

Reversal What happens when the reader has been led to expect a certain development in a story and suddenly circumstances change and just the opposite of what was expected takes place.

In James Thurber's "The Catbird Seat," the protagonist, prim, stiff Mr. Martin, has decided to "rub out" his co-worker, Mrs. Barrows, because he is worried that she plans to get him fired. He goes to her house:

> Mr. Martin looked quickly around the living room for the weapon. He had counted on finding one there. There were andirons and a poker and something in a corner that looked like an Indian club. None of them would do. It couldn't be that way. He began to pace around. He came to a desk. On it lay a metal paper knife with an ornate handle. Would it be sharp enough?

At this point we're expecting a murder scene, but it does not happen. The reversal happens after Mr. Martin suddenly changes his strategy and lies to Mrs. Barrows that he drinks and smokes all the time and that he has no respect for their boss, Mr. Fitweiler—and before leaving, confides that he also takes heroin and plans to kill Mr. Fitweiler. The next day, Mrs. Barrows tells the president of the company what Mr. Martin said to her: Mr. Fitweiler does not believe Mr. Martin could do such a thing and fires Mrs. Barrows. *(See: gimmickry, peripety, surprise ending.)*

Revision The transformation of first drafts to polished, completed work. Revision covers poking about with commas as well as making major adjustments; often, indeed, the activity of pondering every comma leads the writer to realize the need for more extensive changes.

Even after their publication, some writers continue to work on stories. This is a paragraph from the version of Raymond Carver's story "Where I'm Calling From" that appeared in the March 15, 1982, edition of *The New Yorker*. The speaker is Frank Martin, who runs a private detoxification center for alcoholics where the *protagonist is staying:

"Jack London used to have a big place on the other side of the valley. Right over there behind that green hill you're looking at. But alcohol killed him. Let that be a lesson. He was a better man than any of us. But he couldn't handle the stuff, either. . . . You guys want to read something while you're here, read that book of his *The Call of the Wild*. You know the one I'm talking about? We have it inside, if you want to read something. It's about this animal that's half dog and half wolf. They don't write books like that anymore. But we could have helped Jack London, if we'd been here in those days. And if he'd let us. If he'd asked for our help. Hear me? Like we can help you. If. If you ask for it and if you listen. End of sermon. But don't forget it. If," he says again. Then he hitches his pants and tugs his sweater down. "I'm going inside," he says. "See you at lunch."

A revised version appeared as the title story in the 1989 collection, *Where I'm Calling From*:

"Jack London used to have a big place on the other side of the alley. Right over there behind that green hill you're looking at. But alcohol killed him. Let that be a lesson to you. He was a better man than any of us. But he couldn't handle the stuff, either. . . . You guys want to read something while you're here, read that book of his, *The Call of the Wild*. You know the one I'm talking about? We have it inside if you want to read something. It's about this animal that's half dog and half wolf. End of sermon," he says, and then hitches his pants up and tugs his sweater down. "I'm going inside," he says. "See you at lunch."

Note how the cutting short of the anti-alcohol sermon creates a small but definite improvement in the portrayal of Frank Martin. Carver's point about Jack London still is there, but Martin's words seem much more in character, much more in keeping with his laconic, inarticulate strength.

Rising Action *(complication)*　A term taken from drama to describe the part of the plot that occurs after the *exposition, after the reader has been introduced to the characters and knows enough to understand and appreciate the story, when difficulties begin to arise for the protagonist because of conflict with an opposing force.

In Flannery O'Connor's "A Stroke of Good Fortune," the rising action is literal, as the protagonist, Ruby, exhaustedly climbs the stairs to her fourth-floor apartment. She is excited because she has been to a palm reader who has told her that, after a long illness, Ruby is due for a "stroke of good fortune." She thinks that her impending illness will cause her husband Bill to give in and move with her to a house, to preserve her health.

The tension increases as Ruby and the reader ponder the seriousness of Ruby's illness, and her other idea, that she is the only one in her family with any ambition. Just as Ruby's thoughts become morbid about her possible illness ("They'd have to knock her in the head before they'd get her near a hospital, they'd have to—suppose she would die if they did not?") she reaches the apartment of a woman friend who tells her she looks pregnant. Ruby finally is forced to realize that her friend is right, which means the end to her ambitions:

> Ruby slammed the door shut and looked down at herself quickly. She was big there but she had always had a kind of big stomach. She did not stick out there different from the way she did any place else. It was natural when you took on some weight to take it on in the middle and Bill Hill didn't mind her being fat, he was just more happy and didn't know why, . . . She rubbed her hand across her skirt and felt the tightness of it, but hadn't she felt that before? She had. It was the skirt—she had on the tight one that she didn't wear often, she had . . . she didn't have on the tight one. She had on the loose one. But it wasn't very loose. But that didn't make any difference, she was just fat.

The complication phase of the plot ends with the story's *climax, the point in a story when suspense is at its highest and a final turning point is reached.

Roman à Clef (Schlüsselroman) A novel in which all the characters are based on real, usually famous people, whom the perceptive reader can be expected to recognize even if the names are disguised. Occasionally the term is used to comprise other types of autobiographical fiction as well.

An example is Carrie Fisher's *Postcards From the Edge*, in which she includes herself as well as her mother, actress Debbie Reynolds, and former husband Paul Simon as characters.

The roman à clef offers the writer more freedom than the straightforward memoir writer enjoys—freedom to interpret or condense events for clarity, and to spice them up for added drama—since the memoir writer is limited to the literal truth. *(See: autobiographical fiction.)*

Roman-Fleuve A novel or series of novels that follows the lives of a single group of characters over a long period of time, sometimes generations. The term is French, meaning "river novel," and the genre was particularly prevalent in France during the first part of the twentieth century.

Marcel Proust's *In Search of Lost Time* (*A la recherche du temps perdu*) is a classic example of a roman-fleuve. *In Search of Lost Time* (sometimes translated *Remembrance of Things Past*), originally published in seven volumes, follows the life of the narrator, Marcel, from boyhood until old age. The cast of characters, like that in real life, is enormous, but, unlike in many real lives, the same people (and their descendents) turn up from the beginning of the novel to the end.

At the end of the novel, Marcel, suffering from poor health, decides to write the story of the memory of his life, which becomes, apparently, the book the reader is then reading. *(See: chronicle novel.)*

Romance A word with many definitions, but most often used to describe a work in which some element of the fantastic comes into play. This element can be as unrealistic as the creation of characters who either could not ever have lived, or who somehow do not seem completely real, or a setting somewhere outside of the real world, or something as basic as a time frame distant from the present time.

In addition, even major characters in romances often are *types—sometimes expanding into *archetypes—rather than fully developed individuals, as might be the goal in a novel. The emphasis in a romance is more on action—especially on events that are extraordinary, or at least improbable and unusual. Some examples of works generally termed "romances" are Herman Melville's *Moby Dick*, Nathaniel Hawthorne's *The House of Seven Gables*, and the short stories of Edgar Allan Poe.

Because the romance developed long before the *novel, there is a tendency to see the novel as a more developed form than the romance, as an evolved improvement over it. In fact, though, the romance simply is different from the novel, which generally attempts to present a realistic picture of characters and events that take place in the present.

This passage from *Wuthering Heights*, by Emily Brontë, in which she portrays her love for Heathcliff despite her decision to marry Edgar Linton, illustrates one of the strengths of the romance: the portrayal of intense, subjective, passionate emotions that seem more related to the *tale than to the more generally reticent *novel:

> "My great miseries in this world have been Heathcliff's miseries, and I watched and felt each from the beginning: my great thought in living is himself. If all else perished, and he remained, I should still continue to be; and if all else remained, and he were annihilated, the universe would turn to a mighty stranger: I should not seem a part of it. My love for Linton is like the foliage in the woods: time will change it, I'm well aware, as winter changes the trees. My love for Heathcliff resembles the eternal rocks beneath: a source of little visible delight, but necessary. Nelly, I am Heathcliff! He's always, always in my mind: not as a pleasure, any more than I am always a pleasure to myself, but as my own being. . . ."

Other meanings for "romance" have included any work not written in Latin, and the old French tales of chivalry.

Round Character   A character who expresses a number of different character traits, including the kind of contradictory characteristics often seen in real people. The term was coined by E.M. Forster in *Aspects of the Novel.*

Forster's work abounds with round characters; one is Leonard Bast, from *Howard's End*, whom the narrator describes as:

> ... inferior to most rich people, there is not the least doubt of it. He was not as courteous as the average rich man, nor as intelligent, nor as healthy, nor as lovable. His mind and his body had been alike underfed, because he was poor, and because he was modern they were always craving better food.

Yet he has a streak of real poetry in him, too, deciding one night to get away from London to see if he can sleep outside in the real country, desiring to "get back to the earth." Bast takes a train out of town, then leaves the road to walk desolately in the fields. He ends up getting lost and finding himself too tired to enjoy the dawn. He charms the upper-class women he is telling about his trip by his admission:

> I'm glad I did it, and yet at the time it bored me more than I can say. And besides—you can believe me or not as you choose—I was very hungry. That dinner at Wimbledon—I meant it to last me all night like other dinners. I never thought that walking would make such a difference. Why, when you're walking you want, as it were, a breakfast and luncheon and tea during the night as well, and I'd had nothing but a packet of Woodbines. Lord, I did feel bad! Looking back, it wasn't what you may call enjoyment. It was more a case of sticking to it. I did stick. I—I was determined. Oh, hang it all! what's the good—I mean, the good of living in a room for ever? There one goes on day after day, same old game, same up and down to town, until you forget there is any other game. You ought to see once in a way what's going on outside, if it's only nothing particular after all.

The women agree, and the narrator tells us:

Within his cramped little mind dwelt something that was greater than Jefferies's books—the spirit that led Jefferies to write them; and his dawn, though revealing nothing but monotones, was part of the eternal sunrise that shows George Borrow Stonehenge.

(See: flat character.)

S

Satire A work that tries, through strategies including humor, exaggeration, *irony, *caricature, sarcasm and *parody, to expose the evil, or merely the foolishness, of various aspects of society. The goal of the satirist is not simply to inspire scorn, but to reform the aspect of society—and it usually is a whole society rather than a single individual—that is a victim of the satire.

Tom Wolfe's *Bonfire of the Vanities* deals with a rich stockbroker who is in an accident in which an innercity black teenager is killed. During the trial, the protagonist eventually loses everything that is important to him: his high-paying job, his family, his position in society. Here is a passage in which a sleazy tabloid reporter interviews the English teacher of the young man who has been killed. The passage is darkly humorous but at the same time angry at the city's overwhelmed educational system and at the indifferent teacher:

> "Will Henry Lamb graduate, or would he have?"
>
> "As far as I know. As I say, he has a very good attendance record.". . .
>
> "Well, Mr. Rifkind, can you tell me anything at all about Henry Lamb's performance or his aptitude, anything at all?"
>
> "You have to understand that they give me about sixty-five students in each class when the year starts, because they know it'll be down to forty by mid-year and thirty by the end of the year. Even thirty, that's too many, but that's what I get. It's not exactly what you'd call a tutorial system. Henry Lamb's a nice young man who applies himself and

wants an education. What more can I tell you?"

"Let me ask you this. How does he do on his written work?"

Mr. Rifkind let out a whoop. "Written work? There hasn't been any written work at Ruppert High for fifteen years! Maybe twenty! They take multiple-choice tests. Reading comprehension, that's the big thing. That's all the Board of Education cares about."

Satire is divided into two subcategories: direct (or formal) and indirect. Direct satire is further divided into Horatian, the most gentle type, and Juvenalian, which is angry and bitter. With direct satire, the narrative voice, usually in the first person, speaks directly to the reader or to a specific character in the satire. Indirect satire looks more like conventional fiction; the satire comes through as a result of the story, and it is the characters who are the victims of the author's wit.

Some twentieth century satirists include William Burroughs, Evelyn Waugh and Joseph Heller.

Scene Everything that follows in the description of a single drama-tized incident, uninterrupted by change of setting or lengthy sum-mary.

Travel in a scene from one setting to another is fine if the scene takes place, say, on a train. A scene usually will include direct dialogue, as well as careful attention to description of physical actions and other sensory details.

A scene allows the writer to draw out the actions and thoughts of characters, perhaps taking pages to show what might have taken only a few minutes. In "A & P," John Updike creates a scene that lasts the entire story, allowing us to see and feel the narrator's reactions as he watches three attractive girls wearing swimming suits come into the grocery store where he works, buy a jar of pickled herring snacks, and get bawled out by the store manager for being inappro-priately dressed. Suddenly unhappy with what he sees as a long, te-dious future in the grocery store, the narrator abruptly quits his job, but ponders "how hard the world was going to be to me hereafter." Since all these actions occur at the same time (a hot summer afternoon) and in the same place (the grocery store), the entire story is created from a single scene.

Scenic Method   A style used to present the action of a work mainly through a series of discrete *scenes and *episodes rather than through *summary and *exposition. The scenic method is the opposite of the *panoramic method.

An example from a novel that uses the scenic method is Jean-Paul Sartre's *The Age of Reason* (*L'Age de Raison*), whose first scene follows in miniature the *structure of many complete novels, beginning with exposition and *description, followed by *rising action, a *climax, and a short *denouement.

As the novel begins, a young professor, Mathieu, goes to visit his mistress, Marcelle:

> Marcelle opened her door before he had reached the landing. A pink iris-scented haze from her room pervaded the staircase. She was wearing her green chemise. Through it Mathieu could see the soft rich curve of her hips. He went in: he always felt as though he were entering a huge seashell.

Gradually, Mathieu comes to realize something is amiss with Marcelle:

> There was certainly something wrong: her gestures had never been so brusque, nor her voice so curt and masculine. She was sitting on the edge of the bed, blankly naked and defenseless, like a great porcelain vase in that dim pink room, and it was almost painful to hear her speak in that masculine voice, and smell the strong, dark odor of her body.

Eventually the scene comes to a climax, when Marcelle admits to Mathieu that she is pregnant:

> "Well, it's happened."
> "What's happened?"
> "It has happened!"

> Mathieu made a wry face.
>
> "Are you sure?"
>
> "Quite sure. You know I never get panicky: I'm two months late."
>
> "Hell!" said Mathieu.
>
> And he thought: "She ought to have told me at least three weeks ago."

Mathieu and Marcelle agree that she should have an abortion. Marcelle suggests that she go to an old friend who performed an abortion on a friend of hers a year before, although Mathieu objects briefly: "That old woman who messed her up last year? Why, it was six months before she was well again. I won't allow it." He says he wants to see the woman before he agrees that Marcelle should go there.

In the scene's denouement, the couple begins to make love, but Mathieu becomes distracted at the thought of Marcelle's pregnancy, and the scene ends with Marcelle smiling at Mathieu as he leaves, but he is worrying—correctly, as it happens—that "she bore him a grudge." *(See: panoramic method, scene.)*

Second-Person Point of View   Fiction where the protagonist is referred to not as "I" or "he" but as "you."

It used to be rare to find a story written in the second person, and the device still is bound to catch the reader's eye. The difficulty is to make the second-person voice sound like more than a gimmick. Recently this point of view gained popularity in stories from Lorrie Moore's *Self-Help* and in Jay McInerney's novel, *Bright Lights, Big City*, which begins:

> You are not the kind of guy who would be at a place like this at this time of the morning. But here you are, and you cannot say that the terrain is entirely unfamiliar, although the details are fuzzy. You are at a nightclub talking to a girl with a shaved head.

Jamaica Kincaid's two-page, one-sentence short story "Girl" carries the technique still further, using the imperative voice to bully readers (the "you") into submission—or rebellion—as the mother character commands her daughter:

> Wash the white clothes on Monday and put them on the stone heap; wash the color clothes on Tuesday and put them on the clothes-line to dry; don't walk barehead in the hot sun; cook pumpkin fritters in very hot sweet oil; . . . on Sundays try to walk like a lady and not like the slut you are so bent on becoming . . .

Self-Effacing Author   A term used to describe a common type of narrator in *modernist fiction whose goal is the realistic expression of reality. The author himself seems to disappear, offering no particular opinions, showing no particular values.

The self-effacing author frequently appears in fiction using the *scenic method of plotting, as in this opening of D.H. Lawrence's *Sons and Lovers*:

> "The Bottoms" succeeded to "Hell Row." Hell Row was a block of thatched, bulging cottages that stood by the brookside on Greenhill Lane. There lived the colliers who worked in the little gin-pits two fields away. The brook ran under the alder trees, scarcely soiled by these small mines, whose coal was drawn to the surface by donkeys that plodded wearily in a circle round a gin. And all over the countryside were these same pits, some of which had been worked in the time of Charles II, the few colliers and the donkeys burrowing down like ants into the earth, making queer mounds and little black places among the corn-fields and the meadows. And the cottages of these coal-miners, in blocks and pairs here and there, together with odd farms and homes of the stockingers, straying over the parish, formed the village of Bestwood.

The term is easily confused with—to the point that the two phrases often are used interchangeably—the idea of the *effaced narrator, which is more properly used to describe a narrator who is able to deliver more sophisticated observations about the character and scene than can the character through whose eyes we see. *(See: autho-rial-omniscient voice, effaced narrator, objective narrator, scenic method, unintrusive narrator.)*

Sentimentality A term used to describe the effect of fiction whose writers have attempted to make readers feel emotions, usually pity and sadness, without giving the reader something about which to feel them.

Usually sentimental fiction relies on clichés, either of situation (the death of a child or a beloved, heroic pet) or of character (the unremit-tingly evil villain, the Mother-Theresa-like heroine), or simply of lan-guage whose goal is to try to wrest tears from the reader.

Often understatement and restraint are used to avoid the appear-ance of sentimentality—or, indeed, of any strong emotion. In "The Sin-Eater," Margaret Atwood's protagonist feels real grief at the death of her psychiatrist, who fell (or perhaps jumped) from a tree in his yard, but the narrator avoids sentimentality by adopting a consciously restrained tone:

> After the funeral we go back to Joseph's house, to the third wife's house, for what used to be called the wake. Not any more: now it's coffee and refreshments.
>
> The flower beds are tidy, gladioli at this time of year, already fading and a little ragged. The tree branch, the one that broke, is still on the lawn.
>
> "I kept having the feeling he wasn't really there," says Karen as we go up the walk.
>
> "Really where?" I say.
>
> "There," says Karen. "In the coffin."
>
> "For Christ's sake," I say, "don't start that." I can tolerate that kind of sentimental fiction in myself, just barely, as long as I don't do it out loud. "Dead is dead, that's what he'd say. Deal with here and now, remember?"

Sequel A work written to follow another, usually picking up where the first book left off, following the characters from the earlier work into the future. The term usually is used only for the second in a series of two; when the same author writes three books about the same characters, it usually is called a trilogy.

A sequel must pick up almost all of the plot threads left over from the first book; merely using some of the same characters, as John Updike does in his "Rabbit" series, is not sufficient to qualify the second book for sequel status.

As long as the work meets the criterion of being the second in a series of two and follows the fates of the same characters and storyline as the first book did, it does not even matter if the author is the same, as recent sequels to Margaret Mitchell's *Gone With the Wind* and Daphne Du Maurier's *Rebecca* indicate.

Serial Fiction Fiction, published in magazines, that is broken off, generally in a particularly suspenseful spot, and continued in the periodical's next issue.

While serial fiction was most popular in the United States and Great Britain during the last quarter of the nineteenth century, novels sometimes are serialized today. In the 1990s, *The New Yorker*, for example, has published connected stories dealing with the same characters over time by writers including Tom Drury and Julie Hecht.

The concept of seriality raises some interesting issues about the way people read. If we read some works that first appeared in serial form—like Gustave Flaubert's *Madame Bovary*, Leo Tolstoy's *Anna Karenina*, and Thomas Hardy's *Jude the Obscure*—over a maximum period of a couple of weeks, how is our experience different from that of the original readers, who read it over a period of longer than a year, with long breaks between chapters?

In addition, while reading a novel outside of school generally is a private experience today, the reader of serial fiction would have been sharing the experience with hundreds of thousands of other readers who were exactly as far along in the work as they. This shared experience must have broadened the possibilities for discussion and speculation on what would happen next among readers, making the experience something like what we today participate in while watching real-life news events unfold.

Series Fiction *(sequence novels)* While the term sometimes is used to describe *popular or *genre novels that use the same characters from book to book, like Lilian Jackson Braun's *The Cat Who . . .* mysteries, series fiction also encompasses any fiction in which the same character appears over the course of several books.

Harry Rabbit Angstrom, a former basketball hero, is the central character in John Updike's series. In *Rabbit Run* he is wracked with guilt about the bathtub drowning of his infant daughter, and his abandonment of a pregnant lover; in *Rabbit Is Rich* he enjoys success as a Toyota dealer. The series also includes *Rabbit Redux* and *Rabbit at Rest* (presumably the last of the series). *(See: sequel.)*

Setting The time—both the approximate year and the hour of the day—and location during which a story takes place. Some writers also consider the psychological state of mind of the protagonist part of the setting.

Readers generally like to be sure of the setting, but sometimes there can be an advantage in making a story's time or place hard to ascertain in detail, especially in nonrealistic fiction. A conscious disordering of a time sequence and a nonlinear juxtaposition of time sequences is also a possibility often used in *narrative collage.

Since most people believe that a character is strongly influenced by her environment, however, it usually is important to make that environment clear, even in works where character is far more important than setting. Ideally, the setting should be more than decoration: setting, *plot and character should be so naturally intertwined that it would be impossible to imagine the story taking place in any other time and place than the one in which the writer has placed it. *(See: background description, description, exposition.)*

Short-Short Story A complete story of 1,500 words maximum and, practically speaking, around 250 words minimum.

For a short-short story to seem complete in itself and not just an outline for a longer piece, some aspect must be omitted—and often what is omitted is a complex *plot. Many short-short stories, in fact, are built around a *theme or an idea rather than a plot; others basically are composed of *exposition. There is no room in a short-short story for gratuitous *digression or for extra characters—although, of course, no two writers would agree on what constitutes digression or extra characters.

On the other hand, a short-short story also can succeed by leaving out everything that isn't plot, as Maxine Chernoff does in her short-short, "The Spirit of Giving," the story of a woman's generally unsuccessful search to buy gifts for her shallow sister and boyfriend. A calendar of Eskimo prints doesn't work for her sister because, although she is an anthropologist, she can't bear to think about the violence of the seal slaughter that is unstated in the pictures. She gives her boyfriend earmuffs, which he rejects because "I'm a translator"; although they still go out, their relationship palls.

The climax of the story comes when the protagonist must decide what to give her sister as a Christmas present; she finally decides on a food processor, having heard that Eskimos no longer put their elderly parents on ice floes to die but are more likely to have the parent live with an unmarried daughter, who is expected to chew their food for them if they have no teeth. The narrator in her note to her sister tells her that "when Mother needs an ice floe, remember who owns the food processor."

The tone of the story basically is light-hearted, and character is only hinted at; still, one gets the impression that if the story were longer, there already is enough there in the way of characterization that it would be possible to round them out quickly.

Overlapping subgenres of the short-short category are *flash fiction and sudden fiction, with flash fiction comprising fiction from about 250 to 750 words, and sudden fiction including work up to about 1,750 words. *(See: anecdote, flash fiction.)*

Short Story A fictional work of up to about 10,000 words (although anything less than about 1,500 often is called a *short-short story) that is complete in itself, without the complexity of a novel or novella, which needs a much longer period of space and time to reach a conclusion.

The short story in its contemporary form developed during the nineteenth century; American writer and critic Brander Matthews claimed to have invented the phrase "short story" in 1901 and to have clearly differentiated its attributes from those of the novel at that time. Unlike the *prose poem, which developed as a form primarily in Europe, the short story reached particular heights of excellence in the United States. Masters of the form include Edgar Allan Poe, Ernest Hemingway, James Joyce and Raymond Carver.

To be successful, a short story must seem complete no matter how short it is. A story always will be different from a miniature novel; usually there will be only a single major conflict; only one—or at most a few—fully developed characters; and not a lot of room for *description or *digression. *(See: flash fiction, short-short story.)*

Showing Versus Telling A phrase used to express the dilemma a writer faces in deciding whether to dramatize or summarize a scene. Generally the "showing versus telling" phrase is evoked to suggest that it is a better idea to dramatize an incident than simply to describe it.

"Showing versus telling" also can refer to providing the reader with evidence and letting him make up his mind about what is going on, rather than simply asserting it as a given.

Here, in Lionel Trilling's "Of This Time, Of That Place," Professor Howe, an English instructor, does not merely say that he believes a student is insane but gives evidence, by quoting from one of the student's papers, about just what form his madness takes. The paper he quotes is an essay the student writes on the first day of class as a response to the question, "Who am I?"

"Who am I?" he had begun. "Here, in a mundane, not to say commercialized academe, is asked the question which from time long immemorably out of mind has accreted doubts and thoughts in the psyche of man to pester him as a nuisance.

... "Today as ever, in spite of gloomy prophets of the dismal science (economics) the question is uninvalidated. Out of the starry depths of heaven hurtles this spear of query demanding to be caught on the shield of the mind ere it pierces the skull and the limbs be unstrung.

... "Existence without alloy is the question presented. Environment and heredity relegated aside, the rags and old clothes of practical life discarded, the name and the instrumentality of livelihood do not, as the prophets of the dismal science insist on in this connection, give solution to the interrogation which not from the professor merely but veritably from the cosmos is given. I think, therefore I am. (cogito etc.) but who am I?"

Later, in contrast, when Howe suspects that another student is mad, he briefly gives his own opinion of the contents of the student's paper for the reader:

The paper had been fantastic. The paper had been, if he wished to see it so, mad.

(See: scene, summary.)

Simile A figure of speech in which two dissimilar things are compared to each other, generally using either the word "like" or the phrase "as . . . as."

One of the purposes of a simile is to make a strange thing immediately familiar by comparing it with something the reader can understand and appreciate. Another simply is to create language that will delight—and often, for whatever reason on the writer's part, call attention to itself as a piece of writing.

In Flannery O'Connor's "A Good Man Is Hard to Find," we find this sentence:

Bailey didn't look up from his reading so she wheeled around then and faced the children's mother, a young woman in slacks, whose face was as broad and innocent as a cabbage and was tied around with a green head-kerchief that had two points on the top like rabbit's ears.

Here we have two similes; the purpose of the "points on the top like rabbit's ears" simile simply is to explain and clarify the image. Certainly everyone has seen rabbit's ears, and because no one can see this woman, the explanation of exactly how her head-kerchief is tied can become perfectly clear perhaps only through a simile.

The purpose of the "broad and innocent as a cabbage" simile is partly for simple enjoyment. No face truly resembles a cabbage all that closely, but it is amusing to picture one that does. Still, the connotations of cabbage—a plain, unexciting, nutritious food—get mixed up into the simile and help to *characterize the woman. *(See: analogy, metaphor.)*

Simulated Autobiography A work that purports to be the autobiography of a real person, but that the reader will be able to see as a work of fiction, if for no other reason than that the name of the author on the outside of the book has a different name from the narrator.

Here is the first paragraph of Charles Dickens's simulated autobiography *David Copperfield*, which appears in the chapter entitled "I am Born" (which is followed by "I Observe," "I have a Change," "I fall into Disgrace," "I am sent away from Home," and fifty-nine other descriptive titles):

> Whether I shall turn out to be the hero of my own life, or whether that station will be held by anybody else, these pages must show. To begin my life with the beginning of my life, I record that I was born (as I must have been informed and believe) on a Friday, at twelve o'clock at night. It was remarked that the clock began to strike, and I began to cry, simultaneously.
>
> In consideration of the day and hour of my birth, it was declared by the nurse, and by some sage women in the neighbourhood who had taken a lively interest in me several months before there was any possibility of our becoming personally acquainted, first, that I was destined to be unlucky in life; and secondly, that I was privileged to see ghosts and spirits; both these gifts inevitably attaching, as they believed, to all unlucky infants of either gender, born towards the small hours on a Friday night.

In many respects, simulated autobiography functions in the same way as conventional *first-person narration, in which the narrator plays the role of a major character. The difference is in the narrator's insistence that the story is a true document, and in the presumption that the document is being written by the narrator, which ascribes to the narrator a greater sensitivity (usually) and writing ability than the average narrator is likely to possess. *(See: diary fiction, first-person point of view, simulated biography.)*

Simulated Biography *(mock biography)*   A work whose narrator announces that it is a serious biography about a real, living (or formerly living) person, but whose subject, or facts about the subject, turn out to be entirely imaginary.

An example is Tommaso Landolfi's "Gogol's Wife," in which the imaginary author of a dignified, even stuffy biography of Nikolai Gogol reluctantly comes to the point in his book at which he must talk about Gogol's wife:

> Let me say it at once: Nikolai Vassilevitch's wife was not a woman. Nor was she any sort of human being, nor any sort of living creature at all, whether animal or vegetable (although something of the sort has sometimes been hinted). She was quite simply a balloon. Yes, a balloon; and this will explain the perplexity, or even indignation, of certain biographers who were also the personal friends of the Master, and who complained that, although they often went to his house, they never saw her and "never even heard her voice." . . .
>
> Gogol's so-called wife was an ordinary dummy made of thick rubber, naked at all seasons, buff in tint, or as is more commonly said, flesh-colored. But since women's skins are not all of the same color, I should specify that hers was a light-colored, polished skin, like that of certain brunettes.

The simulated biography often serves the function of parodying real biographies—as well as pointing out the philosophical problems that all biographers inevitably face. Steven Millhauser's biographer in the mock biography *Edwin Mullhouse* begins his detailed observations of his subject when Edwin is only eight days old and the biographer, Jeffrey Cartwright, is just six months older. Cartwright is convinced that Mullhouse, who commits suicide at Cartwright's urging on his eleventh birthday, is a truly important American author. He convinces Mullhouse to commit suicide in part because he is worried that Mullhouse's life lacks coherent shape, and that his suicide will provide a satisfying end to Cartwright's biography of Mullhouse. This misguided idea on Cartwright's part mirrors the difficulties all biographers face in trying to build a plot from the life of a real person whose life perhaps contains no logical structure.

Simulated biographies also differ from real biographies in that one of the main purposes of these works generally is to characterize the biographer as well as the subject. In *Edwin Mullhouse*, the normal reader will come to like Cartwright much more than he will the ostensible subject, Mullhouse—which may be Cartwright's conscious intention.

Simulated Scholarly Apparatus Fictional footnotes, endnotes, "works-cited" pages, or bibliographies created to imitate those that appear in nonfiction and scholarly works.

Vladimir Nabokov uses this technique in *Pale Fire*, ostensibly a scholarly essay elucidating a poem, "Pale Fire," by John Shade, a distinguished American poet who has just been murdered. The style of the "essay" is stiff; it clearly is intended by its college-professor author to be published for an audience of academics rather than for the casual reader or poetry lover.

In fact, the real story, which comes through in the strange footnotes to the poem, concerns the life of the psychotic scholar-narrator who stole the draft of the poem from the jacket of the dead poet, and who is for a while convinced that the poem is a disguised history of his life as king of the imaginary country of Zembla. That there is something peculiar about the scholar/commentator is clear by the third paragraph, which starts as a description of Shade's work habits:

> A methodical man, John Shade usually copied out his daily quota of completed lines at midnight but even if he recopied them again later, as I suspect he sometimes did, he marked his card or cards not with the date of his final adjustments, but with that of his Corrected Draft or first Fair Copy. I mean, he preserved the date of actual creation rather than that of second or third thoughts. There is a very loud amusement park right in front of my present lodgings.

Another example of simulated scholarly apparatus, on a lower grade level, is Joyce Carol Oates's "How I Contemplated the World

from the Detroit House of Correction and Began My Life Over Again," subtitled, *"Notes for an Essay for an English Class at Baldwin Country Day School; Poking Around in Debris; Disgust and Curiosity; A Revelation of the Meaning of Life; A Happy Ending . . ."*
This story presents itself as a draft of a personal-experience essay written for an English class at a suburban private school. The writer/ narrator is a student who recently has returned to school after having run away to live in Detroit among drug addicts and prostitutes.

The story is divided into a crude outline of the type that a not particularly gifted high school student might devise:

    I   Events
   II   Characters
  III   World Events
   IV   People and Circumstances Contributing to This
        Delinquency
    V   Sioux Drive
   VI   Detroit
  VII   Events
 VIII   Characters
   IX   That Night
    X   Detroit
   XI   Characters We are Forever Entwined With
  XII   Events

The tone of the story sometimes is much more sophisticated than the high school student could achieve; other times the voice is childish or tentative, as the girl tries different options for her draft of her story, which she, like the narrator of *Pale Fire*, elaborates on for literary effect:

> Clarita. She is twenty, twenty-five, she is thirty or more? Pretty, ugly, what? She is a woman lounging by the side of a road, in jeans and a sweater, hitchhiking, or she is slouched on a stool at a counter in some roadside diner.

In *The Mezzanine*, on the other hand, Nicholson Baker uses footnotes simply as a means of humor as he takes a whole book to discuss his lunch hour, during which he eats his lunch, buys new shoelaces, and tries to read a book.

Situation *(dramatic situation)* The fundamental predicament in which the characters in a work find themselves.

In James Dickey's *Deliverance*, the situation is that four men from the city are trapped while on a white-water boating trip in a remote area and must escape from a group of deranged backwoodsmen who are viciously pursuing them.

The *plot is much more complicated than the situation, involving as it does the city men's initial meeting with the malicious strangers, the apparent reasons for their attack on the boaters, the boaters' attempts to escape, and other events that mark the characters' confrontations.

Devising a situation can be tricky, since many situations have been overused to the point of becoming clichés. However, even a familiar one can become exciting if it is presented in a unique way.

The term "situation" also is sometimes used as a synonym for *donnée. *(See: donnée.)*

Slapstick A type of comedy involving pranks and physical humor.

This example comes from William Faulkner's "Mule in the Yard," which eventually (and inevitably) ends with Mrs. Hait's house burning down. Here, Mrs. Hait, old Het, and Ab Snopes, owner of a renegade mule, are chasing first the mule, and then the mule and a cow, around and around Mrs. Hait's house:

> "Git the rope!" Mrs. Hait said, running again. Snopes glared back at old Het.
>
> "Fore God where is ere rope?" he shouted.
>
> "In de sellar fo God!" old Het shouted also without pausing. "Go roun de udder way en head um." Again she and Mrs. Hait turned the corner in time to see again the still-vanishing mule with the halter once more in the act of floating lightly onward in its cloud of chickens with which, they being able to pass under the house and so on the chord of a circle while it had to go around the arc it had

once more coincided. When they turned the next corner they were in the back yard again.

"Fo God!" old Het cried. "He fixin to misuse de cow!" For they had gained on the mule now, since it had stopped. In fact, they came around the corner on a tableau. The cow now stood in the centre of the yard. She and the mule faced one another a few feet apart. . . . Now and in turn, man and cow and mule vanished around the next corner, Snopes now in the lead . . . They ran on, Mrs. Hait in grim and unflagging silence, old Het with the eager and happy amazement of a child. But when they gained the front again they saw only Snopes. He lay flat on his stomach, his head and shoulders upreared by his outstretched arms, his coat tail swept forward by its own arrested momentum about his head so that from beneath it his slack-jawed face mused in wild repose like that of a burlesqued nun.

Slice of Life   A work that purports to give a *realistic picture of life, generally without an obvious beginning, middle or end. In a slice-of-life work, the narrator or author does not offer opinions or comments about the scene that is being created.

Stephen Dixon's "Signatures" begins with an autograph-seeker asking an unknown painter for his autograph and ends with the painter finally agreeing to give it to him. Along the way, other people are also asked for their autographs and either do or don't give it to the autograph-seeker. There is no real suspense; the story's interest rests primarily on the rhythms of the characters' speech and with the reader's interest in the passersby:

> I'm walking along the streets, on my way from this place to not particularly that, when a man stops me. "You in show business?"
>
> "No."
>
> "You look like you are."
>
> "You made the same mistake a month ago when I was on the subway token line."
>
> "That so? See any stars around?"

"They're probably all inside. You're the guy who collects celebrity signatures."

"That's right." He's looking around, hasn't time to talk.

"Doing all right by it?"

"I make out."

"This your best block?"

The slice-of-life writer is more interested in *mood and *theme than in *plot. The slice-of-life story generally reaches no conclusion and has no particular moral. It is impossible to say what the characters will do after the end of the story, and what their lives were like before the story's beginning.

Socialist Realism *(boy-meets-tractor literature, Soviet realism)* A type of *Utopian fiction, endorsed by officials of the former Soviet Union. The premise of socialist realism was that human beings have a natural urge to reform the State through violent revolution and eventually will attempt to rebuild society as a collective governed by a powerful state rather than through the rule of rich or powerful individuals.

In novels of socialist realism, the protagonist generally is a peasant who appears as a natural leader, aided by what he learns from the directives of the Communist party. This hero is then able to lead other peasants to great social and military victories, following carefully the tenets of communism.

Socialist realism doesn't necessarily involve writing about the Russian Revolution; Alexander Fadeev's *The Young Guard*, for example, concerns Russians fighting the Germans during World War II:

> Forward, forward, comrades, to meet the rising sun!
> We'll fight our way to Liberty with bayonet and gun.
> Let crimson banners be unfurled
> That working men should rule the world.
> To battle, valiant young guard
> From factory and Farm!
>
> *—Youth Song*

In *The Young Guard*, the changes in a coal mining town under the Soviets are presented in positive terms:

These new pits belonged to a lonely landowner called Yarmankin, also known as the Mad Squire. Consequently, the village which grew up round these pits was commonly called Yarmankin, or the Mad village. The squire himself lived in a gray stone single-story house, half of which consisted of a greenhouse containing exotic plants and birds brought from overseas; it stood alone, exposed to the four winds on the high hill beyond the gorge, and was also called "mad."

Under Soviet rule new pits were sunk during the first and second five-year plans and the centre of the Sorokin Coal-Field shifted to this area. Modern dwellings went up, large buildings were built for the various offices, hospitals, schools and clubs. On the hill, by the side of the Mad Squire's house, the attractive winged building of the District Soviet was erected.

Spoonerism A mistake of speech in which a speaker scrambles two words, combining the beginning consonant of the first word with the rest of the second word, and vise versa.

An example is attributed to Oxford Professor W.A. Spooner, from whose name the term comes: "You have hissed my mystery lectures and tasted the whole worm" (instead of, "You have missed my history lectures and wasted the whole term").

Static Character Someone who does not change in character or personality throughout the course of a work. The character's age may change, or her position in life, but she basically is the same person at the end of the story as she is at the beginning.

To call a character "static" is not necessarily to slam the character or the author's abilities. Static characters are common in stories where discussion of character is not the main point and, curiously, they also occur in stories that attempt to imitate reality closely. In real life, major character change ordinarily does not occur in the short period of time that a short story, in particular, encompasses. A static character is not necessarily a *stock character, either, although a stock character always will be a static one.

An example of a well-drawn static character is Paul in Willa Cather's

"Paul's Case." At the beginning of the story Paul desperately desires to escape dull Pittsburgh for more glamorous surroundings. Near the end of the story Paul, having stolen a thousand dollars from his father's business, does, in fact, leave Pittsburgh and move to a hotel room at the Waldorf Astoria. He still is the same confused Paul, though, unable to think of much to do in New York beyond ordering flowers for his room and eating in the hotel restaurant, pleased to give the impression that he belongs. Physically he has made a big change, but internally he still is the same old Paul, a strange but unchanged character. *(See: stock character.)*

Stock Character   A character whose personality and character are so familiar through past exposure in other works that the normal techniques of *characterization hardly are necessary, because the reader already knows all about the character. Some examples of stock characters are the mad scientist, the strong-but-silent cowboy, the dignified butler, the poor little rich girl, the morally bankrupt banker. Often stock characters have moved into the fictional realm via other media like film, or they are characters from fiction who are easily transformed into movie clichés.

A stock character is a *flat character, one with few definite character traits, but all flat characters are not stock characters. Stock characters also differ from *archetypes. The archetypal mother, say, is supposed to encompass all mothers into a single, recognizable image—what T.S. Eliot called a "primordial image"—of the mother. But a stock character is limited to a few broad, stereotypical character traits.

Although stock characters are most easily found in TV and movies, they share some of the same advantages as flat characters—immediate recognizability and frequent usefulness as comic relief. The psychologically repressed nurse in Ken Kesey's *One Flew Over the Cuckoo's Nest* may be the cousin of *M*A*S*H*'s Hot Lips Houllihan, but certainly there is nothing clichéd about Kesey's description of this well-known figure:

> The big nurse tends to get real put out if something keeps her outfit from running like a smooth, accurate, precision-made machine. The slightest thing messy or out of kilter or

in the way ties her into a little white knot of tight-smiled fury. She walks around with that same doll smile crimped between her chin and her nose and that same calm whir coming from her eyes, but down inside of her she's tense as steel. I know, I can feel it. And she don't relax a hair till she gets the nuisance attended to—what she calls "adjusted to surroundings."

(See: flat character, static character, type.)

Stock Situation *(formula)*   A situation that is so familiar that it has become a cliché. Some examples are the reading-of-the-will scene; the father-and-son-coming-of-age-hunting-trip scene (which generally is climaxed by the son's-refusal-to-kill-a-doe scene); the innocent-teen-age-girl-brutalized-in-reform-school scene. As with stock characters, many of the best examples are from genre fiction or from other media, such as TV and movies.

A well-written stock scene, of course, is a lot better than a badly written one. Even in the best novels, however, when the nursing-home resident tediously waits all day in the lobby for relatives who never show up, we are patient only on the hope that the writer eventually will do something new with the concept, to turn a hackneyed situation on its ear.

Stock situations lend themselves easily to parody, one of their main uses in contemporary literary fiction and *metafiction. Here, in *Snow White*, Donald Barthelme transforms the stock situation of a lonely princess waiting for her prince to arrive:

> *"Which prince?"* Snow White wondered brushing her teeth. "Which prince will come? Will it be Prince Andrey? Prince Igor? Prince Alf? Prince Alphonso? Prince Malcolm? Prince Donalbain? Prince Fernando? Prince Siegfried? Prince Philip? Prince Albert? Prince Paul? Prince Akihito? Prince Rainier? Prince Porus? Prince Myshkin? Prince Rupert? Prince Pericles? Prince Karl? Prince Clarence? Prince George? Prince Hal? Prince John? Prince Mamillius? Prince Florizel? Prince Kropotkin? Prince Humphrey? Prince Charlie? Prince Matchabelli? Prince Escalus? Prince Valiant?

Prince Fortinbras?" Then Snow White pulled herself together. "Well it is terrific to be anticipating a prince—to be waiting and knowing that what you are waiting for is a prince, packed with grace—but it is still waiting, and waiting as a mode of existence is, as Brack has noted, a darksome mode. . . . I wonder if he will have the Hapsburg Lip?"

(See: cliché.)

Story   One use of the word is as synonymous with *short story, describing a work of approximately 10,000 words or less, as distinct from a novella or novel.

In another sense, the word "story" first was used by Russian formalist writers to describe the raw material of a work, with its events told chronologically, with little attention paid to the reasons why these events took place.

"Story" is differentiated from *"plot" in that plot organizes the events of the story into a particular order, which may not be chronological, but which may include, for example, *flashbacks and *flashforwards. In arranging a plot, the author might choose to emphasize some details while de-emphasizing others, and might include authorial *digressions or comments on the events. The story, on the other hand, simply is a chronological record of the events that occur over the course of the period covered by the plot.

The story of a novel like Laurence Sterne's *Tristram Shandy* can be summarized in a few paragraphs; the plot, with its many dislocations of chronology, asides, puns and digressions, would take nearly as long as the novel itself to recount.

E.M. Forster defines the difference between plot and story somewhat differently. He calls story the narration of the events told in the chronological sequence in which they occur, while plot is the narration of the events with the emphasis on the reasons for the events' taking place, their cause-and-effect sequence.

"Story" is also sometimes used synonymously with *"tale," something that can be told orally. *(See: plot, short story, tale.)*

Story-Novel *(linked stories, stovel)*   Novels whose chapters stand alone as stories but that also, combined, deal with the same characters and themes and, ultimately, come together to form a complete entity.

An example is Louise Erdrich's *Love Medicine,* in which fourteen stories, all involving members of the Chippewa Kapshaw family but taking place between 1934 and 1984, explore the relationships among the various family members without ever forming a formal plot.

In the first chapter, we learn of the events leading up to the death of June Kapshaw, who, drunk, leaves the truck of a man she has picked up in a bar and walks out onto the plains, freezing in a snowstorm; in the third chapter, we learn about how June Kapshaw's aunt, Marie Lazarre, planned to join a convent and become a nun and falls victim to the psychotic torture of a deranged nun. The two stories are related only in that they tell about incidents in the lives of characters who are related. But with the other chapters, these stories form a bleak picture of life on the reservation that is much richer than the individual stories themselves.

A story-novel can end up forming an impression, rather than a complete plot, as does Sherwood Anderson's *Winesburg, Ohio,* whose main character, the young George Willard, eventually says goodbye to his girlfriend and small town to take a train to a larger city. *Winesburg, Ohio* is divided into stand-alone chapters that, for the most part, create character sketches of the often deeply disturbed people in his hometown, some of whom barely know George, but all of whom leave the impression that George certainly is doing the right thing by getting out of Winesburg.

Story of Initiation *(*Erziehungsroman*)*   A story in which the protagonist, often an adolescent, experiences an event that either leads him to self-discovery or to a change of character, or both, giving evidence that this event will bring him closer to maturity and the adult world than he was before.

In James Joyce's "Araby," the protagonist, telling in retrospect the story of his adolescence, describes his love for a neighbor girl, identified only as "Mangan's Sister," and his determination to attend a bazaar that Mangan's Sister has expressed an interest in attending, in order to buy her a gift.

His uncle returns home, drunk and late on the night of the bazaar, and the boy doesn't arrive at the bazaar until it is about to close. When the lights go off, the protagonist experiences an *epiphany that leads him to the realization that not only was his love of Mangan's Sister false "vanity," but, in fact, that his whole love for her was a kind of defense against the dullness and drabness of his life. The reader leaves the story convinced that the protagonist likely will not try to escape from boredom by developing an infatuation again.

The story of initiation may lead the protagonist to the threshold of some kind of new maturity but not definitely into it; it may leave him enmeshed in a struggle, or it may lead him definitely into adulthood, as we know it does in "Araby."

The story of initiation is closely related to the *bildungsroman, but bildungsroman must be a novel rather than a story. Also, a story of initiation technically relates more to a reaching of emotional maturity than intellectual maturity. *(See: bildungsroman, epiphany.)*

Stream of Consciousness   Language that imitates the unedited, random expressions and feelings that go through the mind before the mind changes them into comprehensible, rational speech. The challenge of stream-of-consciousness writing is to give the impression of unedited thoughts while at the same time being intelligible to the reader.

Although stream-of-consciousness writing often looks strange (odd grammar and paragraphing, abrupt jumps from subject to subject), the intention often is to create the effect of reality, to present people's thoughts as they really occur, to define characters more like the people who exist in real life. One of the best examples of stream of consciousness is Joyce's 30,000-word "Molly Bloom" soliloquy at the end of *Ulysses*:

> Yes because he never did a thing like that before as ask to get his breakfast in bed with a couple of eggs since the City Arms hotel when he used to be pretending to be laid up with a sick voice doing his highness to made himself interesting to that old faggot Mrs Riordan that he thought he had a great leg of and she never left us a farthing all for masses for herself and her soul greatest miser ever was actually afraid to lay out 4d for her methylated spirit telling me all her ailments she had too much old chat in her about politics and earthquakes and the end of the world let us have a bit

of fun first God help the world if all the women were her
sort down on bathingsuits and lownecks of course nobody
wanted her to wear I suppose she was pious because no man
would look at her twice . . .

Structure The general framework into which the plot of a work is
organized.

The structure of any work depends to some degree on the kind
of story the writer creates. A novel where plot and action are most
important, for example, probably will be more intricately structured
than one focusing primarily on development of character. A *picaresque novel may be structured with events taking place presumably
at random, but most novels are not shaped so arbitrarily.

Realistic stories often are told with the events occurring in chronological order; of course, the writer has the option of shifting the chronology through the use of *flashbacks and *flashforwards. Chapters,
paragraphs and sentences can be made long or short; the method of
presenting material can be *scenic or *panoramic; the *pace can be
slow and *digressive or quick and to the point. *(See: form, plot.)*

Style The way the author expresses herself: the words she uses
(whether abstract or concrete, imagistic or straightforward, simple or
ornate, friendly or cold, vivid or bland, excited or blasé). A writer's
decisions about style also will include decisions about sentence
rhythms and even about the order in which the ideas are arranged.

Style cannot be divorced from the subject of a story; the words a
writer chooses are inextricably connected with what she has to say.
Indeed, the word "choice" is important; a writer chooses a style appropriate to create the effects she desires.

Here is the exposition in Ernest Hemingway's "Indian Camp." Notice the short, simple sentences and the recurrence of key words
("boat," "row," "Indian"):

At the lake shore there was another rowboat drawn up. The
two Indians stood waiting.
Nick and his father got in the stern of the boat and the
Indians shoved it off and one of them got in to row. Uncle
George sat in the stern of the camp rowboat. The young

Indian shoved the camp boat off and got in to row Uncle George.

The two boats started off in the dark. Nick heard the oarlocks of the other boat quite a way ahead of them in the mist. The Indians rowed with quick choppy strokes. Nick lay back with his father's arm around him. It was cold on the water. The Indian who was rowing them was working very hard, but the other boat moved further ahead in the mist all the time.

"Where are we going, Dad?" Nick asked.

"Over to the Indian camp. There is an Indian lady very sick."

"Oh," said Nick.

William Faulkner's style, with its long sentences, emotional rhythms, and clauses that tend to elaborate closely on what occurred in the one just previous, could not be transferred to Hemingway's story; and the drama of a Faulkner story like "Barn Burning" would be lost without the verbal excess of its sentences:

The store in which the Justice of the Peace's court was sitting smelled of cheese. The boy, crouched on his nail keg at the back of the crowded room, knew he smelled cheese, and more: from where he sat he could see the ranked shelves close-packed with the solid, squat, dynamic shapes of tin cans whose labels his stomach read, not from the lettering which meant nothing to his mind but from the scarlet devils and the silver curve of fish—this, the cheese which he knew he smelled and the hermetic meat which his intestines believed he smelled coming in intermittent gusts momentary and brief between the other constant one, the smell and sense just a little of fear because mostly of despair and grief, the old fierce pull of blood.

Subject-Dominated Fiction Fiction in which the subject matter takes precedence over other aspects of the work, such as *style, *plot, *theme and *characterization. Writers of subject-dominated fiction usually are interested in convincing a reader to take a certain point of view about the subject, and such works are filled with broadly drawn characters often meant to be taken symbolically or allegorically.

Often the desire of subject-dominated fiction is to express some idea that might be expressed better through nonfiction. Sometimes, ironically, subject-dominated fiction is unsatisfying because it over-simplifies the characters and even its all-important subject.

Curiously, long works of subject-dominated fiction tend to work better than short ones; a plot and cast of characters large and compli-cated enough to deal with many different aspects of the subject can make up for the fact that neither is developed to a realistic degree. Marilyn French's feminist novel *The Women's Room* and Herman Wouk's *The Winds of War* are two examples of fiction in which the sheer breadth and scope of material overcomes the fact that few of the situations and characters stand out as truly individualistic. *(See: didactic fiction, propaganda novel, thesis novel.)*

Subjective Style *(subjective writing)*   A style that portrays the inner convictions, hopes or ideals either of the protagonist or of the writer, placing more importance on these intangibles than on the subject being discussed.

Subjective style is the opposite of *objective style, which concerns itself with the concrete object being described rather than on the opinions and feelings of the writer or of the characters.

The word "subjective" may be used in two distinct ways. It can refer to works in which the author's thoughts and autobiographical feelings come through (as in autobiographical fiction), or it can por-tray the thoughts and emotional responses of a fictional character. Generally it is the second kind of subjectivity—the feelings coming out of the character—that is most admired.

In Doris Betts' "Still Life With Fruit," the protagonist, Gwen, has a baby under particularly unsympathetic hospital conditions: Her hus-band is not present, the nurses are insensitive, the forceps seem mon-strous, the doctors are unpleasant and almost leering. The story ends:

> Gwen touched her own throat to make sure no other hand had grabbed it. Something crawled under her skin, like the spider which webbed her eyelids, tightening all lines. In

both eyes the spider spilled her hot, wet eggs—those on the right for bitterness, and those on the left for joy.

In this story there is not any particular suspense about the outcome of the birth—there is no indication that there will be physical difficulties. The focus is on Gwen's emotional state. After the birth, Gwen feels she will never be the same for reasons other than that she now has a baby: she vows not to live dependent, as she had planned, with her mother-in-law while her husband serves in the Army.

Indeed, in "Still Life With Fruit," we get both the protagonist's feelings and, in the background, what seem to be the author's feelings—outrage at what women go through unnecessarily in bearing children.

John Gardner offers a different definition, talking about subjective fiction as *realistic fiction in which we feel we are actually present in the action, giving the example of Victor Hugo's novels. He calls "objective" the kind of fiction like Henry Fielding's *Tom Jones*, in which we never are allowed for long to forget that we are reading a work of fiction rather than becoming immersed in a real life.

Subplot *(counterplot, secondary plot, underplot)*   A secondary plot in a piece of fiction, less important than the main plot.

Subplots are more often found in novels than in short stories, since a good short story generally is too short to support more than one fully developed plot.

Often the subplot has an important relationship to the main plot, either through providing contrast or parallel with the main plot. In Mary McCarthy's *The Group*, the main plot involves the emotional deterioration of Kay, a young Vassar graduate who at the time of her graduation seems, despite family disapproval of her marriage, to have everything going for her:

> There was to be no honeymoon, they had heard, because Harald (that was the way he spelled it—the old Scandinavian way) was working as an assistant stage manager for a theatrical production and had to be at the theatre as usual this evening to call "half hour" for the actors. This seemed to them very exciting and of course it justified the oddities of

the wedding: Kay and Harald were too busy and dynamic to
let convention cramp their style.

The story follows her husband's infidelity, her divorce, lack of
money, mental breakdown, and suicide at the end of the novel.

The many subplots of the book involve the women Kay went to
school with: prim Dottie's brief affair with a much poorer man; Polly's
difficulties with her mentally ill father; Priss's unsuccessful attempts
to breastfeed her son; and Libby's difficulties with her job in publishing. The subplots usually do not overlap with Kay's story, but they
still are related, as they all contribute to the reader's understanding
of Kay and her world, and the special problems faced by financially
well-off, pampered young college graduates in the changing world of
the 1930s.

Other times, a subplot occurs outside of the main plot, with little
relation to it, existing mainly to provide a change of scene from the
main plot, a different emotion, or comic relief from a serious main
plot. In Mark Twain's *The Adventures of Tom Sawyer*, the main plot
concerns Tom and Huck Finn's witness of the murder of a doctor by
the evil character Injun Joe; Tom and Huck's flight to an island to hide
from Injun Joe, whom they fear will try to kill them; Tom's brave
telling on the witness stand that Injun Joe is the murderer; and Tom's
terrifying adventures with Becky Thatcher when they get lost in the
cave where Injun Joe is hiding.

The subplots involve Tom's clever attempts at wheeling and dealing: his contrivance to get his friends to whitewash the fence his Aunt
Polly has ordered him to paint by convincing them that the chore is
a particularly desirable honor; and his cagey trading of tickets earned
for memorizing Bible verses in Sunday school so that he is awarded
a Bible without actually memorizing anything. These subplots illumi-
nate Tom's character a bit—but they are unrelated to the book's main
plot and primarily provide a kind of comic relief to it.

Subtext   A term, used more often in drama than in fiction, to describe
the author's private, personal thoughts and intentions about the work
that he does not share with his audience. "Subtext" also is sometimes
used to describe the feelings that exist between characters that they
do not acknowledge to each other, or sometimes even to themselves.

Ernest Hemingway remarked about his "The Big Two-Hearted River" that he wanted to write a story about the war without mentioning the war; in this instance, the war becomes a subtext in the story.

In an interview in *The Literary Review*, Vance Bourjaily, author of *Now Playing at Canterbury*, explains that the subtext in this work was the constraints he put on himself to use as many different kinds of "narrative premises" as he could:

> There's a picaresque story, which is Skeats', an account of how he came from Australia to New York and thrived there. There's a political story, which is Shapan's account of the Vietnam protest. The opera, "$4,000" is a melodrama. Billy Hoffman's story, "The Bride of Corinth," another kind of melodrama, a southern melodrama. There is a highly subjective fantasized story that Professor Short tells about Fitzgerald visiting his seminar. Having done all this, it was absolutely necessary, I felt, and my editor went round and round about this, and I finally insisted, that I give Maury Jackstone a puzzle story to tell, a story in which you would have to solve a lot of language puzzles in order to figure out what the hell he's talking about, which is like certain kinds of contemporary fiction a lot of people don't much care for. Close readers find it. That's an example of how the subtext sometimes does become very important to you, so important that you may decide to risk a little reader interest at a certain point in order to complete your subtext.

Knowing the subtext can be helpful for the reader in figuring out the significance of a difficult work; in a poem by Nadezhda Mandel'shtam, "*Voz'me na radost,*" the image of a necklace of dead bees in the final stanza becomes less puzzling if one knows that the image comes from an earlier debate among various schools of poetry about the use of words and imagery in general, and is itself a nod to that debate.

Summary A method of presenting information necessary to a story without interrupting the flow with dialogue or other dramatization. Often summary is used to get the reader quickly through information that it would not be appropriate to develop into a full scene;

summary often is used to speed up the action. In *Jane Eyre,* for example, Charlotte Brontë writes:

> In the course of the day I was enrolled a member of the fourth class and regular tasks and occupations were assigned me.

In a novel where the reader needed to learn a lot about the particulars of the education of ten-year-old orphans in charity schools, this sentence could be expanded into a fully developed scene. Here, though, Brontë has chosen to collapse the events of six or eight hours into a single sentence.

Ernest Hemingway's emphasis on dialogue and action did much to influence writers away from summary in the twentieth century; in general, summary is much less used now than in the last century.

Surprise Ending *(trick ending, twist ending)*   An ending that a reader could not logically anticipate before its occurrence, either because the writer gives no clue as to what is to come or because it depends on some information that the writer has withheld from the reader until the end of the story.

The term generally is negative; stories whose endings are unanticipated but that come as a delightful surprise usually are not put into the "surprise ending" category. Surprise endings often are seen as unfair tricks.

Stories in which the narrator does not reveal some important fact about herself until the end often leave the reader feeling cheated. Mystery novels that neglect to give the reader some important bit of information she must know to solve the crime before the detective does sometimes are called "acroidian," after Agatha Christie's *The Murder of Roger Ackroyd,* in which the *first-person narrator reveals at the end that he is the murderer and has been concealing this fact from the reader while ostensibly attempting to find a solution.

Still, the unexpected ending that works actually can be a delight; Saki, O. Henry, and Guy de Maupassant are particularly known for their successful surprise endings.

Edith Wharton's "Roman Fever" contains a successful surprise ending. Two women, widows in "ripe but well-cared-for middle age," sit at a restaurant in Rome overlooking the city. One of the women, Alida Slade, begins to recount a malicious prank she played in Rome on the other woman, Grace Ansley, about twenty-five years earlier. Worried that her fiancé, Delphin Slade, might become attracted to Grace, she wrote Grace a letter purporting to be from Delphin, asking him to meet her at the Roman Coliseum one evening to watch the moon rise, hoping that waiting outside at the Coliseum in the cold night air would make Grace ill so she would have to spend time away from Delphin. Grace had, in fact, believed the letter was from Delphin and is crushed to hear that he had not written it himself.

As the women sit and talk, Alida Slade reflects on the fact that Grace's daughter Barbara is a much more exciting, vivid person than her own daughter and wonders how two dull people like Grace and her husband could have produced such a delightful child.

As the women get up at last to leave the restaurant, Alida, though disconcerted to learn that Grace had answered Delphin's "letter" and met him at the Coliseum, crows once more that she, Alida, after all, had Delphin all twenty-five years before his death, while all Grace had to remember him by was a letter that Delphin didn't even write. Then Grace smiles and reveals her surprise: "I had Barbara." *(See: reversal.)*

Surrealist Fiction A type of fiction first conceived by André Bréton in 1924, which emphasizes the writer's imaginative expression of dreams and other psychic states reached through the unconscious mind.

Surrealist writing, based on concepts from Freud's theory of the unconscious, is especially notable for the way in which it juxtaposes images and objects that logically would not seem at all related. The merging of these images, ideally, helps reveal something real, on a nonintellectual level, about the human mind and soul. Surrealism's goal is to find a reality different from logical reality, which would come through only if a person's subconscious thoughts were allowed free expression.

Surrealism is an outgrowth of the *dada movement, and like dada is related to a protest over the more scientific, objective, and materialistic world view of the years around World War I. The surrealists were convinced that the intellectual mind alone would not bring about real understanding of the world. Because these early surrealists were much more disciplined than dadaists, their writing generally is more memorable, and the group is seen as more important than the dadaists.

This dreamlike passage comes from André Bréton's *Nadja*; the speaker, a narrator who gives his name as André Bréton, recounts something that Nadja, whom he has only recently met, told him:

> In Lille, her native city when she had left only two or three years ago, she had known a student she may have loved and who loved her. One fine day she decided to leave him when he least expected it, and this "for fear of getting in his way." This is when she came to Paris, writing him at increasingly longer intervals without ever giving her address. Nearly a year later, however, she ran into him in Paris itself and both of them were extremely surprised. Even as he took her hands, he could not help telling her how changed he found her, and then, still holding these hands, he was surprised to see how well manicured they were (though they are not at all so now). Then she too had mechanically looked at one of the hands holding hers and had not been able to restrain an exclamation upon noticing that the last two fingers were joined together. "But you've hurt yourself!" The young man was obliged to show her his other hand, which revealed the same deformity. She questions me about this for some time and with great feeling: "Is such a thing possible?"

(See: automatic writing, stream of consciousness.)

Suspense The reader's feeling of anticipation about how the story will turn out. A reader feels suspense when she is deeply curious about what will happen next, or when she knows what is likely to happen but doesn't know *how* it will happen.

Some writers try to minimize the aspect of suspense on purpose to force the reader to focus on other aspects of the work. In Leo Tolstoy's *The Death of Ivan Ilych*, we know from the title that Ivan Ilych's pain in his side is not a minor problem that will soon go away. Since we know what will happen to Ivan Ilych, our focus moves to more subtle questions. In this case, we wonder whether he will realize that yes, he has lived his life in vain, but no, it is not too late to change even on the last day of his life.

Certainly, it would be hard (and perhaps pointless) to write a piece of fiction in which there was not some issue the reader has a burning wish to find out about. Even in historical fiction, with characters whose life stories are well known, the "why" usually brings suspense to the novel.

Symbol An object in fiction that represents something else, either because it genuinely resembles the other thing, or because it brings about an association in the reader's mind. The use of symbols helps a writer show how two seemingly disparate things actually are related.

There are two different types of symbols. The first is the universal symbol, which everyone will recognize. In Alice Munro's story, "The Found Boat," four children, two boys and two girls, find a boat and take it down the river, where one of the boys and one of the girls have a brief, semiromantic experience. Afterward, the children retreat back into childhood and nervously forget their moment of closeness. In this story, the river serves as a symbol of the passage of time and movement of life, a universal symbol that is not uncommon in fiction.

The other type of symbol uses an object that has no particular meaning on its own but that becomes symbolic only from the way it is used in the work. In Gloria Naylor's *Linden Hills*, one of the characters, Norman, a black man who usually is a sensitive and loving soul, occasionally is overwhelmed by a psychotic frenzy he calls "the pinks," which causes him to destroy everything in his house. This has happened so many times, in fact, that he and his wife have stopped replacing the items he destroys and keep only two Styrofoam cups, for example, to drink from. Here the color pink, which has no universal symbolic significance, comes to symbolize the oppression of white people, which has torn the black household apart.

It also is important that a symbol be relevant and significant on its dull, literal level, as is the description of the muddy, swollen river in "The Found Boat" and the horrifying details of Norman's psychotic episodes in *Linden Hills*. Indeed, it is helpful to remember that many writers whose work has been found to include symbols did not consciously include them.

Systems Novel *(encyclopedic realism)* A type of contemporary novel originating in the 1970s that uses techniques of *postmodern fiction, such as *fabulation and *satire, to create a model of a society that depicts not only personal relations among the characters, but also the history, science, philosophy, and the state of the culture of an imaginary fictional world as a whole. The story in a systems novel comes from the interrelationship of these diverse elements.

Systems novels generally are long and include large casts of characters from all strata of society, involved in a number of ultimately intersecting, often convoluted plots. The systems novel differs from other long forms like the *epic in its attempt to create a world that is recognizably different from the real world, and in its inclusion of subjects like science or philosophy as part of the story.

An example of a systems novel is Kathryn Kramer's *A Handbook for Visitors From Outer Space*, whose intersecting plots include a mysterious war as well as four siblings and an incestuous, hermitlike family of deposed royalty living in New Jersey, which crowns its oldest brother king after the death of his father, Langoustino:

> He forced Sigismund and Constantina (eight and seven respectively) to prove their fealty by washing his feet, lighting his cigarettes, winding up his Victrola; he ordered them to catch frogs in the pond back of the house and to sacrifice them to the Ludwicker god. Dagobert's were not the most inspired tests of allegiance ever conceived, but perhaps this could be blamed on the area in which the Ludwickers lived, hardly a place to encourage belief in the efficacy of the search for such things as the Holy Grail or the missing half of a broken sword. "Still, we have to do something. Keep up the tradition somehow, don't we, Pheupsy?"
>
> Xilipheupia smiled. Tad was her king and liege lord and she never doubted that before long he would recover the throne and then he and she would reign, side by side. He never asked her to attest to her loyalty as he did Sammy and George; he demanded only her adoration and in return

professed to treat her as his confidante and equal. They were only ten months apart in age, and, after all, they had been lovers for over a year.

The novel also includes a group of recent college students called the campers; an apparently normal family whose angry son is the book's protagonist and whose grandfather has been sent to live at a retirement home for old soldiers; and the daughter of Dagobert and Xilipeupia, a violin prodigy, who attempts to come to know the outside world.

The systems novel and *maximal novel are closely related; if there is a difference, it is that the maximal novel generally is more difficult and even longer than the systems novel.

Other systems novelists include William Gaddis (*The Recognitions*), Thomas Pynchon (*Vineland*), Don DeLillo (*White Noise*) and John Barth (*Letters*).

T

Tag A physically descriptive detail, generally a kind of label, repeated almost every time a character enters the story, which serves to identify and characterize him.

Although a tag is not a character trait, it is a quality that makes a character easily identifiable and memorable throughout the story. Tags often include physical attributes, odd names, speech habits and impediments, and distinctive habits. In Charles Dickens' *Great Expectations*, the minor character of "Mrs. Joe," the protagonist Pip's shrewish sister, is "tagged" by her repeated grievance that she never has time to take her apron off. In chapter four, for example, Mrs. Joe observes:

> "Perhaps if I warn't a blacksmith's wife, and (what's the same thing) a slave with her apron never off, *I* should have been to hear the carols," said Mrs. Joe. "I'm rather partial to carols myself, and that's the best of reasons for my never hearing any."

Earlier, of course, Pip has undercut his sister's complaint by observing:

> She made it a powerful merit in herself, and a strong reproach against Joe, that she wore this apron so much. Though I really see no reason why she should have worn it at all: or why, if she did wear it at all, she should not have taken it off every day of her life.

Tags are generally but not always reserved for minor characters who do not warrant more developed characterization. Arthur Conan Doyle's Sherlock Holmes is an example of a major character who has a number of physical tags—his deerstalker's hat, his violin-playing, his ability to deduce specific information from minute details, and his use of injected cocaine, which we see in *A Study in Scarlet*:

> ... now and again a reaction would seize him, and for days on end he would lie upon the sofa in the sitting-room, hardly uttering a word or moving a muscle from morning to night. On these occasions I have noticed such a dreamy, vacant expression in his eyes, that I might have suspected him of being addicted to the use of some narcotic, had not the temperance and cleanliness of his whole life forbidden such a notion.

And later, in *The Sign of the Four*:

> Sherlock Holmes took his bottle from the corner of the mantelpiece, and his hypodermic syringe from its neat morocco case. With his long, white, nervous fingers he adjusted the delicate needle and rolled back his left shirtcuff. For some little time his eyes rested thoughtfully upon the sinewy forearm and wrist, all dotted and scarred with innumerable puncture-marks. Finally, he thrust the sharp point home, pressed down the tiny piston, and sank back into the velvet-lined armchair with a long sigh of satisfaction.

(See: flat character, stock character, type.)

Tale An ancient form, often handed down orally through generations, traditionally told as a way of trying to understand the workings of a confusing world.

The word "tale" sometimes is used simply as a synonym for "story." It has a more precise usage, however, when it describes a story whose details definitely are not realistic, which one must suspend one's disbelief to enjoy. Often "tale" is used as a synonym with *"legend," the difference being that a tale always will include details impossible for a reader to believe, and that the writer must charm or lull the reader into taking as true. The tale is different from a *myth in that it generally is not told from a desire to explain mysterious natural phenomena apparently caused by supernatural forces.

The narrator of a tale, as John Gardner points out in *The Art of Fiction*, often will make a tale's setting indistinct and remote; the *tone, as well, is unlikely to connect the story closely with reality, although the detail of things not-really-of-this-world can be careful and complex, encouraging the reader into belief.

Characters in a tale may have supernatural powers, but even if they do not, they often strive to be convincing without at all seeming like real people.

Isaac Bashevis Singer's "Gimpel the Fool" is told purposely to seem like a tale. The protagonist, Gimpel, lives in an unspecified time and place and is so credulous as to seem completely unreal:

> I am Gimpel the fool. I don't think myself a fool. On the contrary. But that's what folks call me. They gave me the name while I was still in school. I had seven names in all: imbecile, donkey, flax-head, dope, glump, ninny, and fool. The last name stuck. What did my foolishness consist of? I was easy to take in. They said, 'Gimpel, you know the rabbi's wife has been brought to childbed?' So I skipped school. Well, it turned out to be a lie. How was I supposed to know? She hadn't had a big belly. But I never looked at her belly. Was that really so foolish? The gang laughed and hee-hawed, stomped and danced and chanted a good-night prayer. And instead of the raisins they give when a woman's lying in, they stuffed my hand full of goat turds.

(See: legend, myth, romance, tall tale.)

Tall Tale Humorous—sometimes darkly humorous—and often preposterous stories of life on the American frontier. Tall tales often come from an oral tradition; identifying a specific author is not possible.

Tall tales, nevertheless, use all the fictional techniques possible to mimic the truth to try to convince the reader of something that absolutely could never happen (often because it would require superhuman abilities on the part of a character). The setting of a tall tale, unlike a plain *"tale," often is specific; the details seem believable, but the story doesn't.

Although the line between a "tall tale" and a *"legend" is thin, and the categories often overlap, tall tales generally were told for entertainment rather than out of an inner desire to explain mysterious occurrences. Paul Bunyan, Mike Fink and Davy Crockett are the heroes of some typical tall tales. *(See: legend, myth, tale.)*

Tautology A negative term describing the unnecessary repetition of words without adding any kind of clarity or amplification. Some examples: "advance reservation," "overused cliché," "enormous giant," "grotesque monster."

Telephone Fiction Fiction whose entire action consists of real or simulated telephone conversations. The most notable recent example probably is Nicholson Baker's *Vox*, the story, told entirely as over-the-phone dialogue, of a man and a woman talking on a 900 sex line:

> "What are you wearing under your shirt?"
> "A bra."
> "What kind of bra?"
> "A nothing bra. A normal, white bra bra."
> "Oooo!"
> "It's shrunk slightly in the wash but it was my last clean one."
> "It's always impressive to me that bras have to be washed like other clothes. Does it clip on the front or on the back?"
> "The back."

Transcribing telephone calls can be good exercise for any writer interested in the exact representation of real dialogue, as Ed Friedman shows in his *The Telephone Book*, a collection of transcriptions of real-life telephone calls he made over several months, which seems at the same time more real and less coherent than the Nicholson Baker example:

EF. I've also been reading *Tales of Beatnik Glory*.

EB. What's that?

EF. That's Ed Sanders' new book.

EB. Hmm. What's it about?

EF. Well, it seems to be vignettes um . . . about the Beatnik era. It opens with an open poetry reading, for example.

EB. Huh.

EF. With no continuity of characters at this point.

EB. Right.

EF. And then telling about this place, the revolution . . . the revolutionary cantina or something like that, the Total Assault Cantina where they everyday make huge fruit salads in ah a bathtub that they put in the window.

EB. Ha ha.

EF. Ha ha.

Tension The sense of excitement a reader feels when two or more aspects of a work tug her in seemingly opposite directions, helping her to maintain psychological interest in the work.

The tension may be between two characters or, say, between the character and society. The tension also can arise out of a relationship between the writer and the reader. Or it may be between two technical aspects of the work; in an *allegory, for example, there is tension between the work's literal meaning and the allegorical, metaphorical meaning.

In Iris Murdoch's *philosophical novel *A Severed Head*, the *protagonist, Martin Lynch-Gibbon, comes home to his wife, Antonia, after an afternoon with Georgie, his lover. He learns that Antonia plans to leave him for *her* lover, a friend of Martin's who is also Antonia's psychiatrist.

The conflict not only is between Martin and Antonia—whether Martin can persuade Antonia to return to him—but also relates to whether Martin will decide that he wants his wife back, or if he would prefer to remain with Georgie; and also whether he will accede to Antonia and her lover's wishes that he remain on close terms with them. In a broader sense, tension also develops between the style, which is strictly realistic, and the plot, which is full of wildly improbable coincidences.

At the end of the story, presumably, in most works, the tension will be resolved. On the other hand, it also is possible and sometimes desirable to end the story before the tension has dissolved. In *A Severed Head*, Martin ends the story in an apparently loving reunion with a third woman who has caused him nothing but trouble over the course of the book: He is happy, but the reader must continue to wonder if this new relationship could ever work out. *(See: conflict, suspense.)*

Theme   The central idea of a story or novel, a concept that is represented through the *plot and through interaction among the characters. Theme is related to the idea that even though fiction is not a reflection of literal reality, it still may communicate a kind of truth about the way human beings act, think or feel in a way that the word-for-word truth cannot.

"Theme" is a much broader term than "plot," illustrating as it does whatever universal idea the story puts forward, while plot has to do instead with the literal events that occur in the characters' lives.

Stephen Crane's long story "The Open Boat," for example, whose plot deals with the struggle of four shipwrecked men in a flimsy lifeboat to reach land, has a couple of themes. One is that nature is indifferent to the plight of the individual; this theme is openly expressed several times during the story. The men finally are in sight of shore—even of people on the shore—but, ironically, still cannot be rescued because the people on shore either don't see them or don't recognize that they are in trouble, and the surf is too rough to swim through. The story's protagonist finally comes to the realization that fate is indifferent as to whether or not he survives:

> When it occurs to a man that nature does not regard him as important, and that she feels she would not maim the universe by disposing of him, he at first wishes to throw bricks at the temple, and he hates deeply the fact that there are no bricks and no temples. Any visible expression of nature would surely be pelleted with his jeers.

The story, however, also contains another theme, dealing with the idea that people in crisis often form a camaraderie that does not exist elsewhere; this theme also is overtly stated in the story:

It would be difficult to describe the subtle brotherhood of men that was here established on the seas. No one said that it was so. No one mentioned it. But it dwelt in the boat, and each man felt it warm him. They were a captain, an oiler, a cook, and a correspondent, and they were friends—friends in a more curiously iron-bound degree than may be common. . . . And after this devotion to the commander of the boat, there was this comradeship, that the correspondent, for instance, who had been taught to be cynical of men, knew even at the time was the best experience of his life.

A theme generally can be related in a complete sentence—the theme of Nathaniel Hawthorne's "Young Goodman Brown" would not simply be "evil," for example, but, depending on how one views the story, could be expressed as something like "Evil is the nature of mankind" or, alternatively, "Looking for evil, being suspicious where no suspicion is appropriate, will ruin your life."

Before the twentieth century, a word like "moral" generally was used instead of "theme." The change is indicative of one way that fiction has changed since the beginning of the twentieth century, when a story is less likely to ascribe to a definite statement of values or an attempt to offer a moral lesson.

Readers are unlikely to agree on a single theme, especially of a long and complicated work; indeed, a novel with a single, easily identifiable theme often will be criticized as *didactic. In some works it will be impossible, in fact, to identify any theme at all.

While some critics object to the term "theme" as being too broad and vague, the term can be especially useful in talking about the kinds of *postmodern fiction in which plot seems to have been lost; the disparate, juxtaposed images and events in this type of fiction often will be thematically related. *(See: fictional truth.)*

Thesis Novel *(issue fiction, novel of social criticism, problem novel, roman à thèse, sociological novel)* A novel type first initiated during the Industrial Revolution, whose goal is to dramatize a particular social problem, usually with the desire to convince readers to sympathize with the characters' situation and to press them to solve the problem.

This example of graphic dramatization, intended to show the injustices of factory work, comes from Upton Sinclair's *The Jungle*:

> There were the men in the pickle-rooms, for instance, where old Antanas had gotten his death; scarce a one of these that had not some spot of horror on his person. Let a man so much as scrape his finger pushing a truck in the pickle-rooms, and he might have a sore that would put him out of the world; all the joints of his fingers might be eaten by the acid, one by one. Of the butchers and floorsmen, the beefboners and trimmers, and all those who used knives, you could scarcely find a person who had the use of his thumb; time and time again the base of it had been slashed, till it was a mere lump of flesh against which the man pressed the knife to hold it.

The *protest novel and thesis novel categories are very close; a difference is that a thesis novel is obligated to propose a specific solution to the problem, whereas a protest novel only describes the problem and exhorts the reader to take action to solve it, without delineating what that action should be. *(See: didactic fiction, naturalism, philosophical novel, political novel, propaganda novel, socialist novel.)*

Tone   The apparent feeling of the author toward his material and even toward his readers. The tone of a work may be intimate, distant, casual, affectionate, disapproving, cautious, tragic, ironic, skeptical, pessimistic, compassionate, sentimental—the possibilities are endless.

A writer's tone is one of the main elements that establishes the degree of distance a reader feels from the characters. An example of a writer who has achieved a sympathetic, affectionate tone toward a character whom many would condemn is William Faulkner in "A Rose for Emily," the story of a southern woman of the early twentieth century who has lost most of her money and spent her youth looking after her father, who disapproved of all of her suitors.

In the story, Emily poisons her lover, a northerner who apparently did not want to marry her, and sleeps with his corpse for the next forty years. Faulkner makes it clear through his tone, however, that he has more sympathy than anger toward this murderer. Even the title, which suggests that the story itself is a gift—a rose—to Emily, conveys sympathy and particularly the language at the end of the story:

> They held the funeral on the second day, with the town coming to look at Miss Emily beneath a mass of bought flowers, with the crayon face of her father musing profoundly above the bier and the ladies sibilant and macabre; and the very old men—some in their brushed Confederate uniforms—on the porch and the lawn, talking of Miss Emily as if she had been a contemporary of theirs, believing that they had danced with her and courted her perhaps, confusing time with its mathematical progression, as the old do, to whom all the past is not a diminishing road but, instead, a huge meadow which no winter ever quite touches, divided from them now by the narrow bottleneck of the most recent decade of years.

The word "tone" often is mistakenly used in place of *mood or *atmosphere. *(See: aesthetic distance, psychic distance.)*

Type A term coined by Henry James to describe a character who functions as a representative of a particular social class.

Here, in F. Scott Fitzgerald's *The Great Gatsby*, Daisy Buchanan seems like a type character, an insensitive young woman who takes for granted that because of her class she will not get into serious trouble over having killed a woman while driving Gatsby's car:

> Daisy and Tom were sitting opposite each other at the kitchen table, with a plate of cold fried chicken between them, and two bottles of ale. He was talking intently across the table to her, and in his earnestness his hand had fallen upon and covered her own. Once in a while she looked up at him and nodded in agreement.
>
> They weren't happy, and neither of them had touched the chicken or the ale—and yet they weren't unhappy either. There was an unmistakable air of natural intimacy about

the picture, and anybody would have said that they were conspiring together.

Later, the narrator gives his own impression of Daisy:

> For Daisy was young and her artificial world was redolent of orchids and pleasant, cheerful snobbery and orchestras which set the rhythm of the year, summing up the sadness and suggestiveness of life in new tunes. All night the saxophones wailed the hopeless comment of the Beale Street Blues while a hundred pairs of golden and silver slippers shuffled the shining dust. At the gray tea hour there were always rooms that throbbed incessantly with this low, sweet fever, while fresh faces drifted here and there like rose petals blown by the sad horns around the floor.

A type character differs from a *stock character in that a stock character will have certain stereotyped characteristics, but these characteristics do not definitely put him in a particular social class. The danger in trying to create a type character is that the writer may end up creating a *cliché; as Fitzgerald once remarked: "If you set out to create an individual, you may create a type, but if you set out to create a type, you will create nothing." *(See: stock character.)*

Typographical Devices *(graphic techniques)*   Techniques by which a writer makes the looks of the typeset copy relevant to the work's meaning.

There are some works whose physical appearances, as well as what the words mean, make them stand out. Laurence Sterne's *Tristram Shandy*, for example, includes some black, blank or marbled pages. Most instances of this technique come from the second half of the twentieth century, however.

The effect of typographical devices, as with other documents included in fiction, can be a type of *realism, as in Gilbert Sorrentino's *Odd Number*, in which, asked to describe the layout of a certain house, the character responds by providing a blueprint-type diagram of the house. The blueprint looks authentic and gives an exact impression of the floor plan of the house.

Another example of typographical devices used to promote realism can be found in Pamela Walker's young-adult novel *Twyla*, which begins with a reproduction of a newspaper article describing a fifteen-year-old's suicide and then becomes an *epistolary novel, told in the form of Twyla's letters to a college boy she barely knows. The conceit is that Twyla is writing the letters in her typing class, and her pathetic attempts to type and spell are illustrated; the type becomes more faint in the book as the year progresses and Twyla neglects to change the ribbon:

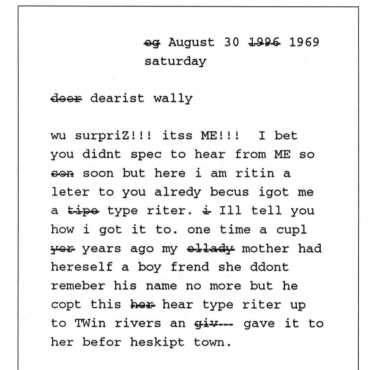

Typographical devices also can have the opposite effect from realism, actually pulling the reader away from the idea that what is going on really happened. The initial response to most typographical devices can be laughter, but the devices also can be a serious attempt by the writer to make sure the reader does not get caught up too much in the words but remains aware that the work is fiction. This is the effect of Raymond Federman's *Double or Nothing,* which is presented as pages of type typed in recognizable shapes—like a Christmas tree, an hourglass and a pyramid—and includes also a page that is printed backward and can be read only by mirror.

The typographical form also can force the writer to think of words and phrases she wouldn't normally, into fresh combinations of words and images. This must have happened in the composition of Raymond Federman's novel *Take It or Leave It,* in which the protagonist, a young French immigrant, writes love letters for hire for his bunkmates in the American Army. The letters are odd—the protagonist's English is not good—and become even more so when the reader notices that each line contains exactly sixty characters of type.

U-V

Understatement Deliberate restraint on the part of a speaker, who makes a comment that seems to make light of whatever the subject is.

After accidentally burning down your neighbor's house, you might understate the problem with a comment like "Sorry about that!" This example of understatement comes from Charles Dickens' *Nicholas Nickleby*:

> Mr. Squeer's appearance was not prepossessing. He had but one eye, and the popular prejudice runs in favour of two.

The purpose of understatement often is, as here, humor; in addition, it can be used to show the character of the *narrator who makes the understatement. Most narrators will not say, after all, that it is merely "popular prejudice" that is responsible for the general preference for two eyes.

Underwriting The act of leaving out aspects of a story that most readers would find significant.

Generally, the aspects of the story that the writer chooses to leave out when underwriting are either descriptive detail and/or emotions. As an exercise, however, the writer might try to leave out nearly anything.

An example of underwriting occurs in Ernest Hemingway's "The Killers." Two gangsters enter a diner and ask for Ole Andreson, a regular patron, announcing that they are going to kill him. Later the protagonist, Nick Adams, goes to Andreson's house to warn him. Andreson says he is tired of running and will just wait for the gangsters to come get him. Later, Nick talks about the visit with the owner of the diner. Here, the underwriting, the blandness of the dialogue, the lack of overt emotion, somehow intensifies the horror of the story:

> "He must have got mixed up in something in Chicago."
> "I guess so," said Nick.
> "It's a hell of a thing."
> "It's an awful thing," Nick said.
> They did not say anything. George reached down for a towel and wiped the counter.
> "I wonder what he did?" Nick said.
> "Double-crossed somebody. That's what they kill them for."
> "I'm going to get out of this town," Nick said.
> "Yes," said George. "That's a good thing to do."
> "I can't stand to think about him waiting in the room and knowing he's going to get it. It's too damned awful."
> "Well," said George, "You better not think about it."

In *A Moveable Feast*, Hemingway discussed this method of leaving out emotion from a story:

> If a writer of prose knows enough about what he is writing about he may omit things that he knows and the reader, if the writer is writing truly enough, will have a feeling of those things as strongly as though the writer had stated them. The dignity of movement in an iceberg is due to only one-eighth of it being above water.

Underwriting frequently is done to avoid falling into the trap of *sentimentality, especially the kind of sentimentality that occurs in the overdramatization of particularly emotional scenes. This underwriting, however, can lead to language inappropriately cool and objective. (See: *frigidity, minimalism, subtext.*)

Unintrusive Narrator   A third-person narrator who reserves judgment on the characters and situations he describes, allowing the reader to intuit the *tone of the story without overtly coming to conclusions about what is going on.

Here, in Richard Wright's "The Man Who Was Almost a Man," the protagonist, Dave, tries to decide what to do after accidentally shooting his employer's mule with a pistol he just bought for two dollars. Although the story is told in third person and the nonparticipant narrator can see into Dave's mind, the narrator does not tell the reader anything that Dave cannot know. The author's feeling about the character comes clear only through the story's title:

> Dave's stomach felt empty, very empty. He picked up the gun and held it gingerly between his thumb and forefinger. He buried it at the foot of a tree. He took a stick and tried to cover the pool of blood with dirt—but what was the use? There was Jenny lying with her mouth open and her eyes walled and glassy. He could not tell Jim Hawkins he had shot his mule. But he had to tell something. Yeah, Ahll tell em Jenny started gittin wil n fell on the joint of the plow. . . . But that would hardly happen to a mule. He walked across the field slowly, head down.

(See: self-effacing author.)

Unreliable Narrator   A narrator whom the reader should not trust to give a reasonable, unbiased version of the story she tells.

While unreliable and *naïve narrators are similar, the term "unreliable" is used to describe narrators who are insane or are purposely trying to mislead the reader; naïve narrators generally are too young or unintelligent to understand the details of the action they describe.

There also is a variety of degrees of unreliability. Consider the narrator in Edgar Allan Poe's "The Tell-Tale Heart":

> True!—nervous—very, very dreadfully nervous I had been and am; but why will you say that I am mad? The disease had sharpened my senses—not destroyed—not dulled them. Above all was the sense of hearing acute. I heard all things in the heaven and in the earth. I heard many things in hell. How, then, am I mad?

A reader does not have to be too careful to realize that this is an unreliable narrator, even before the narrator admits to hearing "many things in hell." No reader would trust this narrator on any important question, and it was a mistake on the old man's part to let the narrator live in his house for a minute.

Other narrators are less obviously deranged than the speaker in "The Tell-Tale Heart" and may be reliable when talking on some subjects but not on others. When the narrator in Raymond Carver's "Where I'm Calling From" describes his fellow patients at the drying-out center where he has been staying, his acute and reasonable observations establish him as a perfectly reliable narrator. When he begins thinking about issues closer to himself, however, he is less trustworthy. He complains frequently about how obnoxious his girlfriend's son had been when he and the girlfriend left him home on Christmas Day and told him to get his own food:

> But right as we were going out the door, this mouthy kid screamed at us. He screamed, "The hell with you! I hope you never come back. I hope you kill yourselves!"

It is easy to see that the son's anger is justifiable by normal standards, which suddenly makes the narrator of the story seem unreliable in his perceptions of what goes on around him.

Utopian Novel A novel that illustrates the author's idea of what a perfect, ideal society should be, often combining fantasy and science fiction elements with some philosophical statement, and including many dramatic scenes that show how the Utopian society would help solve real social problems.

One of the best-known Utopian novels is *Lost Horizon*, by James Hilton. It is the story of Hugh Conway, a British diplomat in 1931, who finds himself, along with several other English-speaking people, transported to an unmapped country high in the Himalayas.

The mysterious new country is called Shangri-La, and Conway and the others find themselves living in a tranquil lamasery whose code of ethics is based on a combination of the Christian and Buddhist religions.

Conway is allowed to meet the high Lama, Father Perrault, a former

Catholic monk, whom he learns actually founded Shangri-La in 1734. He has lived to be over 250 years old because of the purity of the air and some miraculous drugs known only to the local residents.

Conway becomes entranced with the serenity of Shangri-La, where people are free from conflict and strife, live and work harmoniously, and enjoy comforts like central heating generally found only in European society. He falls in love with a young Chinese girl, Lo-Tsen, and is shocked to learn that Lo-Tsen actually is sixty-five years old, but that the serene, peaceful life at Shangri-La has kept her from aging.

After Father Perrault finally dies of old age, the other travelers to Shangri-La decide to trek back to civilization. Against his better judgment, Conway, along with Lo-Tsen, leaves Shangri-La. The novel ends after Conway has been brought to a Western hospital by an ancient Chinese woman—actually, of course, Lo-Tsen. After he recovers from his journey, however, Conway instantly sets out in search again of Shangri-La. *(See: anti-Utopian novel.)*

Verisimilar Fiction   Fiction whose goal is to attain the appearance of truth.

Vivid, idiosyncratic description as well as dialogue that sounds as if it could be taken from life are the tools that make verisimilar fiction seem real.

The term "verisimilar" is not necessarily in complete opposition to science fiction or other types of speculative fiction, however, if the details presented in that kind of work are given in such a way that they *could* be truthful, if certain basic natural laws, for example, were suspended. *(See: mimesis, modernism, realism.)*

Vignette *(sketch)*   A short scene, drawn with specificity and subtlety for the purpose of either illuminating some larger aspect of a work's *theme or simply of creating a vivid, resonant picture. A vignette generally is not related to the development of a story's plot.

In Charlotte Brontë's *Shirley*, the protagonist, Caroline Helstone, resigning herself (prematurely, as it turns out) to an unmarried life of good works and self-denial, visits an older woman who spends her life doing good for others. Here, the author digresses from the main plots of Caroline Helstone's search for happiness and her eventual husband's attempts to keep angry workers from destroying his textile plant, and gives us the picture of Caroline visiting Miss Ainley (who is not a major character in the book), mainly to provide an example of the good that a hard-working person can do:

> Caroline was soon at home in that tiny parlour; a kind hand took from her her shawl and bonnet, and installed her in the most comfortable seat near the fire. The young and the antiquated woman were presently deep in kindly conversation, and soon Caroline became aware of the power a most serene, unselfish and benignant mind could exercise over those to whom it was developed. She talked never of herself—always of others. Their faults she passed over; her theme was their wants, which she sought to supply; their sufferings, which she longed to alleviate. She was religious—a professor of religion—what some would call "a saint," and she referred to religion often in sanctioned phrase—in phrase which those who possess a perception of the ridiculous, without owning the power of exactly testing and truly judging a character, would certainly have esteemed a proper subject for satire—a matter for mimicry and laughter. They would have been hugely mistaken for their pains. Sincerity is never ludicrous; it is always respectable.

(See: episode, slice of life.)

Voice   A term often used since the 1980s that in one sense can refer to an author's *style, his distinctive way of combining words, rhythm and diction that makes his manner of writing unique. In its other meaning, voice is synonymous with *persona, the characteristic speech and thought patterns of any *first-person narrator, or of the *implied author who tells a story.

This paragraph from Frank Conroy's *Stop-Time* shows a voice that is both thoughtful and casual. Any emotion the narrator felt about leaving Fremont seems to have been forgotten; the focus is on the relaxed sense of waiting:

I'd been waiting at the main road since early morning, watching cars. The day was clear and sunny and from my seat on top of a stone gate pillar I could see about a mile. Much of the time the road was empty.... I'm sure that leaving Fremont was an emotional experience—saying goodbye to my friends, tying my duffel bag on top of the car, driving down the gravel road for the last time. Possibly I cried. But I can't really remember. My last image is from on top of the stone pillar, recognizing the car and watching it come toward me. In a sense it's as if it never reached me, as if approaching me, it drove to invisibility. Perhaps children remember only waiting for things.

The writer also has the option of using a more complex, ornate voice, one that will never let the reader forget he is reading a writer's creation rather than stepping directly into the window of another life, as in this example from Nabokov's *Ada*, with its difficult vocabulary and long sentences:

He had written it involuntarily, so to speak, not caring a dry fig for literary fame. Neither did pseudonymity tickle him in reverse—as it did when he danced on his hands. Though "Van Veen's vanity" often cropped up in the drawing-room prattle among fan-wafting ladies, this time his long blue pride feathers remained folded. What, then, moved him to contrive a romance around a subject that had been worried to extinction in all kinds of "Star Rats," and "Space Aces"? We—whoever "we" are—might define the compulsion as a pleasurable urge to express through verbal imagery a compendium of certain inexplicably correlated vagaries observed by him in mental patients, off and on, since his first year at Chose. Van had a passion for the insane as some have for arachnids or orchids.

(See: style, persona.)

W-Z

Waiting-Room Fiction *(desert island fiction)* Fiction in which the characters—strangers often of different ethnic and social backgrounds—are brought together and forced to interact by virtue of the fact that they cannot leave wherever they are either because they are trapped (airplane passengers, or victims of the often-televised "caught-in-the-elevator" story), or because they're waiting for something important to happen (a group of people at a doctor's office, for example.)

In real life, oddly assorted people sitting next to each other on an airplane often do not talk to each other, so it is important that at least some of the characters of waiting-room fiction establish themselves either as unusually outgoing or as psychologically driven to tell some story to a stranger. Of course, the plane's passengers participate in waiting-room fiction only as long as the plane remains quietly in the air; once a terrorist appears, the plot generally will turn into a "thriller." It is difficult to balance the careful depiction of character that waiting-room fiction requires with a *plot containing a lot of action outside the minds of the characters.

An example of waiting-room fiction is Flannery O'Connor's "Revelation," which starts with a description of people in a doctor's office:

> The doctor's waiting room, which was very small, was almost full when the Turpins entered and Mrs. Turpin, who was very large, made it look even smaller by her presence. . . . There was one vacant chair and a place on a sofa occupied by a blond child in a dirty blue romper who should have

been told to move over and make room for the lady. He was five or six, but Mrs. Turpin saw at once that no one was going to tell him to move over. He was slumped down in the seat, his arms idle at his sides and his eyes idle in his head; his nose ran unchecked. . . .

The only man in the room besides Claud was a lean stringy old fellow with a rusty hand spread out on each knee, whose eyes were closed as if he were asleep or dead or pretending to be so as not to get up and offer her his seat. Her gaze settled agreeably on a well-dressed grey-haired lady whose eyes met hers and whose expression said: if that child belonged to me, he would have some manners and move over—there's plenty room there for you and him too.

. . . Next to her was a fat girl of eighteen or nineteen, scowling into a thick blue book which Mrs. Turpin saw was entitled Human Development. The girl raised her head and directed her scowl at Mrs. Turpin as if she did not like her looks. . . .

Writing What You Know The concept that it is best for writers to write about subjects with which they are familiar.

Jerome Stern, in *Making Shapely Fiction*, suggests that a better way to express this idea might be, "Don't write about what you don't know":

> [I]f you know nothing about Zaire, the federal penitentiary system, schizophrenia, or the French Revolution, you're un-likely to write about these things successfully.

This is not to say that writers should write only from their own past experiences. David Madden comments in *A Primer of the Novel for Readers and Writers*, " 'What you know' can be a rich world created out of one's imagination."

As Henry James puts it in *The Art of The Novel*:

> I remember an English novelist, a woman of genius, telling me that she was much commended for the impression she had managed to give in one of her tales of the nature and

way of life of the French Protestant youth. She had been asked where she had learned so much about this recondite being, she had been congratulated on her peculiar opportunities. These opportunities consisted of her having once, in Paris, as she ascended a staircase, passed an open door where, in the household of a pasteur, some of the Protestants were seated at table around a finished meal. The glimpse made a picture; it lasted only a moment, but that moment was experience. She had got her direct personal impression, and she turned out her type. She knew what youth was, and what Protestantism; she also had the advantage of having seen what it was to be French, so that she converted these ideas into a concrete image and produced a reality.

Yarn   An outrageous lie told by a *first-person narrator, either to the reader or to some hapless listener-character, who may or may not believe the story she is being told.

A yarn writer will try to tell the story as convincingly as possible. She will include, as Mark Twain does in the following excerpt from "Baker's Bluejay Yarn," masses of realistic detail and refutations of any counterarguments the reader might have that the story is not true.

Yet because the yarn is so outrageous that no one could ever believe it, the yarn-spinner must be portrayed either as herself deluded into believing that the story is true or laboring under the belief that the listener is credulous enough to believe such an outrageous story.

John Gardner differentiates "yarn" from *"tale" and *"tall tale" in *The Art of Fiction*, commenting that in a yarn, something about the teller and the ostensible hearer of the yarn must be known, whereas with tales and tall tales, the emphasis is on the story rather than on the teller.

Here, the narrator recounts a story that a friend, Jim Baker, told him. While humor is the yarn's main point, questions also present themselves regarding just how crazy Jim Baker was to believe this story. On the other hand, Jim Baker may have been trying to pull the narrator's leg when he told the story, or the narrator himself might disbelieve the story and consciously be trying to pull the reader's leg:

Animals talk to each other, of course. There can be no question about that; but I suppose there are very few people who can understand them. I never knew but one man who could. I knew he could, however, because he told me so himself. . . . According to Jim Baker, some animals have only a limited education, and use only very simple words, and scarcely ever a comparison or a flowery figure; whereas, certain other animals have a large vocabulary, a fine command of language and a ready and fluent delivery; consequently these latter talk a great deal, they like it . . . Said he:—

"There's more to a blue-jay than any other creature. He has got more moods, and more different kinds of feelings than other creature; and mind you, whatever a blue-jay feels, he can put into language. And no mere common-place language, either, but rattling, out-and-out book talk—and bristling with metaphor, too—just bristling! And as for command of language—why you never see a blue-jay get stuck for a word. No man ever did. They just boil out of him! And another thing: I've noticed a good deal, and there's no bird, or cow, or anything that uses as good grammar as a blue-jay. You may say a cat uses good grammar. Well, a cat does— but you let a cat get excited, once; you let a cat get to pulling fur with another cat on a shed, nights, and you'll hear grammar that will give you the lockjaw."

Young-Man-From-the-Provinces Novel   A phrase coined by writer Lionel Trilling to describe a novel whose protagonist is an innocent young person from the country who comes to a big city and must cope with life there.

"Innocent," of course, does not mean lethargic or brainless: The protagonist of *Claudine in Paris*, the second of Colette's "Claudine" novels, has come from the provinces to Paris to live with relatives at age seventeen:

My first outing took place in March. A sharp sun and an acid wind; Papa and myself in a cab with pneumatic tyres. In the red cloak I wore at Montigny and my astrakhan cap I looked like a poor little boy in skirts. (And all my shoes have grown so big!) We took a slow walk in the Luxembourg, where my noble father entertained me with the comparative merits of the Nationale and the Sainte-Geneviève Libraries. The wind dazed me, so did the sun. I thought the big, smooth, tree-lined walks really beautiful but the quantities of children and the absence of weeds shocked me, the one quite as much as the other.

This starts her to thinking about her own life:

What lots of children, what lots of children! Shall I have as many children as that one day? And who is the gentleman who will inspire me to perpetrate them with him? Ugh, ugh! It's odd how chaste my imagination and my feelings are since my illness.

At the end of the novel, of course, Claudine has found love and becomes quite sophisticated about the often-sordid ways of Paris.

INDEX

More From Story Press!

The Poetry Dictionary—by John Drury. This comprehensive book unravels the rich and complex language of poetry with clear, working definitions. Drury uses classic and contemporary examples to illustrate how poets have put theories to work. In many cases, several different poems are used to demonstrate the evolution of the form, making *The Poetry Dictionary* a unique anthology. It's a guide to the poetry of today and yesterday, with intriguing hints as to what tomorrow holds. *#48007/$18.99/336 pages*

Idea Catcher—from the Editors of *Story Press*. This spirited journal will help you open your eyes to the creative possibilities in your everyday world. You'll find something on every page of this journal to stimulate your senses and spark your imagination. *Idea Catcher* will teach you to use rich, surprising sources of inspiration through several writing "prompts." Plus, you'll find insightful quotes from well-known writers and short anecdotes about how authors "caught" the ideas that became great works of literature. *#48011/$14.99/160 pages*

The Best Writing on Writing—edited by Jack Heffron, is the first in a series that will showcase the most provocative new articles, essays and lectures on fiction, nonfiction, poetry, playwriting and the writing life. These 27 illuminating and thought provoking selections are a lively feast of the well-written word and how it is fashioned. *#48001/$16.99/208 pages/paperback*

The Best Writing on Writing, Volume 2—edited by Jack Heffron, is the year's best collection of memorable essays, book excerpts and lectures on fiction, nonfiction, poetry, screenwriting and the writing life, all from 1994. The selections feature such luminaries as Joyce Carol Oates, Margaret Atwood, Justin Kaplan, Charles Baxter and Maxine Kumin to name a few. *#48013/$16.99/paperback*

Fiction Writer's Workshop—by Josip Novakovich. In this interactive workshop, you'll explore each aspect of the art of fiction including point of view, description, revision, voice and more. At the end of each chapter you'll find more than a dozen writing exercises to help you put what you've learned into action. *#48003/$17.99/256 pages*

Turning Life Into Fiction—by Robin Hemley. Writers' lives, those of their friends and family members, newspaper accounts, conversations overheard—these can be the bases for novels and short stories. Here, Robin Hemley shows how to make true stories even better. You'll learn how to turn journal entries into fiction; find good story material within yourself; identify memories that can be developed; and fictionalize other people's stories. Exercises guide writers in honing their skills. *#48000/$17.99/208 pages*

The Art and Craft of Novel Writing—by Oakley Hall. Using examples from classic and contemporary writers ranging from John Steinbeck to Joyce Carol Oates, Hall guides you through the process of crafting a novel. In example-packed discussions, Hall shows what works and why. You will learn the key elements of fiction and gain inspiration along the way. *#48002/$14.99/240 pages/paperback*

Address Unknown—by Kressmann Taylor. Commemorating the 50th anniversary of the liberation of World War II concentration camps, this gripping tale portrays in letters the terror of Nazism as it unfolds between an American and his former business partner in Germany. It serves as a sobering reminder that history can repeat itself. *#48006/$12.99/64 pages*

New York Magazine Crossword Puzzles—by Maura B. Jacobson. One of America's favorite puzzle-constructors brings you an assortment of her witty and inventive puzzles. Each collection contains fifty stimulating puzzles, reprinted from *New York* magazine, with themes ranging from literature and famous films to the Bible and the Oscars. *Volume 1: #48004/$9.99/64 pages/paperback; Volume 2: #48005/ $9.99/64 pages/paperback; Volume 3: #48009/$9.99/64 pages/paperback; Volume 4: #48010/$9.99/64 pages/paperback*

These selections are available at your local bookstore or directly from Story Press. To order from Story Press, send payment, plus $3.50 postage and handling for one book, and $1.00 for each additional. Ohio residents add 5.5% sales tax. Allow 30 days for delivery.

Story Press
1507 Dana Avenue
Cincinnati, Ohio 45207
or call: 1-800-876-0963

VISA/MasterCard orders call TOLL-FREE
1-800-289-0963

Prices subject to change without notice.   Stock may be limited on some books.

Write to this address for information on *Writer's Digest* magazine, *Story* magazine, Writer's Digest Book Club, Writer's Digest School, and Writer's Digest Criticism Service.   6555